The Evolutionary Transition
to Capitalism

The Evolutionary Transition to Capitalism

EDITED BY

Kazimierz Z. Poznanski

Westview Press
BOULDER • SAN FRANCISCO • OXFORD

Permission is gratefully acknowledged to reprint Chapter 8, which is a revised version of Josef Brada, "The Transformation from Communism to Capitalism: How Fast?" *Post-Soviet Affairs* 9, no. 2 (April–June 1993): 87–110.

Published in 1995 in the United States of America by Westview Press, Inc., 5500 Central Avenue, Boulder, Colorado 80301-2877, and in the United Kingdom by Westview Press, 12 Hid's Copse Road, Cumnor Hill, Oxford OX2 9JJ

A CIP catalog record for this book is available from the Library of Congress.
ISBN 0-8133-2270-7 — ISBN 0-8133-2271-5 (pbk.)

Printed and bound in the United States of America

The paper used in this publication meets the requirements of the American National Standard for Permanence of Paper for Printed Library Materials Z39.48-1984.

10   9   8   7   6   5   4   3   2   1

Contents

PART THREE
The Evolutionary Paradigm:
Theoretical Debate

Acknowledgments

This book is a byproduct of two recent U.S.-Polish Economic Round-tables organized by the Henry Jackson School of International Studies, University of Washington, and the Department of Economics at the University of Warsaw (held in Charleston, South Carolina, and Siena, Italy, respectively). The purpose of these annual meetings, initiated in 1991, is to bring together economists working on the issues of transition in the postcommunist world. Financing for the gatherings—and follow-up publications—has been generously provided by the International Research and Exchange Board, by the University of Washington's Provost Office, and by a private gift from Mr. and Mrs. Dekaban, alumni of the University of Washington. I coordinated the roundtable meetings in cooperation with Professor Wojciech Maciejewski (University of Warsaw) and Professor Fabrizio Coricelli (University of Siena).

Kazimierz Z. Poznanski

Introduction

Kazimierz Z. Poznanski

This volume represents a comprehensive inquiry into the evolutionary interpretation of the postcommunist transition process. It is a sequel to a collaborative book, *Constructing Capitalism: The Reemergence of Civil Society and Liberal Economy in the Post-Communist World* (Westview, 1992) by many of the same authors. In the earlier collection, also under my editorship, many contributors analyzed the postcommunist phase, though largely in a speculative fashion since the process was just unfolding at the time of writing. This book has the advantage of drawing from an accumulated body of facts covering the transition process several years long by now, allowing the initial reactions expressed in the previous book to be tested afresh.

Although they build on different factual bases, these two publications are linked analytically in that they are largely placed within the framework of the evolutionary theory. This particular approach was explicitly applied only in a few chapters of the earlier book, most notably those analyzing the transformation of property rights under communism. By contrast, the present collection of studies is shaped almost exclusively in the evolutionary mold, while focused mostly on the postcommunist reforms. As such, this volume should be considered the first coherent statement of the evolutionary perspective on the current process of transition in postcommunist economies (and possibly on the more general issue of comparative economic systems as well).

Although almost all the chapters in this book draw heavily from evolutionary economics, the actual contents of the evolutionary theory are not outlined in any systematic way by any of the individual chapters. This would have not been an easy task anyhow, since the theory is neither complete nor uniform (for a more complete demonstration, see Poznanski 1993). When reading this book one should have, however, little difficulty in getting a good sense of the different set of assumptions and concepts the evolutionary approach brings to the economic debate. It should be particularly easy to relate this way of thinking—and modeling—to the radical approaches to postcommunist transition, to which evolutionary economics is in obvious opposition.

It will be a fair reflection of the ideas expressed in the book to describe this evolutionary theory as one that—following classical economics—considers an individual as central to analysis (rather than class, as in the anti-classical Marxist approach, or nation/state, as in pre-classical mercantilism). However, unlike in classical economics, the evolutionary theory does not assume that the individual is perfectly rational and thus that economic processes are totally deterministic. Within the evolutionary model, an individual operates, as Hayek stresses, in an intentional, rational way under conditions of incomplete information so that results of actions are only quasi-deterministic (with eventual success reflecting effort as well as luck).

Evolutionary economics assumes that most of the information useful in economic processes is possessed by individuals in a form that makes it impossible to communicate it accurately to others. In other words, it is impossible to provide it fully and/or in a timely manner. This type of information is called "tacit" or "technical," and the most practical way to properly utilize it is for individuals to do so themselves. Such information can be partially and with delay transmitted from one individual to another, but only in special circumstances. This can be done best in informal settings, where personal contacts are allowed to develop over time and where frequent observation eventually reveals the information (in a case of learning not by teaching but rather by "assimilation" through frequent intimate contacts).

Given the central role of information in any economic process, the major effort by individual players in any economy is devoted to obtaining information and thus reducing uncertainty involved in decisionmaking. It does follow that it is basically the shortage of information and not so much the scarcity of capital or labor—as assumed by classical theory—that represents the basic problem in economic life as seen by evolutionary theorists. To put it differently, it is not the effective allocation of resources, as understood in classical economics, but getting information that primarily concerns evolutionary economics (since what really prevents individuals from mobilizing their resources is uncertainty over effects of their productive application).

The principal method, or instrument, for maximizing the stream of information (and reducing uncertainty or instability) is building economic institutions, or institutionalization (an assumption that clearly brings evolutionary theory to the neoinstitutional school, with North). Economic organizations can then be defined as sets of routines for decisionmaking, developed to permit their members to reduce informational costs. With routines in place, economic decisions do not always require a time-consuming search for information from zero. Decisions are made, by and large, in a repetitive way, that is, in a less than rational manner, if the classical criterion is taken.

Economic systems within which organizations operate have the same general (rather than specific) purpose as organizational routines—namely to provide for cost-effective information processing. Market (but also central) planning can be then defined as a mechanism for utilization of economic information available to organizations (and individuals acting within them). Given this assumption, the efficiency difference between systems—say, market and central planning—is to be measured in terms of the systems' respective information costs. Evolutionary economic theory argues that the lowest cost system is that of the (voluntary) market, though even here the costs are high (taking the bulk of productive resources).

Although the classical theory does not explain how institutions emerge, change, and decline, evolutionary economics offers an explanation. The major evolutionary thesis with this respect is that, as a rule, economic (as well as political) institutions come into existence and then evolve to eventually undergo a demise at a slow pace. This is a process characterized by incoherence, with the main input coming from individuals acting in a trial-and-error fashion (acting on their initiative but not with a well-defined and calculated end goal or vision of intended institution). The evolutionary perspective on institutionalization as driven by individuals is, of course, consistent with the methodological individualism of the evolutionary economic theory as understood or defined here.

The evolutionary theory, which advocates a natural, organic type of institutionalization, is in contrast to constructivism, which proposes, as Mises points out, a total overhaul followed by the implementation of untested "plans" preconceived by the state. Although the individualistic type of institution-building leads to the emergence of complete markets, constructivism leads to pathologies such as central planning. By making a total assault on existing institutions, such constructivist attempts unnecessarily remove or destroy whatever workable elements exist. Trusting in "plans" produced from abstraction rather than real-life experience, these radical steps invite utopianism, and letting the state take charge creates interest in extending failed measures.

Since such constructivist attempts are generally not practical, they cannot be fully implemented according to the preconceived model. Even at the time of inception, when reform fever is at its highest, some major compromises are being made, bringing ideals closer to the reality of what is possible. Thus, by their own idealized standards, radical institutional changes begin with a "failure" of implementation. This initial compromise is followed by other compromises, so that the real fate of constructed—as opposed to self-grown—institutions is to decline and give way to something else. As such, constructivist reforms—often part of broader social revolution—are sad events, to use the phrase introduced by Dahrendorf.

However excessively costly they are to a given society, such preconceived systems (to mention central planning again) may last for a considerable time. Consequently, the economic burden of constructivism is often very high. This extended life is a result of the fact that at least some of the compromises that go against the original "design" help improve the system. Also, any deviations from a partially—or completely—unworkable system are time consuming, if they are to produce acceptable results. Applying the logic of the evolutionary argument, one has to accept that any particular system can he replaced with an effective substitute only through gradual, organic, institution-building—and not through another constructivist experiment.

It follows that during any transition from one coherent system of rules to another, say, toward the market or away from it, the working mechanism has to combine many elements that come from different end-types (see Poznanski 1993). This is what would distinguish the transition process from that of reforming a well-articulated economic system, where unified rules operate. But one has to keep in mind that even well established economic systems display considerable diversity, or contamination, so that theories built on the notion of unity cannot be correct. The explanation for this diversity is that "competition" between institutions—as in the case of organization—is never perfect, so that certain unorthodox arrangements could be retained for an extended period.

There are few better contemporary cases of institutional change on which to apply the evolutionary theory than the current transition toward markets in the postcommunist world. What makes it a particularly valuable object of analysis is that so many individual (country) cases of transition fall clearly in the category that has been of special interest to evolutionary economists. Specifically, many, if not most, of the cases found among the postcommunist economies involve radical change in existing institutions. Thus, the ongoing transition can be seen as a great testing ground for various evolutionary claims, and this book presents the results of such a testing, focusing primarily on privatization as the core of transition.

As privatization has become the centerpiece of the transition process, outlining approaches to divestment has also been elevated to the focal point of debates on transition. Many of the models of divestment brought into this debate could be classified as constructivist. Janos Kornai, in Chapter 2, puts the early communist model of a simulated capital market into the constructivist category. In this model, state-owned enterprises are allowed to trade their shares directly among themselves or through state-owned holdings. Kornai doubts that such a system would ever emerge on its own, as a consequence of voluntary actions by state-owned enterprises (except as a way of freeing enterprises from central control, though with dire consequences for economic performance).

Another model that Kornai classifies as constructivist is the labor-management type of ownership, as practiced, for instance, in communist Yugoslavia. There was considerable interest among anticommunist opposition in taking this so-called third way, as an alternative to genuine planning or effective markets. (One finds these sentiments particularly active in Poland.) In this model workers are given control over capital allocation, with or without legal ownership of that capital. Kornai argues that however noble the motives behind this model, it lacks coherence, due to the obvious absence of separate representation for capital. Such a model would most likely have to be imposed by the state as it is an inferior alternative to genuine capitalism (but also to state planning—see Kornai 1992).

Kornai also raises objections to the concept of free distribution of state assets through vouchers, a system in which the state offers to citizens, at no charge (or at a nominal price), shares in its enterprises. The major justification for this approach is that it permits the fastest—and the most egalitarian (equitarian)—divestment given the initial conditions (e.g., lack of private savings). Kornai's argument is that there is a danger that in the absence of stock markets, imposition of such a model of "democratic capitalism" will make an effective allocation of capital in these economies impossible. Also, since no assets are really free, workers will have to pay with less access to state services (thus undermining the equitarian objectives of such a free distribution).

Doubts are also raised regarding the belief that if internal privatization (turning assets to domestic actors) is, for whatever reasons, not a very practical option, the state should encourage foreigners to take over whatever represents a good value. Although Kornai sees a legitimate role for foreigners in the transfer of state capital to private hands, particularly in the backward financial sector, he finds it of limited use. He questions the notion that the final proportion of foreign capital accumulated through equity (portfolio) transactions or direct investment is quite immaterial. This is not only for reasons of maintaining economic sovereignty, but also because to build support for capitalist institutions, a strong domestic class of capital owners is needed.

If these experimental schemes are as impractical as they may appear, it would mean that their realization must be difficult, or simply questionable. For Peter Murrell, such programs at best create an illusion of major progress, because formal changes—title transfers—prove easy, while the essence of property rights, or the informal aspect, does not change easily.

For title holders to act as private owners, it would be necessary to provide security of private rights, but this is much more complicated than handing over titles. He further claims that the more radical the formal reforms—seen as an expression of rhetoric—the less is being implemented. To put it differently, the realization of reform programs undertaken by the state is a direct inverse function of their rhetoric.

This inversion reflects the simple fact that economic organizations, seen as sets of routines, can be productive only if their internal—mostly informal rules are not damaged. Organizational memory, which is usually retained through routines, can be overloaded with signals and damaged by excessive change. With substantial loss of organizational memory, productivity has to decline. So, if economic reforms are too radical, organizations may become simply incapable of affording any real change in their behavior. With this comes pressure on the state either to roll back radical programs, or to try to resort to familiar old-fashioned measures that seem most useful in restoring an organization's capability to calculate optimal survival strategies.

Although Irena Grosfeld agrees with the notion that informal structures are the major obstacle to institutional change and that formal ones are relatively easy to accommodate, she takes a different position from Murrell and claims that since the formal component is easier to manage it should be reformed by the state in a radical way. There is no reason, Grosfeld claims, to assume that organizations are going to change their behavior on their own, and even if they do, it would take too long (with extended waste of resources that puts an unacceptable cost burden on society). To trigger substantive change in their behavior within a reasonable timetable—and at a reasonable cost—existing organizations have to be placed in a different set of formal rules without any delay.

It could well be, however, that despite the fact that formal changes are easier to afford than informal ones or that general rules can be changed faster than organizations, it is not necessarily true that the former are suited for radical reform. Thus, it is not only that economic organizations may be unprepared to properly respond to such radical changes in the formal rules of the game, but it is also doubtful that postcommunist states have the strength or the capacity needed to execute massive reform of that kind in a coherent way. There is thus a high risk that such weak bureaucracies may produce a poorly crafted, even contradictory, set of rules, thus increasing the probability that reform will be rejected—or superficially adopted—by organizations.

But even a strong state, with sufficient workers and "morale," may fail to deliver on its promises due to the predictable mismatch between leaders and those at lower levels of bureaucracy. As Murrell stresses, those involved in exact implementation are likely to lack the information on which the leaders base their ambitious programs. Information possessed by those who implement the programs reflects the experience of working within the old system, and their efforts to change rules are going to be molded by that experience. And it is not even certain that principal reform-movers have an adequate understanding of all key aspects that their attempt entails to give proper guidance to subordinate levels.

That a breakthrough in formal rules does not have to trigger major positive, or even any, change in the true working of a given system seems to be, as Murrell contends, supported by the real-life experience of post-communist Mongolia. Starting from 1991, the state dispersed capital assets through free-of-charge distribution, so that formally the economy became private by mid-1992. But severe restrictions on the execution of private rights have been put in place so that in essence very little has changed. One of such constraints is the bureaucratic allocation of materials, which the state felt compelled to undertake in order to head off chaos in production. Taxes are collected from nominally private enterprises very much in the same arbitrary way as they were in the past.

Also, in 1990, Mongolia removed traditional price controls in order to allow prices to be freely determined by demand/supply forces. However, although a complete liberalization policy has been proclaimed, the pricing practices have not changed much, with enterprises forced to comply with a number of requirements and subjected to numerous state impositions. Enterprises have been forced to inform buyers of their price corrections and to register any changes with pricing agencies. Increases that are found excessive can be rolled back, and extra (deemed "unfair") profits can be confiscated by the state. All these interventions have been coming from local pricing agencies, which filled the gap previously held by one unified agency, and with this proliferation of authorities, the extent of interferences in pricing might have actually increased.

Looking for more evidence one may turn to the Czech Republic, which has implemented a radical program of equal distribution of vouchers among adult citizens. In two rounds, starting in 1991, the majority of state assets have been divested in a remarkably orderly fashion in about a three-year period. The purpose of this experimental program was to take control of capital away from the highly centralized state bureaucracy and disperse shares among large numbers of private owners. Although fear was expressed that this form of "democratic capitalism" will produce very weak—and thus disinterested—shareholders, the opposite has happened. The majority of shares has been acquired from individuals by a few investment funds, so that an incredible concentration of capital control has been restored.

The Czech program has been built on the assumption that with turning assets over to private hands, the users of capital—professional managers—will be exposed to more effective external control, or governance, than they were under state planning. This has proven very difficult to accomplish, because the few funds that control the bulk of shares are simply unprepared to execute their rights. Apparently, it has been very difficult to dismiss underperforming managers, so that the old-time practice of fixed jobs has not ceased. Putting deficit-making enterprises into bankruptcy, as an even more deadly threat, has been rare despite a rather tough law passed recently. Survival of these enterprises has been helped, as in the past, by generous state subsidies (including cancellations of bad debts owed to banks).

Although radical reforms generally accomplish little in terms of getting rid of old-time elements, their impact on economic behavior (or the motivation behind it) can be serious and damaging. In fact, even those radical programs that have been canceled before taking effect can negatively affect the motivation of economic players, because simple, credible, announcements of radical intent by the state reformers will make them alter their strategies. The reason is that as long as such an announcement is found by the enterprises to be credible, their management may choose to make a defensive adjustment without waiting to find out whether the state is actually going to take material steps to implement its reform.

When new elements are brought into the existing system and then taken back to make room for traditional arrangements—in their original or somehow modified version—this can have a bad impact on behavior as well. Faced with new elements, enterprises will make appropriate correction in their strategies only to see them go because old-time institutions are eventually restored. Neither of the respective adjustments in behavior can be done instantaneously, and even a return to preexisting routines at the end of this reform cycle is time consuming. This is because any change in behavior takes organizational energies and resources that are limited. With any repetition of such a cycle of aborted reforms, these resources are further depleted.

One possible example of such an adjustment instigated by a radical reform that was announced and then not delivered occurred in Poland, where in 1990, in a move to "construct" a market economy but also to remove excessive welfare demands from the budget, the state declared a plan to complete privatization in three years. Because the state proved to be too weak to muster sufficient political support to put its ambitious plans in action, it eventually settled for a slow process of divestment with enterprises allowed more input. In the meantime, enterprises have been left for an extended period not knowing who is eventually going to acquire state assets in their enterprises. Given this ambiguity, both managers and workers reduced their efforts—including interest in capital formation—and with this came production losses.

Continuing with the case of Poland, one may add that not only enterprises but also banks have initially found themselves in a similar situation of greatly destabilized property status. In 1990, unwilling to further carry the burden of financing state enterprises, the state made its own banks responsible for supplying credit. This was such a sudden change that banks—now left without state backing or assurance that they will be bailed out in a situation of stress—found themselves unprepared to finance enterprises. They had neither the knowledge to assess creditworthiness of their clients nor the instruments to enforce default on payments. This resulted, as I claim in Chapter 1, in a liquidity crisis, which made it difficult even for viable organizations to maintain their production.

It could well be that this weakening of ownership structure is largely what has drawn Poland into the deep post-1990 economic crisis. Many nonsystemic factors could have contributed to that decline, but none probably could have had such a spectacular impact on economic activities as the destabilization of property rights. If this were true for Poland it might be also valid for other postcommunist countries that ended up in sometimes even more severe recession. But to generalize this hypothesis one would have to deal with the fact that the pattern of reforms in Poland has not been identical to that found in many other postcommunist economies. In other words, one would have to explain how diversified reform approaches could have produced a uniform outcome of deep recession.

Turning to Russia, one finds that even though privatization in this country (unlike in Poland) was very swift, the divestment resulted in an increased uncertainty over property status as well. The fact that privatization was so rapid does not mean that the state in Russia was more in control of asset divestment; since it was much more badly hurt by political turmoil, it exercised even less control than the state in Poland. What happened in Russia was that rather than block asset transfer as in Poland, the enterprises decided to take over assets from a weak state. Through a disorganized process of voucher distribution—with little or no state supervision—managers and workers captured their assets, with nobody quite certain of their legal rights.

A credit crunch has also occurred in postcommunist Russia, and with greater weakening of the state has come a more severe liquidity crisis than in Poland. Unlike Poland, Russia has continued to provide subsidies on a large scale, but in contrast with the recent communist past, this has become much less orderly and thus more disruptive to production processes. Importantly, although enterprises were left to secure their supplies from each other, the state has been unable to provide effective enforcement to back up their contracts. Fear of delayed compensation for deliveries or simply of nonpayment has caused managers to deny customary (trade) credit and to resort to barter arrangements, a practice that precipitated the decline of production levels.

Since so many countries pursuing various strategies of transition have found themselves in recession, it might appear that there is sort of a universal cost for getting out of the central-planning system. However, not all transitions have brought on recession in all economies. In China, the shift from central planning has produced extremely strong production growth, combined with a remarkable stability (i.e., domestic inflation and external balance), for a country at China's level of development. This difference in performance would suggest that China has taken course different from that of economies that entered recession and that it has gotten its policies right while others have not.

The above question is addressed by Josef Brada, who argues that many conditions under which Chinese transition has been taking place seem to be so much more favorable than those found in Eastern Europe and Russia that the model of gradual change pursued by China is neither desirable nor feasible for these other economies. One of the fundamental differences is that China is a much less developed country, in which the agricultural sector weighs so much more; this situation apparently makes gradual changes much more appropriate than would be the case in industry-dominated Eastern Europe and Russia. Consequently, to be useful, evolutionary economists would have to stop using China as a ready-made model and develop their own practical alternatives to radical programs.

One of the differences in starting conditions is, as Brada argues, that China's macroeconomic disequilibrium was much less pronounced than, for example, Russia's, and with a larger share of people working in farming, China had fewer problems with removing shortages faced by consumers. However, Barry Naughton finds China's economy at the outset of reforms in enormous disequilibrium, which is reflected by (among other factors) a very extensive rationing of basic consumer goods, more so by far than in communist Russia. Besides, many East European countries, including Hungary, entered into the recent transition with negligible imbalances, and it should also be kept in mind that having relatively less manpower in farming probably did not matter that much, since the greatest imbalances faced by consumers in Eastern Europe were not in food but in industrial products.

Brada goes to Chinese farming to make another point, namely that this sector cannot support claims on the advantages of gradualism, for reforms there were radical. He states that reform in agriculture involved a rapid expansion of private property, something akin to the free distributions of state assets that evolutionists object to. However, leasing state land to families, initially for a limited period and only later for an extended period, with permission for transfer of rights, is by no means radical. Brada also finds the Chinese price reform, with massive freeing of prices for foodstuffs, to be radical, something objectionable to many evolutionists. But this freeing can also be judged as being slow, with control of some consumer products retained for years (and some control recently restored to curb urban inflation).

If initial conditions are critical for the choice of reform strategy, one wonders what would justify the gradual—as we see it—approach taken by China in its agriculture and the radical style of reforms in Eastern Europe. In terms of efficiency, the cooperatives in Hungary or the state farms in Czechoslovakia were probably not that inferior, so one wonders where the sense of urgency would have come from. Why would, for instance, Hungary almost instantly abolish import protection for its agriculture? Also, why would postcommunist Poland do the same, even though its agriculture was almost totally private at the outset of recent reforms (leaving aside the fact that major competitors for food exports from these countries retained subsidies at the level equivalent to one-third of producer cost)?

Thus, it may be that the adoption of radical reforms in East European agriculture was not dictated by initial conditions but simply represents policy errors. So, the difference between China and the other countries is that the former just made a correct choice with respect to farming. But it could well be that China's overall gradualism—applied also in industry—has been a proper choice, while the overall radicalism of East European (and Russian) reforms might have been a mistake. This is exactly the point that Naughton makes in his comparative analysis of China's model. In his view, China outperformed Eastern Europe not only from certain favorable initial conditions but most important from its different reform approach, gradualism, characterized by fragmentation.

This gradualism of Chinese reform is reflected, as Naughton argues, in the fact that stabilization—removing imbalances in product markets—has mostly been accomplished through restructuring of production under the old system. The bulk of restructuring has been executed by reallocation of state-financed investment in products that were in shortage. This state-led restructuring made it possible to eventually bring more market forces into play later, in the mid-1980 phase of reforms. Such an approach greatly differs from that of Eastern Europe, where even now, despite great dislocations in industry, there is very little political—but also intellectual—support for such restructuring (with the ideas presented in Chapter 7 by Jozef van Brabant representing a rare example of such support).

While state-led restructuring was unfolding in China, steps were also taken to systematically increase the access of nonstate actors to the allocation of resources. This has been facilitated by a uniquely Chinese solution called the dual price system, under which most of the goods have both an internal price (fixed by official organs) and an outside—market—price as well. By allowing above-plan production to be sold at higher prices than those allowed for the contingent, the government created incentives to expand production. The greatest differences indicated more severe structural problems because the system caused resources to be steered that way. These price differentials were also helpful in letting the state know where to bring additional budgetary means to achieve the most sizable improvements in the overall structure of production.

Equally important, the room for free pricing and contractual allocation has been permitted to systematically expand, but without denying the state's ability to reverse some of this progress in the potentially disruptive areas. This has been accomplished by taking a firm position that the size of the central plan—setting production targets and fixing various prices—will be fixed in absolute terms. Thus, with production growing upward, as it has, the proportions of the economy controlled by plans and those operating without plans—or under markets—have been allowed to constantly expand. Naughton calls this (unmistakably evolutionary) pattern of systemic changes "growing out of plan" (as opposed to what one could describe as "dropping a plan," as East European economies recently did).

Also important is the fact that China's economy has been allowed to "grow out of the public," in other words, to change its property structure in favor of a private system. Chinese reformers, so far, have refused to permit massive privatization of state-owned enterprises. In a way, they fixed the absolute amount of public capital but at the same time allowed unconstrained formation of private capital. With the public sector growing at a lower rate than the emerging private sector, the proportions between the two have been steadily improving in favor of the private. Thus, China's economy has been allowed to turn from public into private, without troublesome (as one could judge from the East European experience) divestment.

That this unclean, by neoclassical standards, system, with dual pricing and dual ownership, has produced very strong performance—rather than a decline—might suggest that such hybridization can be effective, at least under certain circumstances. Looking at this property dualism, one could say that the expanding private sector might have been exerting positive influence on the state through filling niches that the state was staying away from but also by applying competitive pressure when their areas overlapped. The presence of a viable private sector has also allowed the planner, at central and local levels, to improve monitoring of subordinate enterprises (e.g., by giving a better sense of potential profitability and taxability of various lines of production).

This point on the benefits of mixed arrangements, at least in the sphere of property rights, during transition from one system to another is further stressed by Ronald McKinnon in his comparison of fiscal reforms in China and Russia. He argues that one of the major dangers of rapid privatization is that it may cause a sharp decline in budgetary revenues. Replacing the relatively simple system of direct taxation of state enterprises with the effective system of taxing private entities is very difficult. Consequently, each unit of capital transferred to private hands may initially produce fewer taxes, so that without increasing the burden on still-existing state-owned enterprises, the economy risks an increase in budgetary imbalances—and also an increased pressure on price inflation.

According to McKinnon, even despite the fact that China has avoided massive privatization, it has been unable to escape fiscal imbalances. This fact makes so much more remarkable the fact that China has been able to expand its economy very rapidly without severe price instability. Rapid inflation has been avoided even though the government has been forced to finance its deficits by borrowing from state banks—by itself a reason not to urgently privatize them. This has been possible because private sector households have been generating huge savings and have become major lenders to the state itself. With the phenomenal expansion of savings, the private sector has been able to meet its own needs as well (limiting the crowding-out effect of forced bank lending to the state).

McKinnon's support for gradual transition is quite obvious, but he does not advocate the Chinese model as universally applicable. He states that as far as the detailed implementation of the model is concerned, it could not be applied in contemporary Russia. The state there is too weak to permit dual pricing, which is dependent crucially on forced deliveries at lower prices to enterprises. Consequently, prices have been instantly freed but no meaningful equilibrium in producer prices has been possible, because enterprises were not financially constrained (i.e., continued operating under soft budget). Enterprises showing no interest in holding money tend to overbid on inputs, including foreign currency. Hence, in order to curb raging inflation Russia should, as an intermediate measure, restore price (and wage) controls.

But, as one could argue, returning to price/wage controls, even for a limited time, would require sufficient state authority, which, as McKinnon states, is absent in Russia. While one might agree with his reasoning that such controls should be maintained until a proper fiscal (tax) system is put in place, the implementation of such a policy seems possible only with the backing of an effective state apparatus. Otherwise it will be impossible to enforce tax rules, so that the fiscal system proposed by McKinnon would be paralyzed by corruption and evasion. If so, it becomes quite apparent that the pattern of economic transition—its technical (instrumental) side—is critically dependent on the cohesion and determination of the implementing state power (meaning that transition is a political economic—rather than simply an economic—issue).

Returning to China, one might venture a hypothesis that what critically differentiates its pattern of transition from that of Eastern Europe (and Russia) is that it has been conducted under the supervision of a strong state. No major political turmoil has damaged the state authority in China, nor has there been a desire by the political class to roll back the state rapidly. The only major change allowed was a shift of power from the state to localities, which probably, in itself, contributed to the increase in the state's ability to control. In contrast, Eastern Europe, and particularly Russia, underwent a traumatic political shift that removed communist parties and hence the backbone of the state. Moreover, almost universally, the successors to the party, postcommunist reformers, have endorsed, at least verbally, the concept of rapid state withdrawal.

Often, it is said that it is exactly the political discontinuity—and in many investigated cases, the consequent absence of a strong state—that made it necessary for East European (and Russian) leaders to embark on a radical path of reform. The merit of this argument has to be analyzed carefully, since intuitively it would seem that the radical program—by its very nature global and deeply disruptive—might require, as a condition of success, a strong state. It could be also argued that without a strong state any radical program would inevitably lead to chaos. If that is correct, this line of thinking would lead us to a conclusion that China was better prepared for shock-therapy reform, and since it did not choose shock therapy this would suggest that its choice of strategy was suboptimal.

Alternatively, it could be argued that whether the state is weak or strong, the proper approach is always gradualism, and the difference in states' abilities to guide reforms simply calls for adjustments in slow-paced programs. Stronger states could, presumably, afford more change without provoking the collapse of reform, since they will be better equipped to combat pathologies if and when they appear. Such states will also be in a better position to balance the gains and losses that tend to expand across social groups with the growing reform pace. Weaker states should therefore restrict the scale and depth of changes and should definitely not risk an immediate erosion of their power base by allowing steps that hurt their revenue base or estrange political allies (including those threatened by reforms).

The above point could be better framed in the context of the sequencing problem. Typically this issue of sequencing has been addressed in terms of whether prices should be set right (and stabilized) before changing motivation structure (e.g., through demonopolization, privatization). Another question has been whether prices could be rationalized within a still-closed economy, or whether the streamlining of prices should be assisted by opening markets to foreign competition. Bringing the state to the equation, one could ask whether the proper sequence—allowing for most effective execution of any of these goals—should not start with ensuring that the state's relevant structures (i.e., public administration and the legislative process) are robust enough to sustain the subsequent reform program.

The recognition by the proponents of gradual transition of the key role of the state sounds rather strange given the critical commitment of evolutionary economics to a minimal state. But the goal should not be confused with the method, and in this case the minimal state is the goal, while a strong state is the method. There could not be any other way, since for an economy that was totally dominated by the state in the past, the only sensible strategy is for the state to slowly phase out this dependence. This subtlety is often lost by the critics of the evolutionary view of transition, who claim that any effort to leave the state as a major actor is a form of constructivism, but this is one of the paradoxes of the transition process.

References

Kornai, J. 1992. "The Affinity Between Ownership and Coordination Mechanisms: The Common Experience of Reform in Socialist Countries," in: K. Poznanski, ed., *Constructing Capitalism*, Boulder: Westview Press.

Poznanski, K. 1993. "Restructuring of Property Rights in Poland: A Study in Evolutionary Economics," *East European Politics and Societies*, vol. 7, no. 3.

PART ONE

Paradoxes of Transition:
Eastern Europe

1

Institutional Perspectives on Postcommunist Recession in Eastern Europe

Kazimierz Z. Poznanski

Economic recessions as deep as those in which the countries of post-communist Eastern Europe (as well as most of the members of the former Soviet Union) have found themselves in recent years do not happen often in the developed world. That these recessions are taking place in countries currently trying to replace an inefficient system—state planning—with an efficient one—the competitive market—makes this regionwide phenomenon even more intriguing. (See Tables 1.1 and 1.2.) So does the fact that many of these economies have been sliding for a considerable (though not necessarily equally long) time without any major accompanying political turmoil (not counting the countries recently trapped in civil wars, for example, Yugoslavia and Georgia, which call for separate treatment).

Most commonly, economic explanations for the postcommunist recession have been sought in various exogenous shocks on the aggregate demand side. Downward inventory stock adjustment, related to tightening of financial discipline, is said to be such a recessionary cause (see Berg and Sachs, 1992). Another factor frequently pointed to is the destruction of regional trade, due to the disappearance of the old political formulation, Soviet hegemony (e.g., Rodrik 1992). In both cases, disruption of the economy is seen as an irreversible result of desirable adjustments—the elimination of excess inventory and of welfare-reducing trade.

Alternative views also attacking the problem from the demand side present the postcommunist recessions as the result of macroeconomic mismanagement and therefore avoidable. Deflationary overdose, or excessive contraction in aggregate demand, aimed at removing hidden

3

(or open) inflation, is seen by some economists as a major culprit (Kolodko 1991, 1993). Indecisiveness in deflating these economies in the early postcommunist years, necessitating repeated recessionary contraction in aggregate demand, is another example of such an argument (Crane 1992). Unlike the previous group of arguments, in which recession is seen as a normal price for restoring cost-sensitivity, here the price of warding off inflation is viewed as excessive (also see Nuti and Portes 1993).

In this chapter I try to examine whether there might be some relevant recessionary forces unrelated to demand conditions, that is, operating on the supply side. Describing my approach as supply-side may not be entirely accurate, however, since there is more involved here. The demand arguments either ignore the role of economic institutions or consider them irrelevant because of the lack of substantive reforms at the time of initial output collapse (see Brada and King 1992). Here, institutions are placed at the center of the analysis, since it is they who determine the payoff matrix and shape the behavior of economic agents (i.e., the supply side). Thus, my approach might better be described as institutional.

It is argued in this chapter that all the postcommunist countries inherited an institutional structure unequipped to deal with such radical policy changes as the drastic deflation applied in Poland in 1990 or Czechoslovakia in 1991. Of great importance has been the underdevelopment of banks, not prepared to channel credit to viable enterprises in need of production restructuring. This institutional structure has been further undermined by postcommunist efforts to rapidly alter it or, alternatively, has been weakened through uncontrolled fragmentation. With these systemic changes, the uncertainty faced by economic agents (including banks) has increased, causing some withdrawal from production and reduced interest in capital expansion.

Regional economies may also have been affected by particular patterns of thinking or preferences developed during the communist period, but, contrary to frequent assertions, the absence of a broad-based interest in developing capitalist institutions has not been one of them. Nor has a tendency toward utopian ideas (e.g., of a "third way," where markets and plans are mixed or of a perfect, self-regulated market) been a significant factor. Rather, it has been the inaccurate perception of communist reality as a total failure by the opposition forces—as well as by the public at large—that could be viewed as a detrimental force, since it has encouraged excessive dispensation with many existing, at least temporarily useful, institutions and policies.

I have also attempted in this chapter to explore whether the recent deterioration in institutional structure—and related economic downtown—might reflect a long-term historical pattern rather than a separate recent episode. There are a number of hypotheses to be tested, including the view that Eastern Europe is a "crisis zone," where adjustments to world market shocks are delayed or incomplete and where so-called regressive reforms take place. The recent regionwide recession could instead be a by-product of the demonstration effect, which typifies backward (peripheral) economies where inadequate (inappropriate) institutions are introduced in haste. Alternatively, the recession might be the result of political processes, wherein short-term economic gains have been sacrificed for long-term ones such as national independence.

Production-Side Factors Behind Recession

Liquidity Crisis

Moving outside of the demand-type argumentation, one should recognize that in order to function, markets require more than a correct price structure—that is, undistorted signals of relative scarcities. They also need money to accommodate necessary resource allocation. Thus, for any deflationary shock to produce positive output response to prices, money has to be provided by the financial system in sufficient quantity to allow for restructuring. Thus, the primary cause of the regionwide crisis might have been the overwithdrawal of credit. Alternatively, it could be that even if credit restrictions had not been built into the "shock," the financial system, that is, banks, refused to supply credit to enterprises for production adjustment.

In fact, it has not been unusual for stabilization programs in developing countries outside of Eastern Europe to follow a monetary contraction in combination with unaccommodating credit policy (Kozierkiewicz 1992). This problem exists despite that keeping credit lines open might help to reduce the negative impact of deflationary programs on output. Israel's heterodox stabilization program offers practical evidence that selective access to credit (in this case for export-oriented sectors) greatly contributes to reducing the costs of the price operation as well as to the durability of lower inflation (Blanchard et al. 1991, p. 9).

Indeed, evidence from Eastern Europe suggests that following the monetary shocks, the amount of real credit has drastically declined in most cases. The credit squeeze has been very sharp in Czechoslovakia (26 percent in 1991 [Hncir 1992]) and Poland (e.g., an almost 40 percent reduction in real terms in 1990 [see Poznanski 1993]). An extreme case would be that of Russia, where after a brief contraction of 60 to 75 percent, credit has been allowed to expand with no controls at all. But Hungary has been conducting a much more accommodating credit policy, with the interest rate not necessarily following each price increase (see Coricelli and Milesi-Feretti 1993).

The credit supply decline has been caused by a number of factors, one being the decision by many reformers to use credit restrictions, such as credit ceilings and interest rate directives, as another anchor in monetary shocks. The fall in credit would be simply another manifestation of demand shock if not for the fact that credit has also been restricted by banks, following their own even tighter policies. This has been reflected in very high interest rate spread (often not responding to refinancing rate reductions, as in Hungary), as well as very high collaterals. Increases in interenterprise credit, already widespread before shocks, have often somewhat mitigated shortages of bank credit.

East European industry has not only been largely left with an inadequate amount of credit but has also been poorly served by banks in allocating money. In particular, state banks have been notoriously unable to limit credit supplies to financially defunct state-owned enterprises. Unpayable (bad) debts have been allowed to accumulate, with banks unwilling to execute their credit contracts and bankrupt the defunct enterprises. Collusion between banks and enterprises (see Coricelli and Rocha 1991) has meant an extension of soft financing conditions, so that restructuralization through "exit" (allowing for rational underutilized resource redeployment) has been hampered.

The side effect of financing "bad" borrowers in the state sector has been a shortage of credit for the private sector. The private sector has suffered not only from the ongoing preference of banks to finance state-owned enterprises but also from state pressure on commercialized banks to finance budget deficits. In Poland, less than 10 percent of total bank credit went to the private sector in 1990–1991, and state bonds emerged as the major part of bank balance sheets. Accordingly, the process of restructuralization through "entries" of private enterprises has been restricted as well. (This point is elaborated in Begg and Portes 1993).

However, banks cannot be squarely blamed for the way they have acted since they have found themselves in a situation for which they were ill-prepared. Their experience has been in executing money allocations decided through a budgetary process and with state "insurance" (i.e., bailout by the budget). They lack the skills needed to properly evaluate loan risks, and their recent "commercialization" has left them with inadequate protection against risk. Even less realistic would be to expect banks to engage in restructuring of their defunct customers. Nor have they yet acquired the means, including political clout, to proceed with mass bankruptcies of their customers.

Even a very wellestablished banking system could not properly intermediate capital allocation in the current environment, that is, with the large amount of "informational noise." The size of past debts of state-owned enterprises, for instance, provide very poor guidance for banks, for they often reflect a financial situation inherited from the communist period, with passive money. High inflation, with multiple sources, complicates economic calculations of future cost-effectiveness of projects as well. Frequent changes in state regulations (e.g., taxes, customs duties, depreciation rates), most of which are difficult to predict, have further obscured calculations.

Organization Routines

The above reference to banking leads me to the more general question of the adaptability of various types of economic agents—organizations— to new conditions. In a neoclassical view, the answer is very simple: They can adapt quickly, since agents are assumed to be perfectly rational. Regardless of specific circumstances, economic agents display the same level of full rationality, that is, the ability to recognize and implement both the best productmix and the bestpractice techniques. Thus, the real challenge for reformers is simply to get the prices right, so that complete and cost-free information is available and optimal choices can be made.

Within this neoclassical tradition, whenever agents fail to follow an optimum "trajectory"—meaning that the market fails—it is assumed that the state needs to intervene. With its insistence on achieving perfect, complete markets, the theory provides an ample excuse for state activism. It is also said that for any state intervention to succeed, it has to be credible. Individual agents will regress to previous habits if unpopular, or even just unfamiliar, measures taken by the state appear reversible at low cost to those affected. It follows from this argument that shock-therapy reforms have a greater chance for success than gradual ones (Dornbusch and Fischer, 1990).

In the separate tradition of evolutionary economics, with its roots in the work of Joseph Schumpeter and Frederich von Hayek, individual agents are assumed to have limited adaptability whereas information is viewed as costly. If so, then the true challenge for reformers is not to set prices accurately but rather to carefully affect organizational behavior. It is not imperative to obtain perfect or correct price structure immediately but rather to make sure that all organizations steer prices in that direction. In fact, only by properly altering organizational behavior is there any assurance that prices will stay at their optimal levels for an extended period.

At variance with the neoclassical paradox (intervention in the name of perfect markets), the evolutionary approach presents the state as largely antithetic to the market. The latter theory perceives the state as the true source of "market failures" and not their only remedy. Thus, monopoly rents are related to regulations blocking "entry," whereas, say, above-equilibrium wages (and unemployment) are caused by labor laws tilting bargaining power toward unions. Whenever state intervention is welcomed, the prescription is that action be taken cautiously, since it is not maximum credibility but rather the relative neutrality of an action that is critical (see Hayek 1945).

The root difference between the neoclassical and evolutionary views is their understanding of what type of information is essential. Whereas the former points to prices, the latter holds that the most relevant information is so-called tacit knowledge (Hayek 1945, Oakeshott 1962). This type of organization-specific knowledge is acquired only through repetitive experience and is stored through "routines." The routines, or subconscious patterns of behavior, are the most essential organizational asset, for they allow organization members to "automatically" respond to variable price signals without overloading their limited computing capabilities.

Since, as Hayek argues, such organization-specific knowledge takes a long time to develop, it can be useful only if the environment around a respective organization remains relatively stable. Routines can be changed slowly in response to measured variations, and with a proper allowance of time, they can even be fully transformed. (For more discussion, see Murrell 1992, 1993). But if the amount of change faced by an organization is excessive, then routines are invalidated and the ability to process incoming signals is lost. A decline in efficiency, or even phasingout—bankruptcy—will then follow.

Working within the above paradigm, one might suggest that the crisis in Eastern Europe is a case of imposing too much change on state-owned enterprise. It could well be that rather than producing positive synergy, the simultaneous change of prices on all possible markets—for labor, capital, money, and foreign exchange—has depleted much of enterprise's ability to process information. This would explain not only the abruptness of the initial post-shock declines in production but also the durability of recessions, since recovery can materialize only through the necessarily slow rebuilding of computing capabilities (see Charemza, 1993).

But information overload is not the only means of disarming routines: Adverse organizational changes might have the same effect. For instance, the loss of a segment of organization may reduce an organization's computing capability. Fragmentation of large enterprises has been widespread during the current transition. It has been a common practice to slice off "pieces" of state enterprises for privatization, as in Hungary (for more information see Grosfeld and Hare 1991). This has not necessarily been an all-optimizing reorganization, as blocks of "indivisible" state capital have often been sacrificed to facilitate small-scale acquisitions.

Incapacitation of routines may also be caused by erosion of organization morale: Cooperative behavior is replaced by indifference or sabotage, leading to efficiency loss. The threat of unemployment may stimulate efficiency, but if "rules" of terminating contracts are not well spelled out, response to the threat may be negative. The same dysfunctional behavior may be caused by the presence of rules that reflect the politics of a given workplace rather than its economic imperatives (i.e., labor productivity maximization). Largely unequipped to conduct orderly reductions and often highly politicized, state enterprises might have recently allowed a loss of morale.

Property Vacuum

Although the above behavioral hypothesis offers a broader view of plausible causes of the crisis than does the hypothesis on bank deficiencies, one still might find it too narrow. Economies are built not only of organizations but also of institutions that facilitate the credible commitment necessary for contracts (see North 1993). The principal institution is that of property rights, that is, the recognized (by law or custom) discretion over scarce resources. Property rights determine both the extent to which agents can internalize net benefits of their resource utilization and the level of costs of transacting or contracting.

Although this centrality of property rights was quickly gaining recognition during the final years of communist rule, there was no strong support for radical ownership reforms. The monoparty had no immediate plans for downsizing the state sector except through pocket-size spinoffs to industrious nomenklatura members. The opposition did not object to state ownership either but rather to the lack of genuine "social" control (so that its preference was for a labor-management style like that of Yugoslavia). Both sides agreed on one point, namely, that these economies would benefit if the state sector was supplemented with a thriving private sector (see Milanovic 1992).

The situation dramatically changed when postcommunist elites began formulating their plans for transition. Rapid transfer of state assets to private hands and the elimination of nonviable enterprises were declared priorities. Divestment of at least as much as half of the book value of existing state-owned enterprises within three years was adopted as a policy guideline in Hungary and Poland (Bolton and Roland 1992). Accordingly, preference was given to the least complicated forms of such transfer, that is, giveaway schemes, which bypassed both the barrier of costly asset valuations and that of limited personal savings (see Gomulka 1991, Blanchard and Layard 1992).

In reality, most of the state assets have not yet gone into private hands, and even conversions of state enterprises into jointstock have been limited (except for Hungary and Romania). Proponents of radical transfer find this situation the principal reason for the only partial success of monetary "shocks" and consider it a threat to the gains made (Sachs 1992).

The opposite view (Poznanski 1992) holds that actual transfers of assets have been very slow because such a complicated process could not take place much faster. This means that policies built on the assumption of fast asset transfers could instead be blamed for contributing to the crisis.

Those economists who find the actual pace of divestment a failure place blame squarely on what they consider an ineffective political system. It is argued that giveaway programs or other ideas suitable for transfer acceleration have been captured by political forces, in which personal fortunes take precedence over concern for general wealth. Other economists disagree, saying that however attractive they may be theoretically, programs such as the mass distribution of shares are not well enough tested for politicians to readily agree on them. This seems to be the case when radical projects are too vague to be credible, causing politicians to stall for time and make repeated corrections (Murrel 1993).

Supporters of rapid transfer argue that the slowness of privatization perpetuates old habits of the state-owned sector, so that new "games" are played with old "tricks." This view implies that privatization programs do not affect state-sector enterprises until transfer is complete, as if this were a world of policymaking without "rational expectations" by policymakers. However, those accepting slow pace as a reality argue that because of games of anticipation, strategies of state-owned enterprises might change before actual privatization takes place. Thus, depending on how privatization is executed, old "tricks" could be replaced with new ones even more threatening to economic efficiency (Blanchard et al. 1991, p. 34).

Poznanski (1992) has offered a hypothesis that radical privatization programs declared at the outset of transition, rather than being neutral, have undermined the property structure in the state sector. A peculiar property vacuum has been created since enterprises have been left without any firm deadlines or even clear-cut ideas on the exact form of privatization. Thus, announced as immediate but not realized and claimed to be firm while being fluid, state-directed privatization programs have increased uncertainty over payoffs at the enterprise level. This uncertainty faced by enterprises appears to be directly responsible for output decline as well as for stubbornly high rates of inflation.

The property vacuum, seen basically as an unintended product of radical privatization, could have affected production levels in many negative ways. Thus, faced with additional uncertainty, enterprises could have simply reduced their output. Moreover, it is possible that state enterprises, being unclear about the future, found it advantageous even to allow for decapitalization. Enterprises could have neglected investment for the sake of consumption, that is, wages because of the very short time horizon. In addition they could have also engaged in asset stripping through sheer neglect.

High rates of inflation could also be attributed, in part, to increased uncertainty over property status—compounded by the ever-present threat of financial insolvency. The theory of "incomplete markets" posits that when faced with higher uninsured risks, enterprises will attempt to insure themselves by charging higher prices. These price margins are added as a form of insurance premium whether the enterprise is a monopolist or not (Charemza 1992). This particular explanation of inflation offers an alternative to arguments linking recent pro-inflationary tendencies to an ultramonopolistic industry structure.

The Legacy of the Communist Economy

The most recent past is that of the communist years, and thus there is a natural tendency to see it as the proper background for understanding the realities of the current transition. That this part of the past is closest to us does not mean, however, that our comprehension of it is necessarily any clearer than that of the earlier precommunist period. The distant past is hard to examine for lack of material facts and is often subject to manipulation, but the recent past is obscured by details and is also not yet easy to see objectively. Misinterpretations of real communism may easily lead to false arguments about the communist legacy.

Theoretical Interests

Among the most popular views stressing the negative role of the communist legacy is that one-party rule eliminated capital-based interest groups during the installment of communism and then prevented their reappearance. A capitalist system, resting on capital, has to be built during the transition without those having a real interest in creating conditions for the accumulation of capital. In the absence of strong "real" interests, weaker "theoretical" interests substitute, with the state taking on itself the role of creating the capital-based strata in the name of a preconceived model of "good" economy (for a full exposition, see Staniszkis 1991, Ekiert 1990).

Lacking personal payoffs, the state apparatus cannot be expected to put its full weight behind the cause of building capitalism. As ideas that drive the state are foreign to other social groups, legitimizing procapitalist measures becomes questionable. Unless the public is disjointed and/or the state is in a position to coerce people, execution of the capitalist model becomes highly unstable and inconsequential. Under other circumstances, states quickly give in to even modest pressure from the discontented elements of the public, easily upset by even mild problems in transition.

The problem with the argument that there was an absence of groups promoting the interests of capital is that if taken literally, it leaves us without a clue as to why, at least during early "classical" communism, capital (profits) enjoyed priority over labor (wages). In fact, the main elements of the communist system seemed designed to give priority to capital over labor (e.g., suppression of trade unions, propaganda against luxuries, worknorm–breakers). That this actually worked is documented in very high capital expenditure ratios and a bias toward investment in capital-goods industries as well as in a strong preference for capital-intensive projects in those days.

Since the party monopolized power, one is forced to conclude that only its members could have acted as such a capital-based group (Gomulka 1986). It could be that this bias toward capital reflected the party's interest in maximizing power resources rather than capital itself. But this would really be only a semantic distinction since, from an economic point of view, what makes somebody maximize capital value is irrelevant. That capital was also wasted, and on a large scale, does not necessarily mean that it had no class representation but rather that this "real" interest was imperfectly served by the economic system (which incidentally was frequently "perfected" by the party, presumably not for ritualistic reasons only [see Poznanski 1993]).

Turning to the "baroque" stage of communism, I would like to note that by then the monoparty, an "interest group," was less attached to power itself than to wealth. The entry, during the Brezhnev era, of neotraditionalism with its patronage and corruption (Jowitt 1983) could be seen as reflecting this very shift in "preference curves." It was only a matter of time before major segments of the party realized that this mechanism of enrichment was too capricious. They also could not help but notice that storing durable goods has natural limits and that limitless expansion of personal wealth is possible only through capital.

This is not to say that at the "baroque" phase these motivations for capital accumulation were present only within segments of the monoparty, which was enjoying massive membership (and recruiting mostly from opportunistic elements). Rather, these interests also involved party families, who provided convenient camouflage for "second-economy" activities steered by party members themselves. Finally, there were others within the second-economy, who were closely intertwined with the party apparatus through various parasitic relations. Specifically, the party used the second-economy as a source of additional, unreported income for its members.

Since the growing desires could not be met by informal communism but only by formal capitalism, these elements in the monoparty and in the "dependent" sector of the second economy became interested in restoring capitalism. This is not to say that this protocapitalist group always expressed its aspirations in the language of capitalist "restoration." They could have had some illusions as to whether, say, a third way might satisfy their desire to accumulate capital for themselves. However, it was their own real interest, rather than someone else's "theoretical" interest, that made them shift their support in favor of genuine capitalism once all options had been opened.

The field of communist studies needs a paradigm to explain the collapse of communism, and the above theory seems an attractive first step. Its strength is that by attributing a central role in institutional change to the monoparty, it is consistent with the view of communism being based on an assymetric power structure. Another strength of this theory is that it identifies the same forces—aspirations for private wealth—as the key source of both the decay of communism and the rebirth of capitalism. It is the power advantage that has allowed "greedy" party elements—and their "dependencies"—to help eventually release this force in full (see also Poznanski 1992).

The above view goes beyond the limited perspective on change under communism offered by the dominant theories (for an eloquent review, see Janos 1986). Weber-type theories, which focus on routinization, are helpful in explaining why revolutionaries were replaced by bureaucrats. But the history of real communism is not simply (or mainly) that of communism becoming normal-bureacratic, like the capitalist societies. Modernization theories properly stress that with job-related changes in mentality, communism would have to relax constraints on consumer sovereignty but not be abandoned as a unified structure, as it was.

It seems that to grasp the logic of communist decay, there is little choice but to examine more carefully the literature that appears most appropriate, that is, that on the origins of capitalism. Capital has to be brought back to the analysis of communist dynamics, and thus so do the works that explain its formation as a social process. Marx, who was so impressed with the relentless forces of capitalism, would be one possible reference. Even more appropriate would be the evolutionary economics of Ludwig Mises, Hayek, or Schumpeter, who all explain the formation of capitalism as a natural order of things, called economy.

Utopian Thinking

Another, not unrelated argument on the negative legacy of communism centers on the preference for utopian thinking. It is said that communism, with its utopian elements, is now resurfacing in another form, either that of the "third road," wherein the workers are also capitalists (see Mokrzycki 1991), or that of another utopia, the free market (for more on that phenomenon, see Morawski 1993). The former might be considered a communist legacy in the sense that the third road presumes many of the communist premises. The latter utopia, calling for complete diversity and freedom, is of course foreign to that of the "planned utopia" which praised uniformity and regimentation.

This "market utopia" is a vision of a society where free markets regulate almost everything while the state is left with a subsidiary or rather marginal role. However, it is said that such a society cannot function since markets are too disruptive, if not in economic terms then in a social sense. The work of Polanyi (1944) on capitalism is evoked in this context to remind readers that the free market is a source of alienation of labor (and devastation of land as a common good). Only the state, by restricting the market, can assure social harmony and prevent economic excesses, so the superiority of the state over the market is imperative in the order to be formed in Eastern Europe.

Another feature of this new utopia is that it assumes that markets can emerge on their own. This, apparently, is a utopian assumption because, as we are told, the market economy—capitalism—is the product of state intervention. This is the view that Polanyi (1943) adopted in his famous account of the capitalist "great transformation." He claims that markets were promoted by the state for the sake of revenue increases, to finance "affairs" such as wars and splendor, rather than for purely economic reasons. If so, current transition in the region must be state-led all the way through (Kochanowicz 1993).

Polanyi's view is of course a broad social theory of capitalist transformation into socialism (communism), so before it is resurrected to illuminate the opposite case—which Polanyi did not predict—one has to reexamine the theory itself. For example, if "free" markets produce alienation, then alienation could not be the force that brought the communist system—absent of market—down. The only legitimate way of keeping alienation as an independent variable in a theory of communist decay would be to accept the notion that a "free" state—as under communism—could be a source of alienation, too.

The other problem with Polanyi's perspective is that the fate of communism is the best evidence that nothing as elaborate as an economic system can be "created" by a state and work. Since the command economy was created and did not work, it might then follow that a working market order could not be the creation of a state. In fact, the work of neoinstitutionalists shows that capitalism became possible only when an arbitrary state was shackled. Commercial courts, independently set up by merchants, were the source of rules that extended to the larger legal system, in which the capitalist system then nested (North and Weingast 1998; Milgrom, North and Weingast 1990).

This anti-Polanyi view is consistent with the evolutionary theory of institution formation, claiming that effective institutions are formed most successfully by "spontaneous" efforts, or trial and error, made by low-level economic organizations themselves. Enterprises are seen here as being responsible not only for organizing production but also for developing complex institutions within which production is conducted (see North 1992). Poznanski (1992) generalizes that markets—with independently acting organizations—are not only the most effective mechanisms for allocation of resources but for institution building as well.

Polanyi devoted his treatise to explaining that "free" markets cannot last, but the truth is that nothing close to this utopian construct was ever really advocated by its founders. Certainly philosopher-economists such as Adam Smith, who "discovered" the beauty of markets, had a very realistic view of them. Smith knew that no society can thrive on selfinterest alone and that altruism—compassion—is also a necessary ingredient of any working social order. As far as reality is concerned, capitalism has never come close to "free" market perfection. Price collusions, monopoly rents, kickbacks, wage-fixing, externalities, and so on have diverted the real market from achieving the ideal at any time.

Regarding the transition, it is rather doubtful that societies in the region, or even just their leaders, believe in a "market utopia." Indeed, the rhetoric of reformers is that of allowing only a minimum-state and letting the market put things in order. However, this language is, to a degree, a cover for postcommunist bureaucracy's inability to be a maximum-state. Another very practical reason for withdrawal is that the state found it to be the most effective tactic for defending the budget from demands for handouts by enterprises. The state also falters under pressures from "interest groups" to relinquish control over traditional monopolies and capture rents for themselves.

One area where the role of the state has not been greatly diminished, paradoxically, is systemic reforms, or designing economic institutions. If there is an element of continuity between the communist past and the postcommunist present it is in state "constructivism." Postcommunist reformers have been trying to "create" a market largely in the same fashion communist reformers tried to "design" an economy without a market or to "use" market to meet their particular needs. Whereas late communist reformers tried on their own to "simulate" a capital market (through, say, state holdings), their followers try to form such markets through their own conceived designs, such as the already mentioned giveaway privatization schemes.

Mistaken Identity

The radicalism of postcommunist reform could not be viewed as a communist legacy literally, since in its "baroque" stage communism was rather conservative. Thus, if there is any connection with communism, then it would have to be an indirect one. It could be argued, for instance, that this radicalism of the postcommunist period is a by-product of anti-communism. This could be called a communist legacy in the sense that anticommunism cannot, of course, exist without communism. If anti-communist "images" have survived communism itself, one possibility is that they might have had some influence on the style of postcommunist reforms.

A point could be ventured that during the communist period there were two utopias, not one: that of communism and that of anticommunism. Communism is a positive utopia of things to come, whereas anti-communism is a negative utopia of things to go. What the communist utopia was promising people was unrealistic, but anticommunism's criticism of the communist reality was not realistic either. In a way, it was a battle of two untruths for "truth," and it could not have been otherwise. The communist utopia could not have been fought with reason but only with another utopia. Only at the level of utopian thinking could these two meet and engage each other in battle.

The key assumption of the anticommunist (or totalitarian) utopia is that communism is static, frozen in time. Once power resources are captured by the party, the fear of loss of political control precludes substantive change. This is a situation of unstable equilibrium, where even a slight deviation from the existing balance, which involves power delegation, leads to a total collapse of the political structure. Since power delegation is needed to address increasingly complex issues, this means that unresolved tensions are bound to accumulate. As it is the society—not the party—that suffers from the costs of such inadaptability, resentment toward the party sooner or later turns into a revolutionary attack on the party.

Contrary to the utopian image, nowhere was real communism destroyed through a revolutionary act. Instead, power was given away through negotiations with the opposition, as in Poland or Hungary. Alternatively, power was peacefully reallocated within the party/state structure, as in the Soviet Union. When confronted with this reality, the anticommunist utopia has succeeded, for the recent events have been uniformly named revolutions, even called the first genuine cases in a broader class (e.g., proletarian [Burawoy 1989]). To recognize the lack of violence, the adjective "peaceful" has been added by some, diluting the meaning of the word (as would be the case with the phrase "violent compromise").

This claim of a dramatic ending to communism would be of no great consequence if not for the fact that it implies that with the defeat of communism came a "revolutionary opening," an opportunity for pushing through an unusual amount of change. This is because revolutions—real ones—remove anti-change segments within society, since stubborn minds constitute a major obstacle to change (e.g., Stalin's collectivization program was facilitated by the extermination of resourceful peasants). Moreover, the revolutionary fervor of the pro-change segments brings enthusiasm for radical change and a willingness to endure personal sacrifice, which is likely to be encountered in the process of change.

The image of a "revolutionary opening" encourages policy radicalism for another reason as well, since by claiming the violent rejection of preexisting structures, it implies that everything that follows must be unique. Thus, rather than building on the past's negative experience, searching for an ideal "place" in the future is encouraged. Another element that this notion of "revolutionary opening" introduces is the tendency to reject the existing ways of measuring economic performance as inadequate. Radical reformers therefore invent new meanings and put forward new measures, which can obscure reality if they all try simultaneously to set time forward.

It could well be that what has happened in postcommunist Eastern Europe is that reformers tried to carry out a revolutionary program in the absence of revolutionary conditions. This could explain why they applied market-based monetary "shocks" in economies lacking genuine markets. They assumed that with the party removed from economics, such markets would immediately emerge—which they have not. This could also explain why, when "shocks" have been followed by recessions, this has been perceived by the reformers, at least initially, as evidence of "hidden" progress—since to eventually succeed, state industry, as a remnant of communism, has to contract.

Modernization-Failure Theories

Whatever insight is offered by these theories about the communist legacy, they divert us—sometimes unintentionally—from seeking the roots of particular problems further back in history. Implicit in the legacy theories is the assumption that communism represented, as its ideologues claimed, a completely new epoch. However, even if this was true at the departure point, it cannot be said at the conclusion unless more communism "killed" less communism, which sounds like one paradox too many. Communism was rudimentary at the end, and even at the beginning it assumed many elements of its precommunist past (Tucker 1978).

Inadjustment Cycles

A good point of departure for analysis beyond the communist legacy is the fascinating historical account of East European modernization developed by Berend (1986). Its main point is that Eastern Europe has been particularly susceptible to periodic world crises, assuming here a much more severe form than parallel downturns in the rest of Europe. Berend distinguished two early such failed adjustments during the modernization period, one in the 1870s and another in the 1930s (i.e., the Great Depression), and then adds that in the 1980s (i.e., the energy crisis) the long-term pattern has been repeated.

Western Europe responded to the Great Depression, with a surge in technical change (Great Britain, for instance, introduced the mass production of automobiles). Eastern Europe has not reacted in the same way, so the economic costs of this inadjustment have had to be paid with foreign credit, causing another crisis—that of debt (as documented in, Berend and Rank 1974). During the more recent cycle, Western Europe responded to higher oil/gas prices by largely moving out of energy-intensive production. At the same time, Eastern Europe delayed its adjustment by borrowing on foreign markets, with a similar effect as in the past.

Although Berend does not make direct references to the concept of "long waves" (or "Kondratieff cycles"), it seems that the three downturns he mentions fall in this category. These cycles are commonly recognized for Western Europe (e.g., Great Britain and Germany) in the literature on long waves but not for Eastern Europe (for which the statistical material needed for testing has not been available). Berend's focus on technical change, as proper response, also echoes the core argument in the "long waves" literature which links this long-term rhythm with periodical clusters of techniques (Schumpeter 1942).

Building on Berend, the argument follows that the problem is not that Eastern Europe never responds to world economic crises but that it allows its crises to drag on and therefore its belated reactions tend to be extreme. Severe economic crisis translates into a crisis of public confidence in existing institutions as well as in the ideology that supports them. Consequently, the region responds to major inadjustments with general, total assaults on its economic system. Thus, for instance, the pains of the Great Depression could be viewed as leading to a surge of communist sentiment, which facilitated the postwar dismemberment of capitalism in Soviet-controlled Eastern Europe (for this particular point, see Berend 1993)

The paradox of the postwar systemic response to a production crisis—by replacing the market with a plan—is that it did not really allow for appropriate adjustment either. Rather than initiate necessary restructuring, it created a largely statistical illusion of economic progress. What it really meant was the "extensification" of economic growth by mobilizing (this time) domestic nontechnical resources (i.e., labor and minerals). This response was, in a way, a "regressive reform," a term that Berend (1986) used in another, earlier historical context (late feudalism, when serfdom was reintroduced in response to deteriorating conditions on world grain markets).

That the communist-type economy can only succeed in "extensification" of growth was theoretically worked out by Hayek (1939) as well as by another evolutionary economist, Mises (1939). They argued that at best this system is capable of assuring static efficiency but cannot support dynamic efficiency (i.e., technical change). Murrell (1990) has tested this theoretical point by examining the trade pattern of communist economies. He determined that these economies, while following their comparative advantage, showed considerable competitive edge in "stagnant" products (particularly those offering positive returns to scale) and weakness in "dynamic" (Schumpeterian) ones.

Thus, from Berend's perspective, the recent collapse of communism in Eastern Europe (and Russia, to which Berend extended his theory of the "crisis zone") would not be viewed as a separate, or unrelated, event. The communist economy would be a part of a long pattern of misguided overreactions that are characteristic of this region. This was not a "chance phenomenon," meaning one that did not have to happen, though it was not a logical consequence of "iron laws" either. If I understand the whole concept correctly, it is that following a protracted crisis, the existing order was likely to be replaced by communism or some other order offering an equally inadequate solution.

If, then, one pushes this approach a little further, the current transition could fit into the framework as well, even though I am not sure whether Berend would like his frame to be so used. Of course, replacing an early (and weak) model of capitalism from the precommunist era with an unworkable communist one cannot be compared with a return from real communism to some type of capitalism. But the radical form of the current transition in itself might be seen as similar to the form that the transition to real communism assumed in the past. This could be another case of overreacting to undeniably serious problems and not allowing things to be worked out at their own, if necessary, slow pace.

To experiment with this framework one more time, it could be argued that elements of regressivity might be present in the current systemic transition as well. Thus, allowing the large-scale state sector to free-fall could possibly be justified on the basis that it is a state but not necessarily because it is large scale, since existing units (plants) are not unusually large in comparison with advanced market economies. The welfare system is now being permitted to rapidly deteriorate as a state menace, but efforts to turn it over to private hands clearly go against the pattern that dominates in the majority of advanced capitalist countries.

The Demonstration Effect

The above argument is not really a theory of crises but is a framework in which to analyse them, for it basically says that there is a pattern of periodic regression in the regional economy. To fill this "model" with independent variables, one may turn for help to "global system" theories. These theories explain economic fortunes of economies not in terms of their own past but instead in terms of their past relation to a "core" of economic growth. Economies within a core are at an advantage, whereas those outside—in the periphery—are disadvantaged. Also, once established, such a relation is very difficult, if not impossible, to change; economies are "frozen" in the global system.

Now that Eastern Europe is discovering how far behind Western Europe it really lies, the core-periphery model is making its way into the debate on late communism as well as on the postcommunist present (Szelenyi 1991). If one assumes that contemporary Eastern Europe constitutes a periphery or semi-periphery, this would mean that after the communist episode the region returned to the status it held before. This does not mean that, inbetween, communism ever really took these economies out of this status but rather that it created a "myth" of this happening. This could be called a return only because now the reality—economic backwardness—is being exposed, that is, demythologized.

When looking for a suitable global system framework, one cannot but be attracted to the work of Janos (1982, 1991) who is among the few students of real communism who have employed this paradigm. His is not an example of mainstream global system analysis, which defines problems of periphery in terms of intentional direct surplus—profit—transfer by the core. Instead, relations within the global system are conceptualized in terms of indirect influence exerted by the core. This unintended influence over the periphery is termed by Janos "demonstration effect," a concept widely utilized in developmental economics for some time now.

The above theory of the demonstration effect is based on an observation that the distance between the developed and the backward is reflected in consumption and productivity. If there is communication between two such economies, the periphery will discover the consumption patterns of the well-to-do core. Although learning about this is easy, absorbing the qualities—the motivations and techniques—responsible for the productivity that supports affluent consumption is not. This distance between imported wants and domestic means is of fundamental consequence. To meet their wants, peripheral elites coerce workers into low wages but, since coercion—army, police—costs, the economy suffers and periodic crises become inevitable.

It is not that the periphery imports only models of consumption, but, when domestic barriers to affluent life are recognized, the elite turns to the core for economic institutions. Core institutions are viewed by reform-minded leaders as responsible for proper work habits and technical progress lacking in their economies. But, as with consumption models, not all core institutions are suitable for the periphery. Not only do they belong to a different—and more mature—stage of development but, when imitated, they are often deformed and thus made even less suitable. Since they fail to meet expectations, the transplants stir up political emotions that then disrupt economic performance.

Although Janos has used this framework mostly to analyse precommunist Eastern Europe, in his most recent work he has attempted to extend the model to an analysis of the communist collapse. Janos (1992) argued that the communist system can be viewed as a design to neutralize the influence of core consumption patterns. Insulation from the core countries—limits on foreign travel and the press—served this purpose, as did propaganda against conspicuous consumption. The communist party excluded itself from this austere lifestyle, creating niches of economic privilege wherein it could imitate—like elites in other parts of the periphery—the affluent consumption model of the core.

When applying the "demonstration effect" model to communism, one must be careful, however, not to forget that during its "classic" stage, communist rule did not allow for great disparity in personal consumption between the rulers and the ruled. So, if coercion was widely used, as it was, it was probably not to prevent protest against inequality (particularly since limited privileges were largely kept out of the public eye). Only during the "baroque" phase did the party begin to tolerate larger disparities, so for this period the model might be expected to be fully relevant. This would be the case if not for the fact that, at the same time, the coercion level subsided considerably (see Jowitt 1991).

After describing the communist countries as a periphery, subject to the demonstration effect, Janos (1992) claimed that, directly or indirectly, this effect was the single most important destabilizer of communist countries, without explaining how it worked. But within his model, one would expect the demonstration effect to undermine the communist system through the same mechanism that damaged precommunist Eastern Europe, that is, the diversion of resources to coercion. This is not an implausible hypothesis since the communist systems invested so much of their productive assets into forcing society to comply with the austere "life-style" chosen for them by the party.

Since within the theory in question another possible source of economic problems in the periphery is the importation of incompatible institutions, one should test communism on this account as well. It could be argued that this was a case of misspecification, since, although the Marxist doctrine viewed the communist system as an offspring of mature capitalism, it was tried in a protocapitalist region of Europe (see Bunce 1992). The evolutionary vision of communism growing out of capitalism (Schumpeter 1942) was turned into revolutionary practice and further twisted by adding a despotic meaning. Given all of these misspecifications, the communist order could not have produced economic progress.

As postcommunist economies have been borrowing, as one might like to call them, core institutions on a large scale, the potential for misspecification cannot be ruled out. Without using this language, some economists have argued that efforts to instantly create security markets by the giveaway of shares are premature. Others find security-centered capital market generally inadequate for the part of the world where bank-centered (German) financing has dominated. Doubts have also been expressed as to whether certain policies—such as stabilization programs from Latin America—have been appropriate given the obscure institutional setting existing in the region now.

Patterns of transition—and institution borrowing—have not, however, been uniform, particularly if one takes a longer perspective. Post-1968 reforms in Hungary and in China since 1978 clearly fall into a subcategory of their own. For instance, both have been much more reluctant to take any drastic stabilization measures and instead opted for a dual-track price structure (allowing for controls of sensitive products). Both have also been more willing to let "imperfect" institutions stay around while "perfect" institutions—such as "export zones" in China (Naughton 1993) or profit-oriented cooperatives in Hungary (Marrese 1983)—have been phased in.

Nation-Building

The above discussion suggests limitations of the global system framework, of which there are many more than those just indicated. One important shortcoming not mentioned is that societies are not only defined by their place in the global system but also define themselves as one nation against another. In particular, nations define themselves against their close neighbors, with whom they share the same space, in either a material or symbolic sense. Since space is scarce, societies struggle over it, and being a nation—a coherent unit—is an advantage. This is what gives practical meaning to the nation as a form of social ordering, and also to nationalism, as a motivator.

Studying East European modernization—the shift from an agrarian to an industrial basis—without reference to nation-building and nationalism would be superficial, since they are historically related. The turn to industrialization happens to coincide with the formation of nation-states and with a surge of nationalism (in a form of coevolution of economics and politics, techniques and ideas). The omission of nationalism as a factor in studying Eastern Europe would be especially awkward, because its abortive industrialization has been intertwined with frequently changing national fortunes, that is, incorporations and liberations, partitions and unifications (Rothschild 1989).

Fitting the communist period into this broad historical scheme of national misfortunes does not seem difficult if only one considers that communists in the Soviet Union first recreated much of the empire that their revolution destroyed and then expanded their control into other parts of Eastern Europe (initially by accepting territorial concessions from Nazi Germany and later by defeating it). With its many attributes, the communist system—both its language and structure—can be essentially seen as instrumental in extending Soviet domination to Eastern Europe (as captured in the concept of "two-tiered Stalinism," with the Soviet party using other parties to control other peoples [Bunce 1992]).

One might be tempted to view the communist system as a perfect instrument of Soviet control over the region, but it was not. Although efforts to turn the communist world into a family of nationless atheist workers served this purpose well, they also contributed to national unity in subordinate countries by eradicating class/religious differences. (One might note here that it is an ambition of ultranationalists to establish a nation of simple laborers, speaking with one voice or even looking alike). Compulsory politicization of the working masses was also useful in the propagation of this grand vision, but at the same time, it facilitated the process of nation-building in the region (as captured by Jowitt 1971).

How communism contributed toward nationalism can be observed in Poland, one of the more closely researched cases. Analyzing the worker rebellion of 1980–1981, Malia (1983) observed that the union movement resembled in many ways the insurrections during partition and that it also assumed many features of "gentry democracy." This is what one might expect given communist efforts to instill in workers a sense that they were the nation and given all the rewriting of history to portray simple people as the true heroes. Rather than changing the "script," these efforts resulted in adding new "actors" to play it, which they did with enormous power, since now they were the nation in a sense.

To bring economics into this exploration, one could adopt the argument made by a number of Polish analysts about the negative impact of

TABLE 1.1   Recession in Eastern Europe: Basic Macroeconomic Output
Indicators, 1989–1993 (in percentages annually)

	Albania	Bulgaria	Czech Republic	Hungary	Poland	Slovenia	Latvia	Russia
			Gross Domestic Product					
1989	11.7	−0.3	2.4	0.4	0.2	−0.5	–	–
1990	−13.1	−9.1	−1.2	−3.3	−11.6	−4.7	2.7	−4.0
1991	−29.4	−11.7	−14.2	−11.9	−7.6	−9.3	−8.3	−14.3
1992	−6.0	−7.7	−7.1	−5.0	1.5	−6.0	−33.8	−22.0
1993	11.0	−6.0	−0.5	−2.0	4.0	1.0	−19.9	−13.0
			Gross Industrial Output					
1989	5.0	2.2	1.7	−2.5	−0.5	1.1	3.1	1.4
1990	−7.5	−17.2	−3.3	−4.5	−24.2	−10.5	−0.2	0.1
1991	−30.0	−22.2	−24.4	−19.1	−11.9	−12.4	0.6	−8.0
1992	–	−16.2	−10.6	−9.8	4.2	−13.2	−35.1	−18.0
1993	−1.0	−9.3	−7.1	3.8	7.4	−2.8	−34.6	−16.2
			Gross Agricultural Product					
1989	10.7	1.2	2.3	−1.3	1.5	0.3	3.9	1.7
1990	−6.9	−6.0	−2.3	−3.8	−2.2	1.7	−3.5	−3.6
1991	−24.0	−6.4	−8.9	−5.0	−2.0	−3.3	−3.5	−4.5
1992	–	−12.5	−12.8	−22.7	−11.9	−10.0	−13.8	−9.8
1993	15.0	−20.1	−0.8	−25.0	2.2	−3.5	−11.5	−4.0

Sources: Economic Survey of Europe in 1993–1994, (Geneva: Economic Commission for Europe, UN); K. Dybaanda, J. Svejnar, 1994, An Overview of Recent Economic Developments in the Czech Republic, CERGE Working Paper Series No. 61, Prague.

national struggles on the economy throughout modern history, including the communist episode. In its very specific romantic brand, Polish nationalism mainly calls for patriotic sacrifice (see Walicki 1990). It focuses less on strengthening the nation by economic discipline than on sacrificing oneself (ban, jail, deportation). Although very effective in mobilizing a nation against oppressors, this brand of nationalism has made economic issues secondary—not to mention that the best talents have always been absorbed by, let us say, illegal printmaking rather than legal money-making activities.

TABLE 1.2   Recession in Eastern Europe: Labor, Price, and Wage Indicators, 1989–1993

	Albania	Bulgaria	Czech Republic	Hungary	Poland	Slovenia	Latvia	Russia
				Unemployment Rate (year end)				
1989	–	0.0	0.0	0.3	0.1	–	0.0	0.0
1990	9.8	1.8	0.7	1.7	6.1	5.3	0.0	0.0
1991	9.4	11.5	4.1	7.4	11.8	10.1	–	0.1
1992	26.7	15.6	2.6	12.3	13.6	13.3	2.1	0.8
1993	25.0	16.4	3.5	12.1	15.7	15.4	5.8	1.1
				Inflation (CPI)				
1989	–	6.2	1.4	17.0	244.1	–	–	–
1990	–	19.3	9.7	28.9	584.7	–	–	–
1991	104.0	254.3	56.7	35.0	70.3	117.7	172.2	216.4
1992	266.0	79.4	11.1	23.0	43.0	201.3	949.7	1020.0
1993	–	72..9	20.8	22.7	36.9	32.7	109.1	410
				Real Wages				
1989	–	3.0	–	0.7	8.3	18.4	4.6	–
1990	–	6.9	–	–3.7	–24.4	–26.5	5.3	8.7
1991	–	–39.4	–25.0	–4.0	–0.3	–15.1	–29.2	–7.2
1992	–	19.2	10.1	–4.0	–2.7	–2.8	–22.7	–29.8
1993	–	10.4	0.6	–1.6	–1.8	16.0	6.7	–1.7

Sources: Economic Survey of Europe in 1993–1994, (Geneva: Economic Commission for Europe, UN); K. Dybaanda, J. Svejnar, 1994, An Overview of Recent Economic Developments in the Czech Republic, CERGE Working Paper Series No. 61, Prague.

Conclusions

Spectacular economic occurrences such as the postcommunist recession in Eastern Europe and much of the former Soviet Union call for unconventional analytical approaches. Both the unusual depth of this recession and its almost universal character seem to suggest that structural factors—such as institutional change—rather than accidental ones have most likely caused this downturn. This is the reason why an institutional approach, broadly defined, seems to offer certain advantages compared to the common approach in explaining this recession in demand terms, respective economic policy errors, and/or independent shocks to various components of aggregate demand.

Common to all postcommunist countries in recession (as well as in transition) is the presence of major political dislocations related to the withdrawal of the communist parties and/or opening of space for contested elections. As I argue, with these political changes came fundmental fragmentation of their economic systems and therefore deterioration in economic performance everywhere. This appeared even in those cases where postcommunist governments proceeded with reform programs, that is, privatization (since these programs all called for a radical divestment of public assets and state refusal to closely manage remaining capital).

Although there is often a preference among economists (as well as political scientists) to view the communist period as a deviation from the historical, "normal" path in the region, there is also a tendency to present the postcommunist transition—as well as the accompanying early, or initial, recession—as unique or uncommon. From this intellectual perspective, recent political dislocations are an indispensible development, since to create space for parliamentary structures, the old communist ones have to be first eliminated—and for the same reason systemic fragmentation in the economic sphere is inevitable. In this sense, the postcommunist recessions can be blamed, at least indirectly, on the legacy of the communist detour from the "normal" modernization path rather than on possible policy errors.

However, it is possible that the communist period was not an isolated misstep in the modernization process in the region but just another ill-conceived attempt to speed up the modernization of these economies out of a feeling that regional backwardness is undeserved and correctable. Taking this approach, recognizing the possibility of a secular historical cycle, might offer an interesting insight into the nature of the communist episode in Eastern Europe. Seeking continuity rather than consequences, regularity rather than singularity, could also lead to the view that the postcommunist phase in institutional transformation might not be immune to missteps. This is not to say that endorsing capitalism could ever be such a misstep but rather that the choice of particular patterns (models) and the pace as well as the sequence of the reforms could be.

Bibliography

Berend, I., and G. Ranki. 1974. *Economic Development of East Central Europe in the 19th and 20th Century.* New York: University of Columbia Press.

Berend I. 1986. *The Crisis of Europe: An Interpretation of East Central European History in the First Half of the Twentieth Century.* London: Cambridge University Press.

Berend I. 1993. comments made at the conference: "Can Europe Work?," University of Washington, Seattle, May 21–22.

Begg, D., and R. Portes. 1993 "Enterprise Debt and Financial Restructuring in Central and Eastern Europe," *European Economic Review*, 37: 396–406.

Berg, A., and J. Sachs, 1992. "Structural Adjustment and International Trade in Eastern Europe: The Case of Poland," *Economic Policy* 13.

Blanchard, O., et al. 1991. *Reform in Eastern Europe*. Cambridge: The MIT Press.

Blanchard, O., and R. Layard. 1992, "How to Privatize," in H. Siebert, ed., *The Transformation of Socialist Economies*. Tubingen: Paul Mohr.

Bofinger, P. 1993, *The Output Decline in Central and Eastern Europe: A Classical Explanation*, CEPR Discussion Paper No. 784 (May).

Bolton, P., and G. Roland. 1992. "Privatization in Central and Eastern Europe," *European Economic Review*, vol. 37: 533–540.

Brada, J., and R. King. 1992. "Is There a J-Curve in Economic Transition to Market Economy?" *Economics of Planning* 25, no. 1 (March): 37–53.

Bunce, V. 1992. "Two-Tiered Stalinism: A Cease of Self-Destruction" in K. Poznanski, ed., *Constructing Capitalism: The Reemergence of Civil Society and Liberal Economy in the Post–Communist World*. Boulder, Colo.: Westview Press, 25–46.

Burawoy, M. 1989. "Reflections on the Class Consciousness of Hungarian Steelworkers," *Politics and Society*, vol. 17, no. 1 (March).

Calvo, G., and J. Frenkel. 1991. "The Role of Capital Markets," in P. Marer and S. Zecchini eds., *The Transition to a Market Economy*. Paris: OECD.

Charemza, W. 1992. "Market Failure and Stagnation: Some Aspects of Privatization in Poland, " *Economics of Planning*, vol. 25, no. 1: 21–35.

Clauge, C., and G. Rausser, eds. 1992. *The Emergence of Market Economies in Eastern Europe*. Cambridge: Basil Blackwell.

Commander, S. 1992. "Inflation and the Transition to a Market Economy," *World Bank Economic Review* 6, no. 1.

Coricelli F., and R. Rocha. 1991. "A Comparative Analysis of the Polish and Yugoslav Programs of 1990," in P. Marer and S. Zecchini eds., *The Transition to a Market Economy*. Paris: OECD.

Coricelli, F., and G. Milesi-Feretti. 1993. "On the Credibility of 'Big Bang' Programs," *European Economic Review* 37: 387–395.

Crane, K. 1992. "Taking Stock of the Big Bang " in K. Poznanski, ed., *Stabilization and Privatization in Poland: The Economic Analysis of Shock Therapy*. Boston: Kluver Academic Press.

Deawatripont, M., and G. Roland. 1992."The Virtues of Gradualism and Legitimacy in Transition to a Market Economy," *Economic Journal* 102 (March): 291–300.

Dornbusch, R., and S. Fischer. 1990. *Macroeconomics*. New York: McGraw-Hill.

Ekiert, G. 1990. "Transition from State Socialism in East Central Europe," *State and Social Structures Newsletter*, No. 12, Winter.

Gomulka, S. 1986. *Growth Innovation and Reform in Eastern Europe*. Madison: University of Wisconsin Press.

———. 1991. "The Causes of Recession Following Stabilization," *Comparative Economic Studies* 15: 396–408.

———. 1992. "Polish Economic Reform: Principles, Policies and Surprises," in M. Keren and B. Urf, eds., *Perils of Transition*, Boulder: Westview Press.

———. 1993. "Poland: Glass Half Full," in R. Portes, ed., *Economic Transformation in Central Europe*. London: CEPR.

Grosfeld, I., and P. Hare. 1991. "Privatization of Hungary, Poland and Czechoslovakia," *European Economy* (June).

Grosser, I. 1993. *Shared Aspirations, Divergent Results*, WIIW Forschungberiechte, vol. 191. Vienna: Vienna Institute for Comparative Economic Studies.

Hare, P. 1987. "Economic Reform in Eastern Europe," *Journal of Economic Surveys* 1, no. 1.

Hayek, F. 1945. "The Use of Knowledge in Society," *American Economic Review* 35.

———. 1939. *Collective Economic Planning*, London: Routledge and Kegan Paul.

———. 1944. *The Road to Serfdom*, Chicago University Press.

———. 1988. *The Fatal Conceit: The Errors of Socialism*, Chicago: Chicago University Press.

Hncir, M. 1992. "Money and Credit in Transition of the Czechoslovak Economy," in H. Siebert, ed., *The Transformation of Socialist Economies*. Iubingen: Paul Mohr.

Janos, A. 1986. *Politics and Paradigms: Changing Theories of Change in Social Science*. Stanford: Stanford University Press.

———. 1991. "The Politics of Backwardness in Continental Europe: 1780–1945," *World Politics*, vol. 45: 325–358

———. 1992. "Social Science, Communism and the Dynamism of Political Change," *World Politics*, vol. 44.

Jowitt, K. 1971. *Revolutionary Breakthrough and National Development: The Case of Romania. 1945–1966*, Berkeley: UC–Berkeley Press.

———. 1983. "Soviet Neo -Traditionalism: The Political Corruption of the Leninist Regime," *Soviet Studies*, vol. 35, no. 3: 275–297.

———. 1992. "The Leninist Extinction," in D. Chrot, ed., *The Crisis of Leninism and the Decline of the Left*. Seattle: University of Washington Press: 74–99.

Kirzner, I., ed. 1982. *Method, Process, and Austrian Economics*. Lexington: Lexington Books.

Kochanowicz, J. 1993. "Transition to Market in Comparative Perspective: A Historian's Point of View," in K. Poznanski, ed., *Stabilization and Privatization in Poland: The Economic Analysis of Shock Therapy*. Boston: Kluwer Academic Press.

Kolodko, G. 1991. "Inflation Stabilization in Poland: A Year After," *Working Papers No. 17*, Institute of Finance, Warsaw.

———. 1993. "From Output Collapse to Sustainable Growth in Transition Economies: The Fiscal Implications," *Working Papers No. 35*, Institute of Finance, Warsaw.

Kolodko, G., et al. 1992. *Hyperinflation and Stabilization in Postsocialist Economies*, Boston and Dordrecht: Kluwer Academic Press.

Kornai, J. 1993. *Transformational Recession. A General Phenomenon Examined Through the Example of Hungary's Development*, Collegium Budapest Discussion Papers No. 1 (June).

Kozierkiewicz, D. 1992. "Exchange Rate Policy and Economic Growth," *Working Papers No. 31*, Institute of Finance, Warsaw.

Lipton, D., and J. Sachs. 1990a. *Creating a Market Economy in Eastern Europe: The Case of Poland,* Brookings Papers on Economic Activity, no.1. Washington, D.C.: The Brookings Institution.

—————. 1990b, *Privatization in Eastern Europe: The Case of Poland,* Brookings Papers on Economic Activity, no. 2. Washington, D.C.: The Brookings Institution.

Malia, M. 1983. "Poland's Eternal Return," *New York Review of Books,* vol. 29 (September 26).

—————. 1992. "From Under the Rubble, What?" *Problems of Communism,* (January–April): 89–113.

Marer, P., and S. Zecchini, eds. *The Transition to a Market Economy.* Paris: OECD.

Marresse, M. 1983. "Agricultural Policy and Performance in Hungary," *Journal of Comparative Economics,* vol. 7., no. 3: 329–345.

Mayer, C., and J. Corbett. 1992. *Financial Reform in Eastern Europe: Progress with Wrong Model,* CEPR Discussion Report, no. 306.

Milanovic, B. 1992. "Poland's Quest for Economic Stabilization, 1988–1989," in K. Poznanski, ed., *Constructing Capitalism.* Boulder, Colo.: Westview Press, 43–62.

Milgrom, P., D. North, and B. Weingast. 1990. *The Role of Institutions in Reviving Trade: The Law Merchant, Private Judges and the Champage Fairs,* vol. 2: 1–23.

Mokrzycki, E. 1991. "The Heritage of Real Socialism: Group Interests and the Search for a New Utopia," Polish Academy of Sciences, Warsaw (mimeograph).

Mises, L. 1939. "Economic Calculation in the Socialist Commonwealth," in F. Hayek, ed., *Collectivist Economic Planning.*

Mizsei, K. 1933. "Hungary: Gradualism Needs Strategy," in R. Portes, ed., *Economic Transformation in Central Europe.* London: CEPR.

Morawski, W. 1993. "Narodziny Obywatela," Department of Sociology, University of Warsaw (mimeograph).

Murrell, P. 1990. *The Nature of Socialist Economies: Lessons from Eastern European Foreign Trade.* Princeton: Princeton University Press.

—————. 1992b. "The Evolutionary Approach to Economic Transition," in C. Clauge and G. Rausser, eds., *The Emergence of Market Economies in Eastern Europe.* Cambridge: Basil Blackwell.

—————. 1993. "Evolutionary and Radical Approaches to Economic Reform," in K. Poznanski, ed., *Stabilization and Privatization in Poland,* Boston and Dordrecht: Kluwer Academic Press.

Naughton, D. 1993. "Growing Out of the Olan: Chinese Economic Reform 1978–1990." Seattle, October 4, 1994.

Nelson, R., and S. Winter. 1982. *An Evolutionary Theory of Economics.* Cambridge: Cambridge University Press.

North, D. 1993. "Institutions and Credible Commitment," *Journal of Institutional and Theoretical Economics.* 149, no. 1 (March).

North, D. and B. Weingast. 1989. "The Evolution of Institutions Governing Public Choice in 17th Century England," *Journal of Economic History,* vol. 49: 803–832.

Nuti, D., and R. Portes. 1993. "Central Europe: The Way Forward," in R. Portes, ed., *Economic Transformation in Central Europe: A Progress Report.* London: Center for Economic Policy Research: 1–20.

Oakeshott, M. 1962. *Rationalism in Politics and Other Essays.* New York: Basic Books.

Polanyi, K. 1944. *The Great Transformation: The Political and Economic Origins of Our Times.* Boston: Beacon Press.

Portes, R. 1992. "Structural Reform in Central and Eastern Europe," *European Economic Review* 36.

———. 1992. "Introduction: European Economy," *The Path of Reforms in Central and Eastern Europe.* Brussels: Commission on the European Communities.

Poznanski, K. 1992. "Market Alternative to State Activism in Rebuilding Capitalist Economy," *Economics of Planning* 15, no. 1 (March): 55–77.

Poznanski, K., ed. 1993. *Stabilization and Privatization in Poland: The Economic Analysis of Shock Therapy.* Boston: Kluwer Academic Press.

Rodrik, D. 1992. "Foreign Trade in Europe's Transition: Early Results," CEPR Discussion Paper No. 676 (June) London.

Rothschild, J. 1989. *Return to Diversity: A Political History of East Central Europe Since World War II.* New York: Oxford University Press.

Sachs, J. 1992. "The Economic Transformation of Eastern Europe: The Case of Poland," *Economics of Planning,* vol. 25, no. 1: 5–19.

Schumpeter, P. 1942. *Capitalism, Socialism and Democracy.* New York: Harper and Row.

Staniszkis, J. 1991. *The Dynamics of the Breakthrough in Eastern Europe.* Berkeley: University of California Press.

Szelenyi, I. 1991. "Social and Political Landscape, Central Europe, Fall 1990," in I. Banac, ed., *Revolutions in Eastern Europe.* Ithaca: Cornell University Press.

Tucker, R. 1961. "Towards a Comparative Politics of Movement Regimes," *The American Political Science Review,* vol. LV, no. 2 (June).

———. 1974. "Communist Revolutions, National Cultures, and Divided Nations," *Studies in Comparative Communism,* vol. 7, no. 3 (Autumn): 235–245.

Walicki, A. 1990. 'The Three Traditions in Polish Patriotism" in S. Gomulka, and A. Polonsky, eds., *Polish Paradoxes,* London: Routledge.

2

The Principles of Privatization in Eastern Europe

Janos Kornai

A wide-ranging debate on privatization in Eastern Europe is taking place, both in the region itself and abroad, among Western experts. A hundred different views have been expressed so far and a hundred different specific programs have been put forward for resolving the problems in practice. I make no attempt here to formulate any hundred-and-first program, although I do put forward my own views. My main purpose is to help readers to conduct a methodical analysis of the problem.

I first formulated my own proposal in a book (Kornai 1990). This chapter further develops and expands the ideas I put forward on privatization in light of subsequent debates and practical experience. My earlier proposals on some questions are corrected in this chapter.

In my writings (1990a, 1990b), I expressed severe doubts concerning the viability of any kind of "third way," that is, a system that is neither communist nor capitalist. In particular, I pointed out repeatedly that the great "third way" experiments of Tito's Yugoslavia, Kadar's Hungary, and Gorbachev's Soviet Union are doomed to fail. They serve a certain good purpose in reeducating people, spreading the spirit of a market economy, and, most important, eroding the old structure and the old beliefs. But they are not able to create a society sustainable in the long term.

The much needed affinity between various components of the system is missing in "third way" solutions. The political monopoly of the com-

This chapter is based on the Fourth Tinbergen Lecture, delivered in Utrecht for the Royal Netherlands Economic Association.

munist part and the predominance of state ownership on the one hand cannot have a strong linkage with market coordination on the other hand. Sooner or later, the mutual incompatibility of the components leads to growing tensions and ultimately to collapse. My arguments concerning the failure of the "market-socialistic" experiments are summarized in my 1992 book, *The Socialist System*. The 1990 book envisaged a gradual shrinking of the state owned sector and also a gradual expansion of the private sector. There then would be an extended period of their coexistence, that is, a dual economy composed of these two sectors.

The word "privatization," featured in the chapter title, is used in two senses. In the narrower sense, it means the transfer of assets hitherto owned by the state into private hands. The broader interpretation covers the property relations in the economy *as a whole*, so that privatization of the economy must be understood to mean that the share of the private sector grows until it ultimately becomes the dominant economic sector. This chapter is concerned with the concept of privatization in that broader sense. The chapter title mentions Eastern Europe, and in the main the chapter deals with the group of small countries embarking on the road of postsocialist transition. However, I believe that most of the problems discussed resemble those in the Soviet Union as well.

Values

Some of those taking part in the international debate put forward their practical proposals on privatization without clearly answering some crucial questions: What purposes do they want the process to serve? What values do they seek to implement? What criteria do they intend to apply to the decision?

I share the philosophy of those who argue that the ends and the means must be clearly distinguished in any analysis of practical tasks. Lucid clarification of the criteria for judgment is also required for any subsequent appraisal of processes after they have taken place. Rather than attempting to detail all the values taken into account, I mention only the ones I consider the most important to the subject. I classify these under four aspects.

1. *The sociological aspect*, in longer, historical terms. What is the new democracy's direction of movement in a society inherited from the socialist system? Socialism in its classical, Stalinist form gave rise to a society that was governed bureaucratically and organized hierarchically. Nationalization extended beyond firms in production to cover practically every activity, so that every able-bodied person, with a few exceptions, became an employee of the state. In countries like Hungary, where reforms had begun many years ago, there had been a movement away

from that ultimate form of etatism before democracy arrived in 1989–1990. I shall not deal here with such transitional states but shall turn to the longer-term prospects offered by the process.

It would be desirable for the structure of society to resemble in its main features the structure of the most highly developed capitalist countries. A broad stratum of independent, autonomous businesspeople and entrepreneurs should emerge. Rather than the vast majority of the property being concentrated in the hands of just a small group, there should also be a broad middle class that includes the masses of owners of small and medium-sized enterprises. Society should undergo *embourgeoisement.*[2] The bureaucratic, hierarchical stratification of society should be widely superseded by stratification according to property. In other words, the hyperactive, overgrown role of the state in the economy should be reduced, even though the economic activity of the state will remain considerable.

All this transformation in the structure of society should be coupled with the modernization of production and the other activities of society, through the spread of up-to-date technologies and lifestyles. This "Western-style" image of society is seen as an attainable goal by many East Europeans who think about the prospects of transforming society, but it is not, of course, the sole course envisaged, even among those opposed to the concept of society espoused by the earlier socialist system.

Some people are put off by modern-day Western Europe and North America, with their business mentality, commercialism, profit-mongering, oversized and overcrowded modern cities, the environmental damage caused by industrial civilization, and many other drawbacks. So instead they tend toward an image of another, romantically unsullied society. Those subscribing to this kind of "third-road" weltanschauung are attracted by the proximity of nature in a village, by the peace of a small town, and by the simplicity of small-scale agricultural and industrial economies.

There is another "third-road" image of society where the intention is to blend capitalism with plebeian-cum-socialistic ideas. The goal becomes a "people's capitalism" that would turn all citizens into proprietors. All these images of future society have direct implications for the way the process of privatization is judged. I favor an orientation toward the "Western-style" social structure, even though I am aware that it has many bad features. I am ready to condemn these and advocate efforts to diminish them, but I am also aware that these bad features will inevitably appear. Those who subscribe to "Western-style" social development must accept it, warts and all. I do not consider the "third-road" images of the future just mentioned either practically attainable or desirable.

2. *The economic aspects.* This does not form a single criterion; a variety of economic interests can be taken into account. The most important economic criterion in my view is to arrive at forms of ownership that induce efficient production. One of the most damaging features of bureaucratic state ownership prevailing under the socialist system was that it gave little incentive to efficiency and in fact frequently encouraged waste. One of the missions of privatization must be to bring about a close and overt linkage between the direct financial interest of owners on the one hand and market performance and profit on the other. Let me pick out three other economic requirements which are also worth taking into consideration.

The privatization process should also help to reinforce the security of private property. Moreover, privatization can help to increase state revenue through the proceeds from the sale of state-owned property. In addition, it can provide relief from budgetary expenditure of subsidizing loss-making state-owned firms. Privatization can offer opportunities for finding new sources of tax revenue.

In view of the monetary aspect, the effects of some forms of privatization are anti-inflationary. They help to eliminate the "monetary over-hang" of unspent purchasing power. Other forms have the precisely opposite effect of increasing inflationary pressure.

3. The aspect of *political power.* Although scholars concerned with criteria of economic rationality or ethics may be averse to considering this aspect, the fact must be faced that privatization of any kind is a political issue. Governing political parties and groups want to reinforce and preserve their power, whereas those in opposition see the issue through the lens of their aspirations to form a government. So one cannot ignore the problem of how popular, deservedly or undeservedly, any privatization program will be.

Among the factors considered by those who want to return property confiscated by the state to its earlier owners is the political weight of the group it benefits, that is, how many votes can be won at the next election. Those who support employee ownership would like to win the political support of this broad stratum in society. Finally, advocates of giving free shares or vouchers to all citizens count on the idea being popular with the public as a whole. Those who seek political popularity through some scheme or other often forget to examine carefully and critically whether those whose approval they expect really are enthusiastic about the idea. I could hardly find a convincing public-opinion survey on the subject. I still have doubts, although I must admit that my skepticism is based on insufficiently reliable impressions. Those who receive the property may be disillusioned and angry, not politically grateful, to find what they receive is less than they expected and were promised and that the process is slow and cumbersome.

4. The aspect of *distributive ethics*. This system of criteria is another highly complex one, full of inner contradictions. The ethical principles considered here are confined to those connected directly with the distribution of income and wealth. Those who suffered losses under the previous system must be wholly or partly *compensated* during privatization. Some take the view that, where possible, the actual items of property confiscated should be returned if they still exist in their original physical form. Others support the idea that the compensation should merely be in money or securities. Several versions of the latter approach are conceivable, with various restrictions on redemption and the degree of transferability.

A range of difficult questions arises in this respect. What kind of injuries deserve redress? Should compensation be confined to the economic damage sustained through confiscation or should it cover losses of other kinds as well, ranging from cases of unjust imprisonment or execution to those who lost their jobs or were denied the chance to continue their education or to travel abroad? And what should be the earliest qualifying date? Should it be when the communists came to power or has the time now come to redress the injuries of those who received no compensation under the socialist system for losses sustained in World War II and the period of fascist rule, for instance?

Ultimately, those who espouse the ethical arguments for reprivatization want to apply the ethical principle of just recompensing. An economic argument can also be brought forward in support of reprivatization: Restoring the old property relations is a tangible demonstration of the idea that private property is sacrosanct. But this argument can be countered with another: The protracted process of reprivatization may undermine the security of property relations based on the status quo. A building or business claimed by a former owner may already be in private ownership.

Reprivatization can also conflict with other economic criteria. It robs the treasury of income or actually involves extra public expenditure. If those entitled to compensation are given securities and these can be traded, many will sell them in order to immediately spend the proceeds on the consumer goods market. That means this procedure will increase the inflationary pressure.

A further comment is needed on the programs for compensation through reprivatization. An attempt is made by their supporters to give the impression that the state is granting the compensation to a certain section of the public. But what is the state in this context but the sum of all the taxpayers? Compensation by way of reprivatization is a redistributive action that transfers wealth to the beneficiaries of the compensation from the pockets of nonbeneficiary, taxpaying citizens. There is no question of those who gained at the time from confiscation now recompensing those who suffered losses from it. The members of the present generation receiving no compensation have also lost, suffering like everyone else from all the consequences of the economic losses and backwardness caused by the previous system.

It can be argued on grounds of *moral entitlement* that a specific group has a right to some part of the state or other communal wealth in view of their social position. "Let the land belong to those who till it." "Let factories belong to those who work there." "Let state-owned flats belong to those who live in them." Even if the debate is confined to the ethical plane, it can be objected that the rest of society also contributed to creating these assets. Do today's tillers of good land, today's workers in a profitable factory, or today's tenants of attractive, spacious apartments really deserve more valuable property than those less fortunate? In the last resort, the slogans quoted are redistributive principles that favor some groups in society at the expense of the rest.

There are demands for *fairness* and *equality*. This principle is voiced chiefly by those who want to divide part of the property of the state among all citizens. The old system failed to fulfill its egalitarian promises: Democracy inherits a society marked by unequal distribution of material wealth and intellectual capital. Compared with these initial conditions, little is changed if rich and poor, well educated and unschooled, healthy and sick alike receive a modest free gift. Moreover, the free gift will soon be sold by those in need and bought cheaply by those who are clever and have the capital to buy it. Sincere advocates of a more equal distribution of income and wealth should campaign in the field of fiscal policy, welfare policy and education, and health and housing policy, where the scope for furthering their objectives is greater.

Privatization is intended to introduce a capitalist market economy. Although the market and capitalist properties have many useful qualities, above all the stimulation to efficient economic activity, fairness and equality are not among their virtues. They not only reward good work but also good fortune, and they penalize not just bad work but also ill-fortune. Although they are useful to society as a whole by encouraging exploitation of good fortune and resistance to ill-fortune, they are not "just." I think it is ethically paradoxical to mix slogans of fairness and equality into a program of capitalist privatization.

Mention has been made of a range of criteria whose appraisal can serve as a basis for arriving at a position on the question of privatization. Some of these are compatible and complement one another. But there are also values that conflict with each other in this particular context. Short-term economic interests may clash with the long-term interests behind the transformation of society. Ethical considerations may run up against sociological or economic requirements.

Even though I am an economist, I rate the first aspect, the long-term sociological criterion, as decisive, and I also opt forthe subsequent alternative, as I consider the emergence of a broad stratum of entrepreneurs and businesspeople and widespread *embourgeoisement* to be of paramount importance. I accordingly place the strongest emphasis of the economic arguments on that which maintains that privatization must be accomplished in a way that gives the strongest incentive to efficient production. Although the other economic criteria are also important, I rate them as subordinate to the ones I have mentioned. I acknowledge that aspects of political power also apply, but they do not influence me in my choice of values. I am not indifferent to the moral aspects of distribution, but I would refrain from applying them in the context of privatization.

Naturally I respect the right of others to choose values different from my own. What I would like to recommend to statespeople, legislators, the specialists who suggest legislation, and the journalists who monitor and criticize the plans and their execution is this: Let them analyze and make public the choice of values that justify the privatization programs they support. Let them face up to the conflicts of values and the "trade-offs" between conflicting requirements and admit it openly if they jettison one value in favor of another. Let them refrain from pretending that the practical proposal they prefer is a neutral one that would further all the values for consideration equally well.

The Transformation's Evolutionary Nature and the Role of the State

A view widely spread is that state institutions should play a very large part in privatization. Such a view can be found in governmental circles. In Hungary, for instance, a central authority called the State Property Agency tried for a long time to concentrate almost every act of privatization in its own hands. (A similar kind of centralization could be observed in Germany.)

The Hungarian privatization process has been rather centralized, but to a less extreme degree than at the time of writing the original chapter. Later rules allowed the management and/or the employees of the state-owned enterprise to initiate their own privatization. Either the enterprise or the potential buyer was permitted to use the services of specialized private consulting firms to assist in privatization.

It is remarkable that there is no single scheme emerging as the single (or at least the most frequently used) procedure. There is a huge variety of schemes, legal forms, and formal and informal procedures leading to the final end result: the shrinking of the state-owned sector and the growth of the privately owned sector. The mushrooming of various transformation procedures gives further support to the evolutionist philosophy of privatization.

There is also strong emphasis on the role of the state in the views put forward by many foreign experts, who certainly cannot be accused of wanting to increase their own power. One of such proposals is for the Soviet Union to quickly establish twenty investment funds by state decree. The managers to head them should be appointed by government, with the advice of experts from abroad. The funds should be assigned the shares in the firms formerly owned by the state, and the stock in the investment companies should then be distributed free to all citizens.

I think the inordinate state centralization of Hungary's privatization and the notion of forming investment funds by state decree to manage private property are good illustrations of what Hayek termed a constructivist approach.[3] They are artificially created, whereas the vitality of capitalist development is a result of the fact that its viable institutions arise naturally, without being forced.

During the period of Stalinist collectivization in the Soviet Union, it was possible to eliminate the class of well-to-do farmers, the kulaks, by state decree. But no state decree can create a class of well-to-do farmers; that will emerge only by a process of historical development. The state can decide to implement confiscation, but no state resolution can appoint a Ford, a Rockefeller, or a DuPont. The selection of the class of owners in a capitalist economy takes place by a process of evolution. And the evolutionary process selects among the institutions and organizations that emerge, causing the ones that are not functioning well under the prevailing circumstances to wither away and choosing as survivors the ones truly fit for their task.[4]

The Polish economist J. Kowalik coined the ironic term "etatist liberalism" for the curious school of thought that suggests pursuing liberal objectives (private property, individual autonomy, consumer sovereignty) by artificially creating organizations contrived by officialdom and aims at controlling the transformation of society by bureaucratic state coercion and administrative measures.

The state should primarily be expected to stand aside from the development of the private sector and ensure that its own agencies remove the bureaucratic obstacles, though there are a number of feasible state measures that go beyond this and actively assist in the privatization process. But governments should not be expected to replace the spontaneous, decentralized, organic growth process of the private economy by a web of bureaucratic, excessively regulatory measures and a hive of zealous activity by state officials.

Types of Owners

Personal Owners

First let me give a few examples, to make this concept clear.

One example is a family farm or a family undertaking in another branch of the economy, that does not employ labor apart from family members more than occasionally. Next there is a small or medium-sized firm in which ownership and management have not been separated and the owner remains in charge. Another case is a newly founded firm in Schumpeter's sense, managed by the entrepreneur establishing it and normally employing borrowed capital, not the entrepreneur's own.[5] A further example is a joint-stock company of any size in which an individual or group of individuals has a dominant shareholding. This need not necessarily be a majority of the shares: A holding of 20 to 30 percent is often sufficient to give the dominant owner (or group of owners) a decisive say in the choice and supervision of management and in major financial matters and investment decisions.[6] Dominance of this kind can emerge so long as the other shareholders are sufficiently passive, which can be the case, for instance, if ownership of the shares is fragmented. The situation may be similar if the rest of the shares are held by the state, and the state refrains voluntarily from active intervention in the firm's affairs. Finally, this category includes a firm in which the former chief executive officer or a group of managers have become owners, or at least dominant shareholders, through a management buy-out.

I have not conducted a rigorous classification of mutually exclusive cases, merely listed examples, and these may overlap in some feature or other. The examples can cover small, medium-sized, and large firms alike. They may take legal forms that entail unlimited liability or liability limited to various degrees and may range from a family farm to modern joint-stock companies. So what, in the end, do these cases have in common? They share the presence of a live, visible, and tangible person or group of persons at the head of the firm. This individual, family, or group has a strong and direct proprietorial interest, so that the size of the firm's profits or losses affects the owner's pocket. In addition, the owner either runs the firm directly or plays a dominant role in hiring and firing the managers and overseeing what they do.

A personal owner can enter the stage of the postsocialist economy in two ways. One is by setting up a brand new undertaking. The other is by buying part or all of an existing state-owned firm. The two methods are often combined: A state asset is bought by an existing private firm.

I believe this personal owner to be the key figure in East European privatization. The appearance of personal owners on a mass scale will ensure to the greatest extent the desired transformation of society, the *embourgeoisement*, and the incentive toward efficiency. Moreover, if one constituent of this process is the purchase of state assets, it will also satisfy the fiscal and monetary criteria. It can be stated, therefore, that the vaster the area in which ownership and control pass into the hands of personal owners, the more successfully privatization will proceed. One of the most encouraging features of the transformation in Eastern Europe is the perceptible advance of this evolution.[7]

There is a widespread notion that an upper limit on privatization by purchase is set by the amount of savings accumulated by the general public. Comparisons of the savings at the public's disposal with the value of the state's wealth are used to arrive at alarming forecasts. The early conclusion reached was that it could be 50 or 100 years before the public has managed to buy up the state's wealth. So there is no other solution: The property of the state can be reduced quickly only by distributing state assets free of charge.

In my view this line of argument relies on false premises. The purchasing power intended by the public for investment (including the purchase of state property) can be multiplied several times by suitable credit and deferred payment schemes.[8] The proportion of the down payment to the credit or deferred payments can be as little as 1:10 or 1:20. This proportion determines right from the start how much of the state's wealth can be bought by those wanting to go into business with the savings they initially possess. In addition, the process can speed up as soon as some of the businesses start to show a profit and a greater propensity to invest. Above all, domestic and foreign banks and other financial intermediaries control the range of attractive credit and deferred payment schemes they offer. Moreover, the main way foreign governments and international financial and economic organizations ready to help can contribute to building up the private sector in Eastern Europe is by setting up financing and backing schemes of this kind.

To some extent special "venture-capital" institutions will have to be established, for there is no denying that special risks are attached to lending money to new private businesses in a postsocialist economy. But these risks can be reduced by an appropriate mortgage system to ensure that the property reverts to the lender if there is a default on the payments. Alternatively, the lender can be a co-owner from the outset. And if the state really wants to be active, it should go about it by offering at least partial credit guarantees that lessen the lender's risk. The majority of private entrepreneurs will, in any case, be more reliable borrowers than many inviable state-owned firms that repeatedly bailed out even though they defaulted on their loans.[9] As long as the credit and deferred-payment schemes are devised with sufficient caution, they will not entail a risk of inflation. In fact, the debt repayments and interest will siphon some of the potential consumer spending away from the entrepreneurs.

It is worth drawing particular attention to the question of management buy-outs. The public is ambivalent toward them. It is pleased that experts, rather than dilettantes, take over the factory, but it is displeased to see members of the "nomenklatura" under the old regime transmuted into born-again capitalists. In my view it is not worth legally prohibiting something that will inevitably occur. Experience of the past few years provides ample evidence to support this conclusion. In Hungary there are many cases where management transferred assets informally (and in many instances illegally) to private hands, including their own hands. It is important to recognize that in such changes the main issue is the transfer of intangible assets, such as business connections, marketing experience, skills, routine, and the firm's goodwill. This part of the formerly state-owned firm's wealth can be much more valuable than the physical assets, which are obsolete and get worn out quickly. It is more expedient to bring the occurrence into the open and place it under the supervision of the public, the law, and the appropriate authorities. Clarification of the moral and business rules for management buy-outs is needed, including the normal credit terms. Let a manager or group of managers capable of buying a business property from the state according to these rules do so by legal means.

Special attention should be paid to the question of peasants wanting to farm privately, private small-scale industry and trading, and small business as a whole. It is quite common in the developed market economies for these groups to receive credit on favorable terms and to receive possibly longer or shorter-term tax reductions. This is appropriate in Eastern Europe as well, particularly now, when the aim is to set these groups on their feet and encourage new small businesses on a mass scale. An important ingredient in the process of creating a broad middle class is the speeding up of the development of small and medium-sized firms.

This ties in with another range of problems: how to overcome the distortion in the size distribution of firms. Excessive concentration took place in the socialist economy. Whereas the larger proportion of employment in most West and South European countries is in firms with less than 500 employees, small and medium-sized firms in most East European countries were wound up on a mass scale or artificially merged.[10]

The need for a healthier size distribution is among the reasons for giving favorable consideration to credit applications from small and medium-sized businesses.

Employee Ownership

I am thinking here of the form in which the shares in a state-owned firm that has been converted into a joint-stock company are taken up by its employees. The most commonly used term for this is employee stock-ownership plan (ESOP). The idea comes in a number of variants; in some the employees receive all the shares, and in others only a smaller proportion. The proposals also vary on the conditions under which the employees receive the shares, ranging from entirely free distribution to price and payment conditions that are more favorable than the market terms. Finally, various suggestions have been put forward on what limits to place on the sale of the shares, for instance, restricting transferability either temporarily or permanently.

The decisionmakers are influenced primarily by the political criteria when they consider this form of ownership. So long as the politicians have convinced themselves through reliable research into public opinion that there is a real call for employee stock ownership, and that employees actually demand it, I see no particular danger in accepting some moderate version of it, that is, in offering the employees, on favorable terms, a fairly small proportion, say 10 to 20 percent of the shares in a firm due to be privatized. In my view, it is more expedient to offer the shares for sale to the employees at a large discount than to give them away for nothing. In the case of a smaller firm, it is also conceivable for all the shares to pass into the hands of the employees, in other words, for the form of ownership of the firm in question to come close to a partnership or a true cooperative.

The consistent (or perhaps I should say extreme) advocates of employee ownership go much further. They would like all state-owned firms (or as many as possible) to assume this form of ownership entirely, irrespective of their size. Many of them couple this proposal with the idea of transfer free of charge. They put forward two main arguments for their position. One is that an employee who is also an owner will have a stronger incentive to produce efficiently. I do not see proof of this. On the contrary, if employees choose their own managers, the managers become dependent on their own subordinates, which can undermine wage and labor discipline. Sufficient evidence for this assumption is provided by the experience with workers' self-management in Eastern Europe, particularly Yugoslavia.

The other argument advanced for comprehensive employee ownership is to let the factory belong to those who work in it. I would expect the various forms of employee ownership to gain a position similar to the one they have in the developed West European and North American countries sooner or later; in other words, that they will represent a respectable proportion but they will fall far short of becoming the dominant form.

Institutional Ownership

This large group of property ownership can be divided into subgroups.

Banks and Other Banking Institutions. Some of the post-socialist economies inherited from the socialist economy a two-tier banking system in which there were already commercial banks alongside the central bank. Certain postsocialist countries that entered the postsocialist period directly, skipping the period of reform within socialism, still inherited the monobank system and are now obliged to set up a network of commercial banks. But whichever of the starting positions pertains, the banking sector has the following characteristics at the beginning of postsocialist transition.

The sole owner of the banks is the state. There may have developed what is known as "cross-ownership," under which state-owned firms outside the banking sector are shareholders in the banks, sharing ownership with the institutions nominated for the task by the state administration. Or a bank may hold shares in a state-owned firm that has been converted into a joint-stock company.[11] But cross-ownership remains merely an indirect form of state ownership and is no substitute for privatization.

The various organizations making up the banking sector of Eastern Europe are engaged in a quite narrow range of activities. Developed market economies possess a great many financial institutions that do not qualify as banks according to the strict legal and economic criteria in force, such as credit-card companies, venture-capital companies, investment funds, mutual funds, saving-and-loan associations, exchange bureaus, and so on. There are strong reasons why postsocialist economies need to develop a banking sector with a similarly varied and multiple profile.

Some of these banklike financial intermediaries (which cannot be called banks in the strict sense) may appear in private-ownership form from the outset. A major role in the development of the new quasi-banking institutions can be played by foreign capital. The development of genuine private banks, particularly large private banks, seems more difficult, even though their activity is clearly essential to a modern market economy. On the one hand, foreign banks can be expected to open branches in the East European countries, and of course these will be real private banks. It is possible that one or two institutions performing quasi-banking functions that were privately owned from the start may be converted into true banks. Smaller banks performing local functions could be formed by domestic entrepreneurs. Alongside all these developments, the privatization of the currently state-owned commercial banks will take place. Particularly in the beginning, this will presumably mean only partial private ownership and mainly foreign involvement.

Privatization of the banking sector[12] in the broad sense will not take place all at once. It will take some time before private property becomes the dominant ownership form. Several factors will play a part in this. One bottleneck is shortage of expertise, experience, and up-to-date technical equipment. In these countries where payment by check has yet to spread among the population and in trade and services. Another example of backwardness is that consumer credit is used only sporadically in these economies. Other requirements for development are the creation of requisite legislation and success in building up a system of state regulation and supervision of the banking sector. It would be desirable if state intervention were not on a scale as to stifle individual initiative, but at the same time the sector cannot be left to its own devices. The security of depositors and the financial stability of the country both require legal, insurance, and supervisory guarantees.

The subject so far has been privatization of the banking sector itself. However, this ties in closely with the privatization of other parts of the economy. Reference is often made by debaters on the subject to the German (erstwhile West German) and Japanese examples, where a sizeable proportion of industrial shares is in the hands of large banks. On these grounds the recommendation is presented that a considerable proportion of the shares in the state-owned firms should already have been handed over to the East European banks.

Not much will be achieved if this idea is applied prematurely and hastily; it will be ineffective chiefly in terms of the criterion of *embourgeoisement* and the criterion of ownership inducing efficient production, which I consider the most important. It will not produce a true owner with a strong interest in increasing efficiency. There are many cases at present where a large state-owned firm making heavy losses is closely tied up with a large state-owned bank, which may be a shareholder and is usually its main creditor. If that is the case, the bank and the firm share an interest in seeing the firm bailed out and artificially sustained. The danger is that if a bank, under the present property relations, is also a shareholder in large joint-stock companies, it will fail to apply business criteria adequately.

Another danger is that the state-owned banks will remain the "politicized" institutions they were before. The parties in government will, at any time, treat them as their own backyard and try to plant their own people in leading positions. This is also a warning against the plan to turn the banks in their present state into factory owners, through a deed of gift by the state, even though the banks themselves are owned by the state.

It will become desirable at a later stage for the ownership relations to develop along the lines just mentioned in connection with the Japanese and German examples. As the weight of domestic and foreign private ownership increases among the owners of a bank or a quasi-banking institution,[12] these individuals can become partial owners of formerly state-owned nonfinancial firms. The more a bank or other banklike financial institution operates on a truly commercial basis and is dominated by private ownership, the more it can be expected to satisfy the criterion of exercising strict control over the firm it owns and taking a truly proprietorial attitude. In other words, as privatization of the banking sector advances as an organic process, so, at the same rate, can whole blocks of shares and portfolios of holdings in various firms previously owned by the state pass into the ownership of the banks. For instance, such blocks and portfolios could form part of the state's capital contribution to joint ventures established in the banking sector.

Pension Funds. The pension funds have become one of the main holders of corporate shares in several developed capitalist countries. Notable in this respect is Britain, where more than half the shares are in the hands of the pension system.[13] The provision of pensions was a task of the state under the socialist system. Pension contributions were paid as tax and pensions were a liability on the state budget. Even where pension provision was in the hands of a separate institution and the sum received in pension contributions was nominally treated as a separate fund, any surplus in the fund was utilized in practice by the state and the state covered any deficit. Although the real value of pensions was always quite low, and further reduced by the effects of inflation, the nominal sum was guaranteed by law. No other decentralized pension system operated in the socialist economy.

Radical alteration of the pension system came on the agenda during the postsocialist transition, but the final forms it will take have yet to be developed in many East European countries. The pension systems of the developed capitalist countries are not uniform in any case, and no consensus has emerged in Eastern Europe on which Western country's pattern to follow. The role of pension funds cannot be avoided in connection with institutional shareholdings. I therefore start out from the following assumptions.

Sooner or later a mixed system emerges. One of its segments is a state scheme with the task of guaranteeing a pension on at least a subsistence level for those qualifying for it. Of course a guaranteed state pension above this minimum level can be laid down by law, but this must be done only in the knowledge that the ultimate financial source is taxation or social security contributions collected in the same way as taxation.

The other segment of the pension system is private in nature, and its primary source of funding is the payment of voluntary contributions. Their cost is shared between employers and employees according to legal stipulations and labor contracts. The network of pension funds is decentralized, and it can be joined by both nonprofit organizations, whose sole task is to provide their members with pensions, and profit-oriented insurance companies, which undertake to pay annuities similar to pensions.

The revenue and expenditure of the state segment rest on compulsory legal stipulations. Membership of the private segment, however, is voluntary. Employers and employees are free to decide whether to join. In the case of a developed decentralized pension system, every employer or employee can choose between several kinds of private pension schemes.

There is no way of telling beforehand exactly what the future pension system in Eastern Europe will be like, but it seems quite realistic to assume that it will resemble the system just outlined. Nominally the idea came through in Hungary: A centralized, state-supported social security system based on mandatory contributions and decentralized pension funds based on voluntary contribution do exist side by side. Their shares are, however, quite disproportional, as the first one is huge and the second one miniscule. The transfer of formerly state-owned assets to the centralized fund had been promised; the initial capitalization of the weak decentralized pension funds did not even start. It is also clear that the transition to a mixed system (containing a private segment) can only be gradual, for the starting point differs among generations. Those already on pension or approaching pensionable age no longer have a choice: They must be provided with a guaranteed pension. The longer the life expectancy for individuals, the more possible it becomes, in this respect as well, to offer them freedom of choice. They may decide at their own risk whether to devote part of their savings to some private pension scheme or other. It will clearly be a long time before a mature, responsible, decentralized private pension-fund sector develops. This also belongs to the type of process I termed organic development.

Let us now return to the question of shares. Numerous private pension funds in the West invest the capital accumulated from contributions in shares and other securities.[14] The funds employ professional managers who try to build up the most favorable portfolios, paying close attention to the interests of their members. Although they are able to control all purchases and sales of this enormous fortune, they can assert

privatization. A municipality is part of
property is passing from one arm of the
tioning this because the first four above
ownership, which can really imply priv
in debate with the fifth type, which is n
state, not privatization at all.[16]

It is inadvisable to create the institut
ership in a bureaucratic way, by state de
being inexpedient, it is not usually poss
will arise through processes of evoluti
develop depends on several factors,
domestic and foreign capital to invest ir
institutions, insurance companies), and
foreign professional staff capable of mar
lios (banking institutions, pension fund
and educational institutions, charitable
it also depends on the activities of the
apparatus: on how fast the right legal fra
tutions develop, how much initiative the
the requisite new institutions into being,
is a free transfer of state property to crea
nizations serving as institutional owners.

Anonymous Shareholders

An important part in modern, mature
mous shareholders who do not possess
selves heard directly at the general meeti
are able to vote with their feet. If they do
the future profitability of a firm in comp
alternate investments, they sell their shar
buy shares. The trend in the demand, sup
exerts indirect influence on both the maj
the general meeting and the managemen
influence is applied through a broad netw
exchange, the brokers, and the banks
dealing with the purchase and sale of shar

These institutions of ownership are b
European economies as well. Stock exch
capitals of a few countries and they issu
daily prices of the publicly traded shares. I
It will take time before this form of owne
and secondary markets for securities, bec
of organic development. A great many

their influence only indirectly, by buying certain securities and selling others. Their transactions influence market prices, which are then reflected in the valuation of the companies. This ultimately has a disciplinary effect on company managers, as a sharp drop in the valuation of their company sheds a bad light on them and a conspicuous rise in valuation is evidence, of varying accuracy, of their success. In all events, this kind of ownership only partially satisfies the criterion of providing an inducement to company managers and effective control over them.

Starting out from the value premises put forward in the first section of this chapter, the conclusions in relation to privatization are obvious: It is worth aiming to turn the decentralized pension funds into shareholders. There is no need to rely exclusively on them investing part of their accumulated contributions in shares at some future date. The establishment of nonprofit, private pension funds could be helped in the first place if each were assigned a portfolio of previously state-owned shares as a constituent of their initial capital. The transfer can even be free of charge, for there is an implicit offset: They are taking over some of the pension commitments that have hitherto been borne exclusively by the state budget.

Legislation is needed, of course, to lay down the conditions for such transfers. Care must also be taken to provide them with portfolios of shares that can be expected to have a positive yield. Otherwise the transaction will be fraudulent, for the ones who suffer will be the pensioners whose pension expectations include the prospective yield from the fund's shareholdings.

Moreover, the difference between pensions from the state and pensions from the private segment must be made clear to the voluntary members of the decentralized pension systems. There is a degree of exposure in either case. Pensioners in the state segment are at the mercy of those who devise and apply the legislation on pensions provisions, whereas pensioners in the private segment are exposed to the fluctuations of the security market and to the degree of success with which the private pension fund manages its securities.

The value premises also show what plans should be rejected. The idea has come up that the state pension system should receive shares before any decentralization and privatization of the pension system take place. In Hungary, for instance, the transfer has actually begun. This move, in my opinion, is a pretense, from which no particular benefit can be expected. The centralized, state pension system is a branch of the state bureaucracy, and so it should be. But if its function is to provide pensions guaranteed by law, its sources of income should not be exposed to the fluctuations of the stock market or the fortunate or unfortunate trends in corporate profits.

Insurance Companies. Here th[
the pension system, so the conclu[
previous point. So long as the insu[
tic institutions exclusively owne[
measure to transfer shares to the[
cross-ownership since one state-o[
another.

The value premises I have mad[
partial privatization of the insura[
state and private segments opera[
both nonprofit and profit-oriented[
panies should be encouraged to in[
in shares. With suitable legal guar[
hand share portfolios over to no[
charge, as a way of encouraging t[
This again is a kind of ownershi[
offset: The private insurance secto[
development can steadily take o[
guaranteed state insurance system.[

*Cultural and Educational In[
Foundations, Churches.* The list co[
developed market economy may[
savings in shares or other securiti[
Eastern Europe. The tighter the bo[
tution to the institution itself, the s[
the responsibility they feel for the p[
financial position, the more they ca[
ans of the wealth placed in their c[
such institutions must find financia[
of handling their securities professi[
potential buyers of state property:[
purchase shares.

But the process can be speeded [
advance any argument against suc[
lios even free of charge. The only[
and supervisory guarantees. And[
there are the vital social conditions[
ing the gift of state property will[
those running it have the institution[

Local Governments. Some of[
managed centrally is likely to be tra[
ernment authorities. This is a necess[
motes the decentralization of po[

happen: expertise and routine, confidence, a large corpus of competent staff, the right legal regulations, effective state supervision, and so on.

Let us take a look into the more distant future. One can expect the role of joint-stock companies and the distribution of their ownership to develop in a direction similar to the one in the developed capitalist countries. So what are the characteristics of the situation there? In a range of European countries where the capitalist market economy has operated continuously, without the interruption of the socialist system, only part of the total productive wealth operates in the corporate sector, composed of joint-stock companies, and only a proportion of the corporate sector is accounted for by companies whose shares are publicly traded.[17] This proportion is smaller in continental Europe than in the United States or the U.K.

Some people are prepared to invest their savings in shares voluntarily. But others will not take the associated risk and prefer other kinds of investment. That is one explanation for the concentration in the distribution of share ownership. In the United States, for instance, the Securities and Exchange Commission has demonstrated that 87 percent of the population on the lower level of income distribution owns only 1 percent of the shares, while those in higher income brackets own 99 percent. Within this group, the richest 1 percent own 80 percent of the shares, and the very richest 0.1 percent own 40 percent of the shares.[18]

So real capitalism is not "people's capitalism." In light of the U.S. figures, it seems a curious idea to turn all citizens into shareholders overnight by a free distribution of shares. To use Hayek's terminology again, this is a constructivist idea, artificial, contrived, and therefore quite alien to the real development of capitalism. I do not think the whole population treasures an inward desire to own a little piece of share capital. Moreover, there is a danger that the expert, honest, and adequately supervised institutions and staff required for a primary and a secondary market in shares of such a giant extent will be absent.

I expect only one benefit to come from mass share-distribution campaigns, and that is a drastic reduction in the proportion of state ownership. This reduction may facilitate the expansion of a dominant group inside a joint-stock company, because it will no longer be confronted with a predominant state owner. This advantage in itself should not be underestimated, but one cannot expect too much of it either. Ownership of share or voucher allocations for every citizen will do little to further the two purposes to which I gave particular emphasis in the section on value criteria: development of broad strata of entrepreneurs and businesspeople and strengthening of the incentive toward efficiency.

At the same time, I fear there will be negative effects for the other economic criteria. The state treasury, hard pressed in any case, loses the potential income from sales. Some recipients of the gift soon pass on their shares or vouchers and appear on the consumer market with the proceeds, which raises the inflationary pressure. In all events, this is a trade-off in which the advantages of speeding up privatization are opposed by drawbacks which merit serious consideration. It seems there will not be a general, free distribution of shares or vouchers in East Germany or Hungary, but implementation of such ideas are quite far advanced in Poland and particularly the Czech Republic. Experience may refute the skepticism expressed above, in which case I am prepared to review my position.

As mentioned before, the justifications given for schemes that distribute shares or vouchers to all citizens free of charge include arguments based on distributive ethics as well: This is considered to be a start for the new capitalism that is fair and offers equal opportunities. Those who really want to improve the equality of opportunity and approve of distributing state property free of charge should press for the donation of truly profit-yielding shares to charities, health and educational institutes, foundations offering scholarships and other similar, nonstate, autonomous institutions. This would help improve the position of those way down on the distribution scale of income and wealth, and it would do so more effectively than a handout of shares or vouchers to rich and poor alike.

There is a case for a gratuitous transfer of part of the wealth formerly owned by the state to new private owners. The following can be included among them: private, nonprofit pension and insurance institutions; cultural and educational institutions; charitable societies; foundations; and churches. In effect, the discount price of shares purchased by employees also contains a gift element. These transfers should be made only under specified conditions, mentioned earlier in this chapter. I do not see a justification for any distribution of gifts beyond that.

Domestic and Foreign Ownership

The question arises with all forms of ownership and institutions discussed so far as to whether the owner is domestic or foreign. Let me first put forward two extreme points of view. One is a position of narrow-minded nationalism and xenophobia, whose exponents want to exclude all foreign imports of capital, seeing in them a threat to national independence and the specific national character of the emerging economy.

This position causes serious damage. Eastern Europe has a huge need for foreign support in all forms. It is particularly important to have direct foreign investment of capital in all sectors of the economy, but most of all in the financial sector. It is desirable that foreign capital should take part in the purchase of the firms formerly owned by the state. When a large-scale, experienced foreign firm buys property, it enters as a real owner, providing incentive toward efficiency and strict control over management.

I also do not agree with the other extreme: the position that the proportion of foreign capital in any sector is quite immaterial. The economy contains key positions that are expedient to keep in national hands because they are indispensable to sovereignty. It is worth ensuring, through a circumspect policy, that the source of all capital investments from abroad should not be concentrated in a single country but should be spread among various countries. This gives the recipient country more scope for maneuver and so reinforces its independence. Apart from those considerations, there is a need for the country's own citizens to take part in the forming of a large business class, as that will strengthen the domestic base for a market economy founded on private property. For society to be transformed in the direction of *embourgeoisement*, capitalism should strike root primarily in domestic soil.

Concluding Remarks:
The Pace of Privatization

Those who take part in the debates on privatization are frequently asked whether they recommend fast or slow privatization. The question is phrased in the wrong way. No one would call oneself an advocate of slowness. The debate should not be about the speed but about the choice of values, the role assigned to the state, and the assessment of the importance of the various forms of ownership and types of owner. Once anyone takes a position on these points at issue, the speed to be expected arises as a result of that decision. I am a believer in the process of privatization proceeding as fast as possible. But it cannot be accelerated by some artful trick. Finding some clever organizational form plus bureaucratic aggressiveness in enforcement are not sufficient conditions for fast privatization.

The key issue is not the pace at which the wealth hitherto owned by the state is transferred into private hands. The most important thing is the pace at which the private sector grows in the form of newly established firms or through the transfer of state wealth or by combinations of both these forms. The following calculation is easy to check. Let us assume that at the start of the privatization process, the state sector accounts for 75 percent of the actual GDP and the private sector for 25 percent.[19] Production by the private sector then rises by 25 percent a year and production by the state-owned sector falls by 10 percent a year. Under those conditions, the private sector will dominate production at the end of the fourth year. Privatization in the broader sense depends on the difference in pace between the two processes and above all on the vitality of the private sector, not on a cunning way of transferring state-owned shares into private hands.[20]

There are grounds for optimism in that. The course of privatization is not ultimately set by the wisdom or stupidity or the strength or weakness of East European governments, opposition forces, foreign governments, international organizations, or advisers at home or abroad. At most, these groups may slow down or speed up the events. The process is directed by an irresistible inner force: the inherent motivation of the present and future private owners.

Notes

1. There is a very extensive literature on the subject. I have selected here just a few of the studies in English that deal with East European privatization: Fischer and Gelb 1990, Frydman and Rapaczynski 1990, Lipton and Sachs 1990, Lewandowski and Szomburg 1989, and Hinds 1990. An excellent survey of the polemic is provided by Stark 1990. This brief list does not include works concerned with privatization in the capitalist countries.

2. See Szelényi 1988.

3. See Hayek 1960 and 1973, ch. 1.

4. The idea that the market performs a natural selection among organizations already appeared in Schumpeter [1911] (1968) and was later elaborated upon in more detail by Alchian (1950). Schumpeter's idea of selection is strongly emphasized in connection with the transformation of the socialist countries in the works of Murrell (1990a, 1990b).

5. Schumpeter [1949] (1989, p. 266) wrote that "the original nucleus of means has been but rarely acquired by the entrepreneur's own saving activity..." He then went on to catalogue the various sources of finance, including the credit system. One of the sources was tapping the savings of other people and "created credit"... "'Credit creation' introduces banks and quasi-banking activities..." In this study and several others, Schumpeter analysed the connection between the credit system and entrepreneurs in detail.

6. The term *noyau stable* (stable core) has become widespread, following French literature. See Friedmann 1989.

7. Statistics in the East European countries have reached a critical situation. All previous statistics were based on detailed information provided by the large state-owned firms. Their proportion is shrinking. At the same time, the statistical offices are not equipped, neither organizationally nor methodologically, to observe and measure the activity of the private sector, least of all under circumstances in which the private sector tries to disguise as much of its activities as possible in order to escape taxation. So it is impossible to give reliable estimates for the scales of expansion of various types of private ownership as a whole.

8. Here again I draw attention to Schumpeter's statement on the relation between the entrepreneur and the credit system, quoted in note 4. Schumpeter

attributed such importance to this that he incorporated it into the definition of capitalism that he formulated: "Capitalism is that form of private property economy in which innovations are carried out by means of borrowed money." (Schumpeter 1939, p. 223).

9. These suggestions were followed in Hungary, but the implementation was slow, hesitant, and inconsistent. Exactly here could unfold the proper role of the state, but that role was performed rather inefficiently. As for savings, later experience shows clearly the flaw of the calculation quoted earlier, namely, to count the number of years needed for buying all state-owned assets from the initial stock of savings. Household savings rapidly increase. Nowadays accumulated household savings in Hungary would be large enough to buy a large share of state-owned property. The problem is that the household does not use it to the desirable extent for that purpose.

10. Ehrlich (1985), using data for 1970, made a comparison between the size distributions of industrial firms in a group of West European capitalist and East European socialist countries. According to her calculation, only 32 percent of those employed in capitalist industry worked in firms with more than 500 employees, whereas 66 percent of those in socialist industry did.

11. Cross-ownership was discussed in my book (Kornai 1990b). Detailed descriptions of the phenomenon, based on experiences in Hungary, can be found in the studies of Mora (1991) and Voszka (1991).

12. Again the key issue is not the percentage of the shares in some private owner's hands but whether the private owner has a decisive say. It is possible that a reputed foreign bank might become the dominant owner of a Hungarian bank even though it is only a minority shareholder.

13. According to Schaffer (1990), 32 percent of British shares were in the hands of pension funds in 1987 and 25 percent in the hands of insurance companies. As for the role of pension funds and insurance companies, Schaffer's proposals resemble in many respects the idea put forward in this chapter

14. Many pension funds in the United States, for instance, leave it to the contributors to decide what proportions of their contributions are to be invested on the stock market, the bond market, and the money market.

15. Let me draw special attention to the need for this transfer of commitments to be conducted fairly. Under no circumstances should the individual citizen (in some cases the pensioner and in some cases the sick or other insured person) suffer losses. Nor should it happen that the state segment hastens to shed its commitments, arguing that the private segment has now received free shares, if in fact such shares do not yet ensure enough income to cover the outgoing pensions and insurance claims. In this respect particular attention, foresight, and caution are required to guard private citizens, already troubled by uncertainties, from further worry.

16. It is another matter that the transfer of some of the state wealth previously handled centrally to the ownership of local authorities may speed up the privatization. Of course, this effect ensues only if the local authority is legally authorized to place property in its possession in private hands and if it has an economic incentive to do so as well. Also important may be whether the elected local

authority officers and councillors think their assistance to privatization will be popular with their voters.

17. This should be understood to mean the shares that are quoted and traded on the stock exchange.

18. The figures are from Light and White 1979, p. 338.

19. This includes the second economy which was not considered in the official statistics.

20. The calculation was based on the optimistic assumption of overall growth. For many reasons, output declined in all postsocialist economies. In practice, the shrinking of the state-owned sector seems to be somewhat slower, but unfortunately also the growth of the private sector turned out to be slower. Yet the key issue is still the relative pace of the dynamics of the two sectors.

References

Alchian, A. A. 1950. "Uncertainty, Evolution, and Economic Theory," *Journal of Political Economy* 58, no. 3 pp. 211–221.

Ehrlich, E. 1985. "The Size Structure of Manufacturing Establishments and Enterprises: An International Comparison," *Journal of Comparative Economics* 9, pp. 267–295.

Fischer, S., and A. Gelb 1990. "Issues in Socialist Economy Reform." Mimeo, MIT, Cambridge.

Friedmann, J. 1989. "Sur l'experience de privatization et sur les noyaux stables," *Commentaire*, pp. 11–18.

Frydman, R., and A. Rapaczynski 1990. *Markets and Institutions in Large Scale Privatizations*, Economic Research Report 90-420. New York: New York University.

Hayek, F. A. 1960. *The Constitution of Liberty*, Chicago: University of Chicago Press.

———. 1973. *Law Legislation and Liberty*, Chicago: University of Chicago Press.

Hinds, M., 1990, *Issues in the Introduction of Market Forces in Eastern European Socialist Countries*, Internal Discussion Paper, Report No. IDP-0057. Washington D.C.: World Bank.

Kornai, J. 1990. "The Affinity Between Ownership Forms and Coordination Mechanisms: The Common Experience of Reform in Socialist Countries," *Journal of Economic Perspectives*, 4, no. 2 pp. 131–148.

———. 1990b. *The Road to a Free Economy: Shifting from a Socialist System. The Example of Hungary.* New York: Norton.

———. 1992, *The Socialist System: The Political Economy of Socialism*, Oxford: Oxford University Press; Princeton: Princeton University Press.

Lewandowski, J., and J. Szomburg, 1989. "Property Reform as a Basis for Social and Economic Reform," *Communist Economies* 1, no. 3 pp. 257–268.

Light, J. O., and W.L. White. 1979. *The Financial System*, Homewood, Ill.

Lipton, D., and J. Sachs 1990. "Privatization in Eastern Europe: The Case of Poland," Brookings Papers, no. 2 pp. 293–333.

Mora, M. 1991, "The (Pseudo)-Privatization of State-Owned Enterprises," *Acta Oeconomica*, 43, pp. 37–58.

Murrell, P. 1990a. *The Nature of Socialist Economies: Lessons from Eastern European Foreign Trade*, Princeton: Princeton University Press.

————. 1990b. "An Evolutionary Perspective on Reform of the Eastern European Economies." Mimeo, University of Maryland, College Park.

Schaffer, M. E., 1990. *On the Use of Pension Funds in the Privatization of Polish State-Owned Enterprises.* Mimeo, London School of Economics: London.

Schumpeter, J. A., [1911] 1968.The *Theory of Economic Development: An Inquiry into Profits, Capital, Credit, Interest, and Business Cycles.* Cambridge, Mass.: Harvard University Press.

————. 1939. *Business Cycles: A Theoretical, Historical and Statistical Analysis of the Capitalist Process.* New York.

————. [1949] (1989). "Economic Theory and Entrepreneurial History," pp. 63–84 in *Change and the Entrepreneur.* Research Center in Entrepreneurial History, Harvard University, Reprinted in J. A. Schumpeter, *Essays.* New Brunswick and Oxford, R. V. Clemence, pp. 253–271.

Stark, D. 1990. "Privatization in Hungary: From Plan to Market or from Plan to Clan?" *East European Politics and Societies,* 4, no. 3, pp. 351–392.

Szelenyi, I. 1988. *Socialist Entrepreneurs: Embourgeoisement in Rural Hungary.* Madison: University of Wisconsin Press.

Tinbergen, J. 1952. *On the Theory of Economic Policy.* Amsterdam.

Voszka, E. 1991. "Tulajdonreform vagy privatiz cio?" (Reform of Ownership or Privatization?), Kozgazdasgi Szemle 38, no. 2 (February), pp. 117–133.

3

Evolutionary Economic Reform and Policy Issues: A Structural VAR Approach

Maria Blangiewicz and Wojciech W. Charemza

Periods of economic transition are generally regarded as being particularly difficult for econometric modeling. The collapse of existing relationships creates uncertainty and makes the entire system virtually unforecastable. Also, during the period of transition from a centrally planned to a market economy, there is rarely a single, rigid plan for such transition. Usually various concepts are tried, more or less successfully, according to economic remedies presented by enthusiastic theoreticians. In the case of East European reform there have been theories presented supporting fast and slow speed of privatization, rapid or slow monetary reform, price liberalization prior to privatization or the other way around and so on. Hence in such circumstances confusion concerning the appropriate theory of reform is generated in addition to the normal informational uncertainty.

An econometrician who attempts to model such a process of reform faces not only the problem of modeling a system with time-varying parameters (sometimes changing very fast) but also faces an informational mess concerning the theory he or she is supposed to use as a foundation for the model. Even if he or she believes in, say, a neo-classical approach to economic reform, there is surely not enough empirical information available to support a particular choice of a consumption function of factors affecting money demand and similar constructions traditionally included in an econometric model. If one rejects the extreme conclusion that no econometric modeling is possible in such a situation (too many econometricians would have to be made redundant if this were true), the other extreme, namely that a full structural model can be successfully constructed, is equally unlikely. The debate on the possibility of structural modeling of the early stage of East European economic reform, where the changes were relatively mild (see Charemza 1991, Klein 1991, Welfe 1992), pales in significance to the growing confusion and disbelief in econometric inference at its later, more volatile stages of economic transition.

In this chapter we suggest a compromise by constructing a time-varying parameters (TVP) model built to evaluate changes in and effectiveness of East European economic reform within a structural vector autoregressive (SVAR) framework. This allows us to deal, to some extent, with the problem of rapidly but continuously changing short- and long-run relations and also to impose a relatively small number of economic restrictions.These restrictions do not concern the dynamics and exogeneity of particular variables in the modelled system but only immediate (simultaneous) relations between some of these variables.

We present below the results of modeling a system explaining interrelations between prices (both state controlled and free market), money demand, households' incomes, and internal foreign exchange rates. The five-equation structural VAR system is formulated and estimated using quarterly data for the period from 1971 to 1992. The next section presents the general specification of the model and discusses the structural restrictions imposed. Then we give an overview of the estimation results for two estimated forms of the model: in levels and in first differences with identified fragmentary cointegrating vectors (that is, vectors that, for at least one subsample of the investigated period, can be positively identified as cointegrating vectors). The fourth section includes some exemplary simulation results.

TVP-VAR Nonstationary Models: An Overview

Following Bernanke (1986) and Blanchard (1989), a SVAR model might be derived from a simultaneous equations "shock-induced" model (SEM), in our case with time-varying parameters:

$$A_t \, y_t = A_t \, (L) \, y_{t-1} + B_t \, z_t + e_t \tag{1}$$

where y_t is a vector of n modelled variables, z_t is a vector of strongly exogenous variables, e_t is a vector of unitary system shocks (with a diagonal covariance matrix with units on main diagonal), $A_t \, (L) = \sum_{i=0}^{p-1} A_{t,\,i+1} L^i$ is a time series of $n \times n$ matrices with elements that are polynomials in the lag operator L, and A_t is a time series of matrices of coefficients describing simultaneity of the vector y_t. The number of lags in (1) is p. A SVAR representation of this system can be obtained by premultiplying (1) by A_t^{-1}:

$$y_t = A_t^* (L) y_{t-1} + B_t^* z_t + \varepsilon_t \tag{2}$$

where $A_t^* (L) = A_t^{-1} A_t (L)$, $B_t^* = A_t^{-1} B_t$, $\varepsilon_t = A_t^{-1} e_t$. There are no restrictions imposed on matrices $A_t^* (L)$. In the terminology introduced by Giannini (1992), equation (2) is a TVP generalization of the SVAR-K model, since relations between the unitary shocks and SVAR errors are usually described as:

$$e_t = K_t \varepsilon_t \tag{3}$$

hence $K_t = A_t$. Apart from moving SVAR-K modeling to a time-varying parameters environment, another modification consists in considering nonstationarity of (2). Generally, if (2) is of a lag length p, the system (2) is regarded as being nonstationary for a given set of matrices $A_{1,t}^*$, $A_{2,t}^*$, ... , $A_{p,t}^*$, if the determinant of $(I_n - A_{1,t}^* \xi - A_{2,t}^* \xi - ... - A_{p,t}^* \xi)$ has a root on and inside the complex unit circle. Allowing for time-varying parameters (that is, for any t) complicates the formalization and interpretation of nonstationarity of (2). Usually there exists a reparametrization of (2) from a sequence of models defined for $t = s, s+1, ... , S, S \leq T$:

$$y_t = A_S^* (L) y_{t-1} + B_S^* z_t + \varepsilon_{St} \tag{4}$$

and,

$$e_{St} = K_S \varepsilon_{St} \tag{5}$$

where $A_S^* (L)$, B_S^*, K_S are constant (for $t = s, s+1, ... , S$) matrices of coefficients that can be reparametrised to $A_t^* (L)$, B_t^* and K_t respectively and ε_{St}, e_{St} are the corresponding error and shock terms. It is conjectured that the variables in vector y_t are weakly integrated of order 1, if there exists at least one subsample $\{ t = s, s+1, ..., S \}$, $S < T$ for which first differences of the variables are stationary (see Charemza 1992c).

In a constant parameters framework if it is found that variables are integrated of order 1, the usual procedure has been to estimate a SVAR model in first differences (see, e.g., Blanchard 1989, Kaminsky 1991). This is appropriate if the variables in y_t are not cointegrated. If they are, omission of the cointegrating restriction (error correction mechanism) may lead to substantial misspecification.

Whether the variables in y_t are cointegrated or not, estimation of a nonstationary equation (4) for a given S by unconstrained ordinary least squares gives an estimator with the same asymptotic properties as the maximum likelihood estimator of the model with a fully specified cointe-grating restriction (see Park and Phillips 1989 , Sims Stock , and Watson 1990). The form usually used for maximum likelihood inference is (see Johansen 1989, Lütkepohl 1991, pp. 356–368):

$$\Delta y_t = \Gamma_S (L)\Delta y_{t-1} + \alpha_S \, \beta_S' \, y_{t-p} + B_{St}^* z_t + \varepsilon_{St} \tag{6}$$

for any VAR model with a lag length p. Matrices $\Gamma_S \, (L)$ are functions of $A_S^* \, (L)$ such as $\Gamma_{S,i} = -I + \sum_{j=1}^{i} A_{S,j}^{*i}$, $\Gamma_S \, (L) = \sum_{i=0}^{p-2} \Gamma_{S,i+1} \, L^i$, I being an identity matrix and, if there are r cointegrating vectors in the model, α_S and β_S are matrices with r columns, called respectively loading matrices and matrices of cointegrating vectors.[1]

Formulation and Estimation of the Model

A TVP SVAR model has been built for Poland using quarterly data for the period 1970(1) to 1991(4). This period covers various stages of devel-opment of an East European economy, from a typical centrally planned regime, through various types of its modifications, to an early postcom-munist economy with its hyperinflation and stagflation periods. For a concise description of East European economies in their centrally planned period, see, for example, Jeffries (1990). For a more analytical evaluation see Nove (1983) and Kornai (1992), and for the postcommu-nist development see Kolodko, Gotz-Kozierkiewicz, and Skrzeczewska-Paczek (1992). Using the notation introduced in the second section of the chapter, we are defining vector y_t as containing five variables:

in_t households disposable income
m_t nominal money balances *(M0)*
p_{1t} official price index
p_{2t} free (black) market price index
x_{2t} internal free (black) market foreign exchange rate

Strongly exogenous variables in vector z_t are:

x_{1t} official foreign exchange rate
d_t nominal savings deposit rate
dm_t dummy variable marking the martial law period in Poland,
       imposed at the end of 1981, equal to one for 1982(1) to 1983(2)
       and zero otherwise
ds_t dummy variable marking the postcommunist period in
       Poland, equal to one for 1989(3)–1991(4) and zero otherwise

Data for all the variables but d_t and the dummy variables are in logarithms and additionally the data for y_t have been seasonally adjusted.

Since the economic policy of Poland in the period investigated is full of more or less radical changes (with the most radical one being a switch from a centrally planned to a market economy), it is assumed here that the process of change is of limited memory. That is, relatively old economic information becomes forgotten with the availability of new information. This gives rise to estimation of the model in windows rather than in a recursive way. We have used an estimation window of the size of 44. With the first five observations retained for lags, the first window contains quarterly observations from 1971(2) to 1982(2), the second window from 1971(3) to 1982(3) and so on. According to the notation introduced in the second section of the chapter, we have forty subsamples, forty different information sets for each S (and consequently forty separate matrices on each of A_S^* (L), B_S^*, Γ_S (L) and α_S, β_S), which corresponds to the number of estimation windows.

Charemza (1992b) analyzed long-run relationships between the variables in y_t. He also evaluated the order of integration for each of these variables in a TVP framework, using the same data set as that in this study, and found that all the variables are weakly integrated of order 1 (with the exception of x_{2t} which is strongly integrated), showing a pattern typical to that of an economic transformation. Periods of lack of integration are for 1989 to 1990, that is, for the period of the collapse of the old regime and the emergence of the open market economy. It has also been discovered that for the periods where the variables in y_t are cointegrated, the most likely number of cointegrating vectors is two. This suggests that the usual practice of estimation of the model in first differences is not applicable since this would lead to an efficiency loss resulting from misspecification. Consequently it has been decided to estimate the model in levels—that is directly in the form of (4) and then (5)—by ordinary least squares (OLS) and, alternatively, in the form of (6) and then (5) by the Johansen (1989) maximum likelihood (ML) method. Although asymptotically both methods are equivalent in terms of their efficiency, the OLS method is more robust to the possible misspecification of the number of cointegrating vectors in (6). However, if the number of cointegrating vectors is properly specified, in finite samples OLS is less efficient than ML.

Figure 3.1 shows time paths of the generally used criteria for evaluation of VAR models: the logarithm of the likelihood function *(logl)*, the Akaike Information Criterion (AIC), and the Schwartz Bayesian Information Criterion (SBIC) computed for the OLS estimated model (4). These time paths are relatively stable in time, although one can observe a visible deterioration of the quality of the model (measured both by the

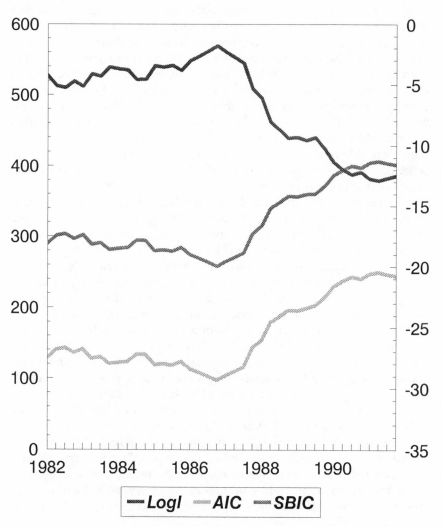

FIGURE 3.1   VAR Evaluation Criteria

likelihood and the information criteria) starting in 1988. Unlike the integration and cointegration statistics, there are no signs of improvement at the end of the sample period, where the economic situation in Poland has stabilized.

In (4) the total number of parameters to be estimated in each window is 125 (25 for each equation: 20 for four lags on five variables plus four for exogenous variables and one for a constant term). In (6), if there are two cointegrating vectors, there are 95 parameters in each window: 15 in each equation for the differenced variables, 2 for each equation for the loadings matrix and additionally 10 for the entire system for two cointegrating vectors. To reduce the computational burden, after initial estimation those parameters that have not been significant at least at the 20 percent level of significance in any one of 40 windows has been restricted to zero. This reduces the number of parameters to 36 in (4), that is, in the OLS version of the model.

The OLS series of residuals have been in turn used for estimation of matrices K_S in (5). A priori restrictions on the parameters of this matrix are formulated as follows (for notational simplification, subscripts S relating to particular subsamples and t are omitted; we dealt with 40 separate matrices K_S):

$$
\begin{bmatrix} e_{in} \\ e_m \\ e_{p1} \\ e_{p2} \\ e_{x2} \end{bmatrix} =
\begin{bmatrix}
1 & 0 & 0 & 0 & 0 \\
0 & 1 & k_{m,p} & 1-k_{m,p} & k_{m,x2} \\
0 & 0 & 1 & 0 & 0 \\
0 & k_{p2,m} & -k_{p2,m} & 1 & k_{p2,x2} \\
0 & k_{p2,m} & -k_{p2,m} & k_{x2,p2} & 1
\end{bmatrix}
\times
\begin{bmatrix} \varepsilon_{in} \\ \varepsilon_m \\ \varepsilon_{p1} \\ \varepsilon_{p2} \\ \varepsilon_{x2} \end{bmatrix}
\quad (7)
$$

where $e_{in}, e_m, e_{p1}, e_{p2}, e_{x2}$ and $\varepsilon_{in}, \varepsilon_m, \varepsilon_{p1}, \varepsilon_{p2}, \varepsilon_{x2}$ denote appropriate elements of and respectively. Restrictions in (7) reflect our belief concerning the simultaneous interactions between particular elements of vector y_t. Variables in_t and p_{1t} are, according to our assumptions, weakly exogenous in (4)–(5) and (6)–(5) for the remaining variables, with the parameters of interest those in (4) or (6). They are not, however, weakly exogenous for the parameters of conditional processes for the remaining variables, if there is at least one cointegrating vector and more than one non-zero row in the loadings matrix (see Urbain 1992). The reason for allowing for lack of simultaneity for in_t is the assumption of a delayed rather than contemporary feedback resulting from an income shock.

Analogously, since p_{1t} represents those prices that are controlled by the government and these were not revised frequently, it seems reasonable to assume lack of immediate response in p_{1t} for shocks in other analyzed variables.

For the money variable, it is assumed that there is an immediate reaction of real domestic money balances to changes in the internal foreign exchange rate (coefficient $k_{m,p}$ weights two domestic price variables p_{1t} and p_{2t} in order to obtain an aggregate). The immediate impact of shocks on real money balances can either be negative, where foreign currencies work as a parallel currency substituting for domestic money, or positive, in the postcommunist period, where its role is more as an additional asset rather than a means of payment (see Charemza and Ghatak 1990, Charemza 1992b). There is simultaneity assumed for p_{1t} and x_{2t}. Since for a long period of time where there was a repressed inflation regime in Poland both p_{2t} and x_{2t} acted complementarily as market domestic prices on the free (black) market, they should react to immediate changes in excess demand on the official market. If total factor productivity is constant, this excess demand can be closely approximated by suppressed money balances, that is real money balances in which the official, suppressed price is used: $m_t - p_{1t}$ (see Nuti 1986, Charemza 1992a). In the postcommunist period, where p_{1t} has no longer been suppressed, it is regarded as just another measure of price for evaluation of real money balances, alternative to a weighted average of p_{1t} and p_{2t}. The role of the relationship between p_{2t} and x_{2t} changes with the switch from the centrally planned to postcommunist regime from complementary to substitutive. Hence, a change of sign of appropriate coefficients in K_S is expected.

Since in (7) there are imposed orthogonality conditions (because of standard assumptions for error terms) and there is simultaneity among particular elements of K_S, its estimation is not trivial. Bernanke (1986) suggested using the method of moments. In this chapter we apply the generalized methods of moments (GMM), which, as shown by Hansen (1982), should be strongly consistent and asymptotically normal for such S for which variables in y_t are cointegrated or, in another words, all elements in ε_{St} are stationary. However, the properties of GMM are not known if the terms ε_{St} are nonstationary. Results of estimation for 40 windows are summarised in Figure 3.2 by the time plot of the loglikelihood function.[2]

The time path of the loglikelihood function for the GMM estimates of the matrices K_S is similar to that for model (4), presented in Figure 3.1. This also shows a decline of informational power of the model for the postcommunist period of 1989 to 1991. As expected, the coefficients $k_{m,x2}$, $k_{p2,x2}$, and $k_{x2,p2}$ have changed signs for the postcommunist regime. Also,

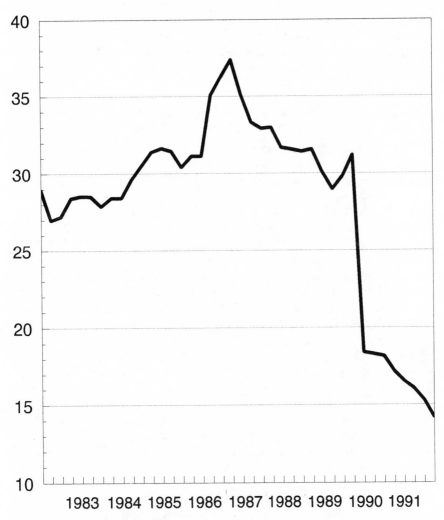

FIGURE 3.2   Loglikelihood Function for the GMM Estimates

the coefficient $k_{x2,m}$ has changed its sign, which reflects the different role of p_{1t} in the period after repressed inflation. There is also an interesting symmetry between $k_{m,x2}$ and $k_{p2,x2}$.

The estimated standard errors of the coefficients (not reported here) are in 80 percent of the cases smaller than the estimated parameters. Most of the results for which standard errors were relatively high are for the late centrally planned and the transition period of 1987 to 1990. Generally, 65 percent of the total of 234 estimated parameters were significant, that is, twice as large as their standard errors.[3]

Reparametrization, Ex-Post Evaluation and Impulse Response Analysis

The analyzed SVAR model has been estimated in form (4) and (5), that is, for a sequence of subsamples (windows) $\{s, s+1, \ldots, S\}$ where the parameters for each subsample have been held constant and they have changed only with a change in $s(S)$. Nevertheless, we are primarily interested in model (2)–(3) rather than (4)–(5). Hence, it is necessary to reparametrize the estimated parameters from S to t. One straightforward operation is simply to replace S by t for all t greater than or equal to the smallest S. This, however, does not seem to be an efficient procedure since for most ts there is more than one estimate of a parameter, because of the rolling in time nature of the estimation in windows. For instance, for the smallest t for the first window there is only one estimate of a parameter; for the second smallest t, however, there are two estimates, since the second smallest t is included in the first and second window, and so on. Consequently, it seems reasonable to average all the available estimates of a given parameter for a given t, maximizing in that way the amount of information used for each estimate.

The model fitted with these smoothed estimates is compared with that with the more popular $S \Rightarrow t$ reparametrization. The model corresponding to the $S \Rightarrow t$ reparametrization is herewith called the "raw"-model, as opposed to the "smoothed" model, in which the smoothed estimates of the parameters have been used.

The properties of smooth and raw models are compared by running ex-post goodness-of-fit simulations for the period of 1983:1 to 1991:4 (See Table 3.1). The model has been solved statically (including the VAR parameters and the estimated elements of matrices K_S) and the fitted values have been compared to the observed ones using the standard set of goodness-of-fit measures (root mean square error, [RMSE], mean error, [ME], and Theil's inequality coefficient U).[4] Also, the Bhargava (1986) unit root statistics R_1 for testing the random walk null hypothesis against the stationary alternative have been computed (in fact, the whole set of

TABLE 3.1   Ex-Post Goodness-of-Fit and Stationarity Measures

	RMSE	ME	U	R_1	DW
Smoothed Model					
in_t	0.253	0.163	0.020	1.15	1.22
m_t	0.609	0.463	0.076	0.04	0.05
$m_t(alt)$	0.012	−0.001	0.015	1.01	1.07
p_{1t}	0.088	−0.005	0.012	1.99	2.11
p_{2t}	0.146	−0.001	0.017	1.12	1.19
x_{2t}	0.117	0.003	0.015	2.11	2.24
Raw Model					
in_t	0.101	0.019	0.011	1.63	1.73
m_t	1.668	0.829	0.208	0.29	0.31
$m_t(alt)$	0.907	0.012	0.113	1.36	1.44
p_{1t}	0.086	0.027	0.012	1.49	1.58
p_{2t}	0.225	−0.096	0.027	0.99	1.05
x_{2t}	0.137	−0.011	0.018	1.73	1.83

the Bhargava statistics has been calculated for testing unit roots with and without drift against stationary and explosive alternatives; they are not reported here since they do not add a lot to the conclusions). For comparison, a standard Durbin-Watson statistic is also presented.

It can be immediately noticed that the worst fits for both the smoothed and raw models is the simulation for m_t. Apart from the bad fit, residuals (that is, the differences between the fitted and the observed values) are clearly nonstationary, as shown by the low values of the Bhargava and Durbin-Watson statistics. This may result from questionable stationarity of first differences of the m_t variable (see Charemza 1992b). This resulted in the implementation of a somewhat heuristic correction mechanism for m_t. Since, in the case of nonstationarity of residuals, they have to depend on the previous values of both forecasts and realizations, the residuals have been regressed on observed values and forecasts on m_t lagged by one period. The fitted values of this regression have been used as a correction factor for the current forecasts. These results are summarized in Table 3.1 as $m_t(alt)$.

These results indicate that, with the exception of in_t the smoothed model gives generally better results than the raw one. The smoothed model provides better goodness-of-fit measures and, probably more

important, the stationarity statistics show a greater degree of randomness for the residuals. Imposing the heuristic correction for m_t visibly
improves fit and randomness of the residuals for the smoothed model,
but for the raw model the $m_t(alt)$ statistics are still not satisfactory. It can
be concluded that, for simulation purposes, the smoothed model should
be preferred over the raw one.

The model with the smoothed parameters has been used for simulation of a response analysis for a single shock. The Appendix to this
chapter gives time paths of simulated responses of particular variables to
a single shock induced in each of the variables separately and equal to its
standard deviation. Unlike the constant parameters system, these simulated responses are time sensitive in the sense that since the parameters
vary for particular periods of time, the simulated responses would also
vary, depending on the simulation period. In our case the simulation
period has been chosen as 12 quarters from 1989:1 to 1991:4. The results
reveal a long-memory pattern of nonstationarity of the analyzed system.
Most of the dynamic multiplies do not converge monotonically to zero.
However, they also do not explode monotonically. This seems to be a
usual feature of nonstationary VAR systems (see Lütkepohl 1991, pp.
139–140). For most of the time paths shown in the Appendix there is a
period in which the effect of a shock dies out for a few quarters and, after
that, begins to rise. In a number of cases some type of periodic oscilla-
tions can be observed.

An Example of Simulation:
The Computation of Virtual Prices

As an example of the application of the model for the analysis of the
Polish economy we have chosen a simulation of virtual prices. The
concept of virtual prices was introduced by Neary and Roberts (1980)
and has been used since in various studies for the analysis of households' behavior under rationing and disequilibrium modeling (see Lee
1986, Quandt 1988, pp. 171–172, Charemza 1990). Virtual prices are
usually defined as prices that would have appeared if the unconstrained
consumption demand was equal to the constraints imposed. Charemza
(1990) estimated virtual prices by solving a single equation autoregres-
sive-distributed lags model for price, allowing for $p_{1t} = p_{2t}$. Following
this concept, it seems reasonable to simulate virtual prices from the estimated VAR model by substituting lagged p_{1t} by lagged p_{2t} and solving
for $p_{1t} = p_{vt}$, where p_{vt} stands for the virtual prices.

Figure 3.3 shows the annual observed and virtual inflation, in logarithms, where virtual inflation has been recalculated from the simulated
p_{vt} data. It indicates the substantial positive difference between the open

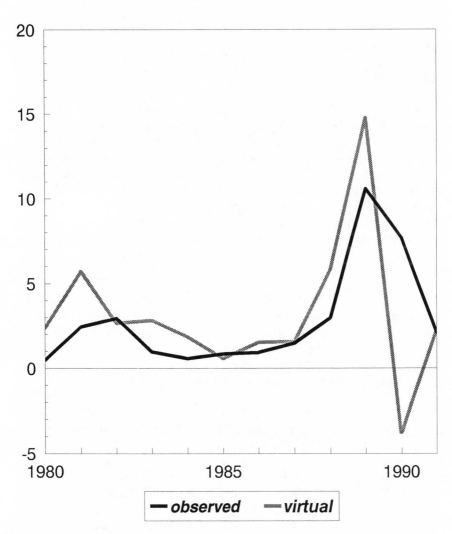

FIGURE 3.3   Observed and Virtual Inflation

(official) and virtual inflation during the 1980s which shows the persistence of positive excess demand in the economy. Generally, in the 1980s there was a negative relation between the official and virtual inflation. A substantial rise in prices in 1982 brought the virtual inflation down and the efforts in 1983 and 1984 to stabilize the official economy caused virtual inflation to increase. This pattern was broken in 1987, 1988, and 1989, when both official and virtual inflation rose. This corresponds to the stage of "shortageflation" of East European reform (see Kolodko and McMahon 1987), when efforts of the government to stabilize the internal market through price increases were accompanied by neither a restrictive monetary policy nor a supply-side policy. This caused shortages to rise and generated inflationary expectations that stimulated consumption demand even further (the so-called "hot money" syndrome). Since official prices finally reached their equilibrium point, at the beginning of 1990, virtual prices have been drastically falling because the consumers' quantity constraints have disappeared. This has led some authors to argue that the officially reported inflation overstates the actual price rise, since it does not take into account the possible disinflation of those prices that has been related to the virtual price behavior of households (see Lipton and Sachs 1990, Lane 1992 and Osband 1992).

Conclusions and Reflections

The TVP SVAR methodology seems to provide a useful tool for modeling the East European transition process. It requires a minimal amount of a priori restrictions, which is useful in the case where the economic theory of transition is not well established and its precise formulas are disputable. It also does not require access to very detailed and diseggregated data that, for Eastern Europe, might be difficult to obtain. Finally, the TVP SVAR models are computationally simple and therefore straightforward to update and to extend by the inclusion of additional available series of data. Because of the autoregressive structure of the model, its use for forecasting and policy analysis causes relatively few problems.

However, as for the modeling of all East European economies, the problem of an adequate data quality is of a primarily importance. This chapter uses an artificially created time series for p_{2t}, and it is quite possible that with some other estimates of the free market prices, the results would be difficult. Also, there is a problem of the quality of the narrow money data, m_t, which, at the moment of conducting this research, were the only data available. It is likely that the forecast stability problems for m_t were caused by the use of narrow money data rather than $M1$. There may be a chance to use some estimates for $M1$ in further studies (new monetary data has been recently used by Chawluk 1992).

Appendix:
Simulation of One Standard Deviation
Impulse Response (in Percentages)

	in_t				
	in_t	m_t	p_{1t}	p_{2t}	x_{2t}
1989:1	1.90955	0.00000	0.00000	0.00000	0.00000
1989:2	0.00000	0.00000	0.000001	0.27135	0.21084
1989:3	0.46964	0.13995	0.046975	0.21708	0.50459
1989:4	0.17208	0.040586	0.32534	0.58924	0.12828
1990:1	0.12238	0.036723	0.41954	−0.66363	0.21427
1990:2	0.14595	0.014002	0.26335	0.29853	0.14613
1990:3	0.066693	0.055916	0.22164	0.10271	0.14685
1990:4	0.22227	−0.030674	0.16731	0.26453	0.14819
1991:1	0.33216	−0.12579	0.16707	0.25472	0.15239
1991:2	0.13172	−0.15304	0.16571	0.24361	0.21115
1991:3	0.12994	−0.18500	0.18912	0.30900	0.22783
1991:4	0.095296	−0.24006	0.24150	0.25061	0.17793

	m_t				
	in_t	m_t	p_{1t}	p_{2t}	x_{2t}
1989:1	1.90955	4.05795	0.00000	0.41498	0.00000
1989:2	−0.07179	2.76881	0.071525	0.70315	0.21084
1989:3	0.44025	1.99501	0.9936	0.60100	0.50459
1989:4	0.11932	2.52094	0.52545	0.94274	0.12828
1990:1	−3.96443	2.53366	0.62975	−0.25342	0.21427
1990:2	−2.58428	2.35580	0.48134	0.16042	0.14613
1990:3	−2.79722	2.17455	0.34953	−0.42374	0.14685
1990:4	−3.20335	2.14108	−0.40492	−1.48702	0.14819
1991:1	−2.80580	2.06719	−1.13447	0.63614	0.15239
1991:2	−2.95157	2.04584	−1.23400	−0.27320	0.21115
1991:3	−2.98058	1.96510	−1.42378	−0.72337	0.22783
1991:4	−3.17107	2.11365	−1.54450	−0.86320	0.17793

			p_{1t}		
	in_t	m_t	p_{1t}	p_{2t}	x_{2t}
1989:1	1.90955	4.04226	1.24206	0.29907	0.29584
1989:2	-0.051736	2.76462	1.34972	0.58253	0.48650
1989:3	0.44846	2.00759	1.08861	0.49377	0.75067
1989:4	0.55632	2.54410	0.98159	1.21962	0.36619
1990:1	-3.45220	2.34614	0.87281	0.15175	0.49055
1990:2	-2.01421	1.99768	0.66220	0.48825	0.068108
1990:3	-2.32560	1.74063	0.56599	-0.073963	-0.87030
1990:4	-2.86038	1.66782	-0.11628	-1.36350	-0.65439
1991:1	-2.39126	1.54241	-0.81561	0.70882	-0.90827
1991:2	-2.41083	1.47785	-0.92868	-0.22998	-1.11927
1991:3	-2.32877	1.35006	-1.16582	-0.59569	-1.11915
1991:4	-2.39028	1.43482	-1.30126	-0.57962	-1.23385

			p_{2t}		
	in_t	m_t	p_{1t}	p_{2t}	x_{2t}
1989:1	1.90955	6.25481	1.24206	4.27664	4.81725
1989:2	-0.84245	4.02665	2.03523	5.33853	4.69962
1989:3	0.055419	2.29881	2.66265	4.72235	4.51167
1989:4	-0.024896	2.68319	3.11333	5.10415	3.99442
1990:1	-5.73670	2.12193	3.14547	4.62467	3.97762
1990:2	-3.12622	1.18224	3.02466	5.34967	3.21205
1990:3	-2.84760	0.18916	3.00258	4.62780	1.87166
1990:4	-3.14714	-0.60595	2.09788	3.05559	2.32767
1991:1	-2.36437	-1.49835	1.28949	6.26021	2.14298
1991:2	-1.98790	-2.36646	1.43005	4.91692	1.89169
1991:3	-1.43991	-3.41080	1.41217	4.26678	1.93372
1991:4	-1.05579	-4.18464	1.42155	4.26950	1.91727

			x_{2t}		
	in_t	m_t	p_{1t}	p_{2t}	x_{2t}
1989:1	1.90955	6.29363	1.24206	6.40747	9.72920
1989:2	-1.70146	3.77032	2.40246	10.50533	9.27664
1989:3	-0.62785	1.65178	3.98698	9.31617	8.59752
1989:4	-0.65630	1.43521	5.16189	9.29082	7.90713
1990:1	-6.20922	0.40219	5.45647	9.31679	7.69835
1990:2	-2.92447	-1.01920	5.44854	10.71573	6.85127
1990:3	-2.10136	-2.66506	5.56692	10.25061	5.57447
1990:4	-1.68099	-4.28089	4.82291	8.88903	6.19748
1991:1	-0.66474	-6.05306	4.29869	12.28944	6.18084
1991:2	0.085254	-7.79899	4.77168	10.89364	6.06545
1991:3	1.12127	-9.82476	5.10981	10.35083	6.19523
1991:4	2.10639	-11.66246	5.40922	10.30838	6.34302

Notes

The financial support of the A.C.E. Project *Structural Change and Spillovers in the East European Reform Process* is gratefully acknowledged. We are indebted to Ali-Nowaihi and Derek Deadman for their helpful comments on an earlier draft of the chapter. We are solely responsible for any remaining errors.

1. It is important to note that the error correction representation (4) of a TVP VAR model is possible only prior to reparametrization from β_S to β_t. After reparametrization it is no longer valid, because of the time inconsistency problem (see Charemza 1992a).

2. Estimates were obtained with the use of *TSP-386* package, by *GMM* command. For the static case this corresponds to the three-stage least squares method.

3. In some cases, however, the estimated standard errors of the parameters were suspiciously small, indicating some numerical problems of the applied *GMM* routine.

4. The inequality coefficient applied herein is that given by Theil (1966, pp. 27–33) and differs from its earlier formulations. It can be interpreted as a measure comparing an accuracy of simulation with the accuracy of the naive no-change forecast. There is a huge literature criticising and defending the use and interpretation of the U coefficients and indeed all the ex-post, static and dynamic, goodness-of-fit measures (see, e.g. Bliemel 1973, Granger and Newbold 1986, pp. 279–280).

References

Bernanke, B. 1986. "Alternative Explanations of the Money-Income Correlation," in K. Brunner and A. Melzer, eds., *Carnegie-Rochester Conference Series on Public Policy*, vol. 25. Amsterdam: North Holland.

Bhargava, A. 1986. "On the theory of testing for unit roots in observed time series," *Review of Economic Studies* 53, pp. 369–384.

Blanchard, O. 1989. "A Traditional Interpretation of the Money-income Causality," *American Economic Review* 79, pp. 1146–1164.

Bliemel, F. 1973. "Theil's forecast accuracy coefficient: a clarification," *Journal of Marketing Research* 10, pp. 444–446.

Charemza, W. W. 1990. "Parallel Markets, Excess Demand and Virtual Prices: An Empirical Approach," *European Economic Review* 34, pp. 331–339.

———. 1991. "Large Econometric Models of an East European Economy: A Critique of the Methodology," *Economic Modeling* 8, pp. 45–62.

———. 1992a. "East Europe in Wonderland; or, What Happened to the Money?" Discussion Paper in European Economic Studies No. 92/8, University of Leicester.

———. 1992b. "Economic Transformation and Long-Run Relationships: The Case of Poland." Mimeo, University of Leicester.

———. 1992c. "Time Varying Parameters and Long-Run Behaviour: Some Definitions." Mimeo, University of Leicester.

Charemza, W. W., and S. Ghatak. 1990. "Demand for Money in a Dual-Currency, Quantity-Constrained Economy: Hungary and Poland 1956–1985," *Economic Journal* 100, pp. 1159–1172.

Chawluk, A. 1992. "Estimating the Demand for Money, Poland 1965–1992," paper presented at the Economic Reform Seminar, London School of Economics.

Giannini, C. 1992. *Topics in Structural VAR Econometrics*, Lecture Notes in Economics and mathematical Systems No. 381, Berlin: Springer-Verlag.

Granger, C. W. J., and P. Newbold. 1986. *Forecasting Economic Time Series*, 2d, San Diego: Academic Press.

Hansen, L. P. 1982. "Large Sample Properties of Generalised Method Of Moments Estimators," *Econometrica* 50, pp. 1029–1054.

Jeffries, I. 1990. *A Guide to the Socialist Economies*. London: Routledge.

Johansen, S. 1989. *Likelihood Based Inferences on Cointegration. Theory and Applications*. Bologna: Centro Interuniversitario di Economeria (CIDE).

Kaminsky, G. 1991. "Dual Exchange Rates: The Mexican Experience 1982–1987. Mimeo, University of California at San Diego.

Klein, L. R. 1991. "Model Building for a Planned System," *Economic Modeling* 8, pp. 418–423.

Kolodko, G. W., D. Gotz-Kozierkiewicz, and E. Skrzeczewska-Paczek. 1992. *Hyperinflation and Stabilization in Postsocialist Economies*. Boston: Kluwer.

Kolodko, G. W., and W. W. McMahon. 1987. "Stagflation and Shortageflation: A Comparative Approach," *Kyklos* 40, pp. 176–197.

Kornai, J. 1992. *The Socialist System: The Political Economy of Communism*, Clarendon Press, Oxford.

Lane, T. D. 1992. "Inflation Stabilization and Economic Transformation in Poland: The First Year," in A. H. Melzer and C. Plosser, eds., *Carnegie-Rochester Conference Series on Public Policy*, vol. 37. Amsterdam: North-Holland.

Lee, L.-F. 1986. "The Specification and Estimation of Multi-Market Disequilibrium Econometric Models, *Journal of Econometrics* 32, pp. 297–332.

Lipton, D., and J. Sachs. 1990. "Creating a Market Economy in Eastern Europe: The Case of Poland," *Brookings Papers on Economic Activity*, no. 1, pp. 75–133.

Lütkepohl, H. 1991. *Introduction to Multiple Time Series Analysis*. Berlin: Springer-Verlag, .

Neary, J. P. and K. W. S. Roberts. 1980. "The Theory of Household Behaviour Under Rationing," *European Economic Review* 13, pp. 25–42.

Nove, A. 1983. *The Economics of Feasible Socialism*. London: Allen & Unwin.

Nuti, D. M. 1986. "Hidden and Repressed Inflation in Soviet-Type Economies," *Contributions to Political Economy* 5, pp. 37–82.

Osband, K. 1992. "Index Number Biases During Price Liberalization," *IMF Staff Papers* 39, pp. 287–309.

Park, J. Y., and P. C. B. Phillips. 1989. "StatisticalInference in Regressions with Integrated Processes: Part 2," *Econometric Theory* 5, pp. 95–131.

Quandt, R. E. 1988. *The Econometrics of Disequilibrium*. Oxford: Basil Blackwell.

Sims, C. A., J. H. Stock, and M. W. Watson. 1990. "Inference in Linear Time Series Models with Some Unit Roots," *Econometrica* 58, pp. 113–144.

Theil, H. 1966. *Applied Economic Forecasting*, Amsterdam: North-Holland.

Urbain, J-P. 1992. "On Weak Exogeneity in Error Correction Models," *Oxford Bulletin of Economics and Statistics* 54, pp. 187–207.

Welfe, W., with J. Gajda, and E. Zoltowska. 1992. "On the Methodology of Constructing Large Econometric Models of an East European Economy Poland)," *Economic Modeling* 9, pp. 137–145.

PART TWO

Radicalism Versus Gradualism: The Asian Experience

4

Reform's Rhetoric-Realization Relationship: The Experience of Mongolia

Peter Murrell

Despite its over-alliteration, the title of this chapter is a serious one. These reforms are occurring in the former socialist countries, from Budapest to Beijing. The rhetoric of reform refers to the tenor and the level of ambition embodied in the government's initial comprehensive statements of its approach to reform. Thus, the rhetoric of reform is primarily its philosophy at the outset together with the character of the set of policy measures that the government initially aims to implement. Realization connotes the nature and effectiveness of the measures that are actually implemented. In this chapter I examine the relationship between rhetoric and realization, arguing that it is not a simple monotonic one. At some point, advances in rhetoric can be counterproductive for realization.

Although the argument of this chapter is purely positive, it does have normative implications. A basic tenet of the radical approach to reform is that the implementation of reforms will be more effective the more ambitious their rhetoric.[1] If this is the case, little is to be gained from considering society's existing institutional structure and its knowledge base when formulating overall reform strategy. But if this tenet does not hold, the

The research for this chapter was supported by the IRIS Center at the University of Maryland and benefitted from the productive environment of the Woodrow Wilson International Center for Scholars. I would like to thank Kazimierz Poznanski for helpful comments. I am grateful to the many Mongolians who were willing to share information and ideas on the reform process under way in their country. The chapter draws on related work undertaken with Georges Korsun and Karen Turner Dunn.

existing state of society becomes central in guiding the overall philosophy of reform. The design of reforms will not be a simple matter of picking complete, ready-made programs off the shelf. Rather, although lessons from the experiences of other countries will be helpful, even the broad agenda of reform has to be carefully calibrated to the existing features of society.[2]

The argument is conducted in two modes. The first section proceeds on an a priori basis, making connections between rhetoric and realization on the basis of simple theoretical arguments. The separate elements of that section contain a common component arising from the view that society's stock of knowledge is an important determinant of the effects of reforms. This stock of knowledge is a critical ingredient of the informal structures of society that must support the institutional and logistical arrangements necessary for the productive progress of reforms. Because political leaders can change only the formal structures in the short run, whereas the informal elements are historically derived and change slowly, there arises the problem of a possible mismatch between these two.

The second section establishes a data point supporting the a priori argument by examining the progress of reforms in Mongolia. Until the end of 1990, Mongolia was under the hegemony of the Soviet Union and the economies of the two countries were integrated. Hence, there are strong parallels between the case of Mongolia and those of the successor states of the Soviet Union, with events in Mongolia ahead by one year. In 1991, Mongolia aimed to implement extremely ambitious reforms, but in a very unfavorable economic environment. This section focuses on the realization of these reforms in four important areas: price liberalization, privatization, the legal system, and the development of the nascent private sector.

Can More Haste Mean Less Speed?

The following arguments are suggestive rather than conclusive. The purpose is simply to show the theoretical possibility that rhetoric and realization can be inversely related. Ultimately, whether this possibility comes to fruition is an empirical question, which is addressed for one country in the section on Mongolia.

Personal Knowledge

Society's stock of knowledge is a crucial input into reform—the knowledge held by policy-makers deciding on major goals, by officials implementing economic measures, and by the populace at large. The relevant knowledge stock includes a broad range of phenomena.[3] There are the judgments of policymakers on the trade-offs available to society, for example, between inflation and efficiency when using price controls. There are the implicit models that officials use when interpreting the results of policies, for example, in deciding whether a perceived increase in the money supply is a reflection of statistical inadequacies or of important problems in monetary control. There are society's general attitudes on the nature of economic activities, for example, on the role of speculation and speculators in a market economy.[4]

It would not be so important to focus on the role of knowledge in reforms if all knowledge were acquired through straightforward technical learning. But this is not the case. Knowledge is a product of history as much as of formal lessons. An important component of intellectual capacity is "personal knowledge," acquired in practical situations, in learning by doing, in apprenticeship (Polanyi 1962). Such knowledge cannot be transferred simply in a formal process; it is learned in, and applicable to, a specific context.

Politics, policymaking, and policy implementation are as much skills as techniques and as such they employ the application of personal knowledge.[5] These activities require personal knowledge in the very framing of questions, the diagnosis of problems, and the interpretation of the activity of others. Thus, the whole process of reform uses this historically derived knowledge.

To see the implications of the forgoing points for reforms, let us take a simple example. Suppose that the architects of a radical reform have sufficiently escaped the historical specificities of their own country's knowledge base, that they are able to design a workable market system de novo.[6] In contrast, the implementers of reform have a knowledge stock that is more reflective of the history of their own society. There will thus be more error in interpretation, and less accurate implementation of the reforms, the farther the rhetoric of reform from the scenario in which the personal knowledge of the implementers was acquired. Hence, it is plausible that the effectiveness of implementation will decrease as the level of rhetoric increases above some level. In an extreme case, a policy measure might seem so theoretical to its interpreters that implementation is simply impossible.

The argument here is simply stated as the possibility that there can be mismatches between the rhetoric of reform and the extant personal knowledge. Some reforms simply cannot be implemented given the knowledge base of society. A rhetoric with too much ambition might immobilize implementers from looking for reasonable alternative reforms. The severity of these problems will increase the greater the gap between the programs envisioned in the reform rhetoric and the historical experiences that have provided the greatest inputs into the personal knowledge of society.

Customs, Habits, Routines

Consider an activity such as the generation of revenues for the budget (that is, tax collecting in market economies). This activity is invariably conducted by large, complex organizations. Here I emphasize three elements of the behavior of such organizations noted by Nelson and Winter (1982, especially ch. 5). First, these organizations function by carrying out a fairly constant set of activities, or routines. Second, organizational memory, and therefore organizational productivity, are retained by the use of the routines: Organizations remember by doing (Nelson and Winter 1992, p. 99). Third, routines are used as control and monitoring devices within the organizations—they are instruments of organization, as well as instruments of production.

Reforms inevitably imply a change in the functioning and behavior of a large number of such organizations. For example, the authorities charged with generating budgetary revenues in former socialist countries will have to turn to the collection of explicit sales and income taxes, rather than the implicit trade and turnover taxes of the old regime. Thus, there is the question of how much of an advance, and how quick a move, one should ask of such organizations.

Asking an organization to adopt a wholly new mode of behavior might lead to such a deterioration in organizational memory and organizational controls that the advantages of a potentially more efficient mode of operation are outweighed. The rhetoric of a radical advance brings the existing routines into immediate disrepute, which leads to a deterioration in the instruments of organizational control. The rhetoric's stigmatizing of existing modes of behavior means that potentially productive elements of present routines cannot be salvaged. Innovation in the neighborhood of the present structure, perhaps the only innovation possible for a large complex organization, is disdained. Therefore, routines are rejected rather than invested with a new content that might well produce significant reforms because some reforms might not measure up to the rhetoric.[7]

There are obvious parallels between the arguments here and that of the subsection pertaining to personal knowledge. Indeed, both arguments might be cast in a wider framework, in which customs, habits, routines, and inherited personal knowledge are alternative means of describing related phenomena (North 1990). Each of these phenomena rely on different underpinnings, but the terminology and theoretical background are not as important here as the general conclusion. Rather, the general result relies upon noting that when there is a large component to knowledge and behavior that is historically derived, the attempt to impose change becomes vastly less productive the farther the theory and philosophy guiding change from the domain of experience.

Pressure from Society

Almost by definition, radical reforms are implemented in a top-down process by an elite, whose knowledge base and concerns are very different from those of the rest of society. Given its revealed preference for the radical model, the leadership will almost certainly have a much more favorable view of the benefit-cost ratio of the new arrangements than does the rest of society. The preference for and the understanding of the new arrangements will diminish the further one moves from the governing elite.[8]

Reforms generate rather large up-front costs. In fact, this might be the very essence of radical reforms.[9] Hence, public protests are most likely to arise early on in the reform process. Given the informational asymmetries previously postulated, it is quite possible that these protests might come to focus on the ambitious but as yet not implemented rhetoric of the leadership. The progress of reforms might be halted before the genuinely constructive elements can be implemented.

The dynamics of rhetoric, protest, and retreat arises if the populace cannot adequately distinguish the rhetoric of reforms from the extent of the implementation of reforms. Such discernment is unlikely. The public at large faces a rather difficult signal-extraction problem. It is in the process of observing attempts to implement a new system. Only observations of the early effects of reform are available as data. The rhetoric of reform offered by the leadership simply complicates the signal-extraction problem. By attempting to persuade the public that a new economic system can be put in place quickly, the leadership might diminish the public's ability to differentiate between the costs of change and the benefits of the new system that is the goal of reforms. As a result, public pressure might cause a rejection of the new system even before its main elements have been put into place.

In Mongolia, protests against the effects of reforms focused on the supposed behavior of the private sector even before it had risen to any level of significance. Top political leaders viewed the public as believing that the emergence of the private sector was a cause of inflation and that the decline of living standards was a result of the exploitative behavior of the new private sector. Independent of the veracity of this belief, politicians had to react because of popular pressures. They introduced anti-reform measures.[10] The popular reaction against the reforms culminated in Mongolia's second parliamentary election of June 1992, when seventy-one out of seventy-six seats went to members of the old Mongolian People's Revolutionary Party (MPRP), whose substantial conservative wing was advocating a slower reform than were other elements of the political spectrum. A common interpretation of that result was offered by the *Economist*: "The coalition [of Democratic parties] offered accelerated economic reform to an electorate that associates two years of free-market reforms with hunger and unemployment."[11]

An Example: Mongolia

An examination of developments in Mongolia provides some modest empirical support for the proposition that there can be an inverse relationship between rhetoric and realization. I begin by positioning the Mongolian reforms on the rhetoric scale. I turn to the realization of reforms in four key areas.[12]

For the seven decades preceding its democratic revolution of 1990, Mongolia was the de facto sixteenth republic of the Soviet Union. Mongolia's industrial base was created by the Soviet Union and its international trade was carried out almost wholly within the Council for Mutual Economic Assistance (CMEA). The Mongolian elite was educated primarily in the Soviet Union; Mongolian educational institutions and their economics curricula were based on the standard Soviet model. The reformist government, formed after the country's first free elections in 1990, therefore faced all the problems of reform that are typical of the other countries of the old Soviet bloc.

The new reform government was a coalition, numerically dominated by the former communist party, the MPRP. However, in the first years of reform, political parties had little cohesion and personal relationships among the elite were as important as party loyalties. Therefore, it was possible in late 1990 for the prime minister, a member of the MPRP, to hand over the reins of overall reform strategy to a group of ambitious young economists, most of whom were no longer members of the MPRP. One year later, it was possible for the MPRP to disclaim responsibility for economic matters and for the new democratic parties to claim the reform policies as their own.[13]

In the months following the prime minister's announcement of reforms, enthusiasm over the pace of reforms almost reached euphoria. The common interpretation of events was provided by *Far Eastern Economic Review*: "The vigour with which Mongolia's landscape is being transformed derives from a group of young, forceful economists, who occupy key positions in the new government ... and who embrace the views of prominent Western economists such as Harvard's Jeffrey Sachs, who has helped to devise fast-track reforms in Eastern Europe. With the help of the IMF and the World Bank, they hope to establish a market economy in two years of what is certain to be a wrenching transition."[14] The enthusiasm spread from the chief architect of the reforms ("The change in Mongolia is not as rapid as we would like, but comparatively on an international basis it is phenomenal"), to the Western press ("a lightning programme to introduce capitalism"), to experts lending technical help ("the speed and competence with which Mongolia is striving towards a free-market economy"), and to aid donors.[15]

This then was the rhetoric. Realization proved to be different, even at the time of greatest euphoria concerning the events in Mongolia. I now turn to some of the policy developments. There is no attempt to provide a systematic overview of the Mongolian reforms but rather an attempt to provide synopses of developments in four crucial functional areas of reform.

The Progress of Price Liberalization

Price reform—and other serious reform—began in January 1991 with the enactment of a resolution that officially freed the prices of a reported 60 percent of goods and listed a number of products and services whose prices were to remain controlled "at the initial stage of the economic transition."[16] Even before this measure, the government had announced a commitment to move to a free-price system, with only temporary controls on some goods aiming at protecting the poorest segments of the population.[17] The spirit with which this measure was introduced was captured in the statement that the resolution would "leave its traces in the history of Mongolian society."[18]

As reforms proceeded, the government reaffirmed its intention to continue a program of rapid price liberalization. It announced that farmgate prices of all agricultural products would be freed following the fulfillment of the 1991 state orders. A measure passed in September 1991 was said to have halved the number of prices subject to government control.[19] The head of the Ministry of Trade and Industry's Price Policy Office claimed in November 1991 that the prices of more than 90 percent of Mongolia's goods and services had been freed and that the prices of fuel, power, and agricultural products had almost reached world-market levels.[20] In early 1992, more steps toward decontrol were announced, culminating in a March resolution that left only flour products, transportation, utilities, fuels, and medicines formally subject to controls.[21] The rhetoric of official announcements therefore tells a story of a transformation from almost total price control to almost total decontrol within fourteen months.

The actual implementation of price control was somewhat different from the official picture. In fact, each of the arguments of the previous section of this chapter seems relevant for price policy. The basic instruments of fiscal and monetary control were not in place and the top personnel in the relevant departments had none of the practical experience necessary to implement new systems of control in a rapidly changing market environment. Those in control of policy, even the radical reformers themselves, were willing to use the familiar old techniques that were thoroughly inconsistent with the new policy.[22] The populace had little understanding of the sources of inflation in a market economy. As a consequence of each of these factors, the developments in price policy deviated a great deal from the ambitious announcements.

Despite the successive central government resolutions on price liberalization, measures that interfered in price setting abounded. For example, in a reflection of the argument that personal knowledge is important in the implementation of policy, the implementing order issued in connection with the initial price-decontrol measure required all economic entities, public and private, to comply with rigid procedures in pricing all products and services whether or not these prices officially remained under government control. These procedures included registering prices with "price-setting bodies" and the establishment of price committees within economic units, which would include representatives of buyers and of central or local agencies.[23]

In response to the political pressures arising from the perception that economic problems were caused by price decontrols, new forms of controls were issued. Some important measures gave local governments new authority over prices. In a reflection of the old practice of using enterprise surpluses as revenue sources, a measure introduced in October 1991 ordered the confiscation of all profits resulting from price increases that were deemed excessive.[24] The government commission responsible for implementing this measure interpreted it as applying to all producing entities, whatever their legal status, and to all prices.

Before reforms began, Mongolia had a fairly consistent and integrated set of price controls administered by a single hierarchy. After eighteen months of reform, a host of organizations and individuals had become involved in matters of price policy. Individual politicians at the highest levels intervened to control specific prices.[25] In companion with tax collection activities, the Ministry of Finance assumed responsibility for the collection of profits deemed to result from excessive price increases. The Ministry of Agriculture and the Ministry of Trade and Industry ran the old agricultural procurement system using fixed prices, in apparent contradiction with official government policy. Even new organizations, set up to aid in the transition, participated. Commodity exchanges, instituted to replace the old distribution system, provide an example: Flows of goods were forced through them and they were used to influence the prices of goods produced by supposed monopolies.

Hence, although the Mongolians have abandoned their old system of price control, prices are certainly far from being free. There are more individuals in the government directly influencing prices than ever before. The prices of the private sector, which had not been previously controlled, are now subject to controls. Thus, it is plausible that the Mongolians might have greater intervention now into market pricing than if the top leaders had advocated a less precipitate route. But even more important is that there has been the creation of new price-controlling institutions that might attain some degree of permanence given their embeddedness in the new power structures.

Privatization and the Security of Property Rights

The central objective of privatization is to create a group of actors in society whose power, goals, and decisions are fundamentally separate from those of the state. There are two interrelated reasons why such separation is desirable. First, efficiency and growth are enhanced by the autonomy of economic units. Second, the independent power base of the autonomous units leads to pressure on the government for the further pursuit of reforms and for the maintenance of efficient market-oriented policies. The goal is not privatization per se but rather an economy and polity propelled by autonomous private property rights.

In pursuing these objectives, privatization must satisfy two necessary conditions. First, there must be formal transfer of clear ownership title from the government to individuals. Second, the recipient of the title must have a clear understanding of the nature of the property rights received and should feel that these rights are secure, especially against arbitrary government intervention. If the nominal transfer has been accomplished but the second condition has not been satisfied, then little might distinguish the "privatized" economy from the old one. This second aspect of privatization is then a matter of the functioning of the institutions of society and the character of the informal aspects of society on which these institutions rest. The formal transfer of property rights is, in some senses, a simple extension of the rhetoric. The recognition of those property rights by society and the use of them by their owners are the realization of reforms.

Acknowledging the importance of the second aspect of privatization leads to an emphasis on the detailed arrangements of society, for example, social and political predispositions on the protection of property rights rather than on the higher-level operation of the formal transfer of title. There is no question that privatization can go very fast in its formal aspects. But there is a question of whether speed on that dimension can retard society's acceptance and defense of a private property rights regime, which is so necessary for property holders to use their rights efficiently.

Privatization was at the center of Mongolian reform efforts: The Privatization Commission was designated as the vanguard of reforms and charged with overall coordination of reform efforts. Privatization was considered by the leading reformists to be the sine qua non of a successful transition. Leading members of the new democratic parties planned to carry out privatization within a matter of two years.

Privatization in the first sense—the nominal transfer of title—has proceeded as fast in Mongolia as in any reforming country. By mid-1992, just eighteen months after the beginnings of reforms, the reformers were well on their way to their two-year goal. Approximately 90 percent (3,500) of small and medium enterprises were already privatized. Five hundred large entities—200 industrial and 300 agricultural—had been through the privatization process. Seventy percent of all livestock was owned by individuals in an agricultural sector that had been completely privatized. Most manufacturing industries were now more than half privatized, as was the overwhelming proportion of the service sector.[26]

But privatization in the second sense has only just begun in Mongolia. A single story, but one that is hardly unique, captures the present situation. After the decontrol of the price of an important food, there were demonstrations in Ulaan Baatar. A top government official was dispatched by the highest political leaders to the major producer of this food, a company that had been privatized six months previously. The government official audited the accounts of this company. On the basis of this audit and a reworking of the cost-accounting data, the company was ordered to lower its price (even though this price was one that had been officially freed by the government). The reason given by government officials was that the cost of production did not warrant the price that was being charged by the entity.

This incident highlights several elements of the general discussion of the first section of this chapter. There were demonstrations, causing the government to react immediately. In their reactions, officials used a policy that derived its essentials from the old system. The government officials believed that detailed intervention into the affairs of the privatized company was appropriate. Cost-based pricing was invoked as the rule to follow. Old habits and a historically derived understanding of the nature of economic processes combined to produce behavior that was at odds with the operation of the economy as envisaged in the rhetoric of reform. Given that this move by the government drew few objections and accomplished its immediate objectives, there is every possibility that such behavior will be accepted as part of the new order of business. To the extent that institutions are secured by society itself, locked in by the beliefs and habits arising out of events, the development of private property rights might well have been significantly retarded.

The preceding example is typical of the extent to which privatization in Mongolia has been only nominal. The old system of materials allocation still exists and is still supported by the compulsory requisition of output by state bodies. Within this system, privatized companies are treated symmetrically with their erstwhile partners in the old state system rather than with new private companies, which are not given official allocations. Intervention in the production decisions of privatized concerns is rife.[27] As the preceding subsection makes clear, interventions into pricing decisions are still pervasive: The nominal privatization of enterprises does not give them access to a due process mechanism that allows them to challenge presumed violations of "price discipline" that can be followed by immediate confiscation of goods. If the legal dictum is correct that there are no rights without remedies, private property rights do not yet exist in Mongolia.

As a result of the attempt to implement the rhetoric but not the substances of privatization, the status of private property rights is absolutely unclear. Many of the old structures of state intervention are still functioning while the new legal titles are in existence. No formal tax collection mechanisms existed, which forced the authorities to use the old methods of tax collection in a way inconsistent with private-sector activity. The absence of a system of monetary and credit control meant that price intervention was almost inevitable. The focus on swift privatization occurred at a time when there were few voices in the country pressuring for the creation of the standard legal instruments necessary for the protection of property rights.

The privatization process in Mongolia has not yet created a group of autonomous actors whose power, goals, and decisions are fundamentally separate from those of the state. The process of swift formal privatization precluded any attempts at addressing the second aspect of privatization—developments within society and in its institutions that would secure the separation between the state and the new owners. Indeed, as the following statement from the Government Privatization Commission attests, there was probably little recognition of the necessity for such separation within society: "From the very beginning, it is necessary to pay special attention to setting control over the contracts of privatized shops, caterings, utility services and other enterprises on issues relating to maintenance of the types and size of services, the supply and price regimes, and the number of employees, and supervision over the implementation of these contracts."[28] (As this statement reveals, some of the inconsistencies that resulted in the attempts to implement the rhetoric might have indeed resulted from the mismatch between the personal knowledge of the framers of the reform program and the rhetoric itself. In the long run, the success of privatization will depend upon whether the present ad hoc government intervention into the privatized sector that is a result of such mismatches is established as a norm in society, locked in by the habits and understandings gained in these first years of reform.

Laws and the Legal System

An essential element of the transition is the establishment of "the Rule of Law, [which] means that government in all its actions is bound by rules which make it possible to foresee with fair certainty how the authority will use its coercive power in given circumstances and to plan one's affairs on the basis of this knowledge" (Hayek 1944, p. 72). To Hayek, the rule of law is so much the essence of a liberal society that "it may even be said that for the Rule of Law to be effective, it is more important that there should be a rule applied always without exceptions than what this rule is" (Hayek, 1944, p. 80). The creation of the rule of law gives us another yardstick with which to judge the effect of rhetoric on the realization of reforms.

That the pursuit of speed in reform can conflict with the rule of law was obvious from the beginning in Mongolia. Two examples provide some of the flavor of the situation. In the very first privatization, land was sold in violation of the constitution of the country.[29] This act was justified by the leading reformers as a way to secure fast privatization.

The second example is the passage of a new tax law at the very beginnings of reform. A central aim of this law was to create a code that would be appropriate for the market economy. As a consequence, the framers of the law brooked no accommodation for the realities of Mongolia, the status of its bureaucracy, and the ability of the implementers to understand and use the law. The law was a fine piece of rhetoric concerning the aims of the reform process.

The result was a law described, by even one of the leading reformers, as "too theoretical" and by an implementer of the law in a rural district as "impossible to interpret for the case of private herders."[30] Given the budgetary catastrophe that was occurring at the time that the new tax law was to take effect, tax collection was conducted outside the framework of the law, using many of the old methods of confiscation. With privatization proceeding apace, these actions violated Article 5 of the new constitution, which instructed the state to protect the rights of all owners and dictated that these rights be limited only through due process of law. Applying the rhetoric of radical reform to the tax law and privatization simultaneously was incompatible with the establishment of a law-governed state under a new democratic constitution.

These two examples were consistent with the overall spirit with which the reform program was pursued. Legislation had virtually no role in governing economic life, which was regulated by the unconstrained day-to-day decisions of the government.[31] This was a result of a conscious decision made early in the reform process to move fast and to sidestep the procedural and political constraints of parliament. Parliament itself handed over the task of reform to the government and agreed that government resolutions would have the force of law. Even though the government's actions were therefore lawful, they did not produce a rule-of-law state: "'[The] belief that, so long as all the actions of the state are duly authorized by legislation, the Rule of Law will be preserved [is] completely to misconceive the meaning of the Rule of Law. The fact that someone has full legal authority to act in the way that he does gives no answer to the question of whether the law gives him power to act arbitrarily or whether the law prescribes unequivocally how he has to act" (Hayek 1944, p. 82).

If, following Hayek, it is the establishment of the rule of law that is the hallmark of a successful realization of market-oriented reforms, then the ambition embodied in the government's program might have slowed the transition. Perhaps, given the lack of the rule of law under the old system, it is not the present place of law in society that is most troubling. Rather, the danger is that present behavior will be interpreted as consistent with the new system and locked into the informal structures of society. As Aristotle recognized, early behavior is all important: "Legislators make their citizens good by habituation; this is the intention of every legislator, and those who do not carry it out fail in their object. ... So it is a matter of no little importance what sort of habits we form from the earliest age—it makes a vast difference, or rather all the difference in the world."[32]

The Development of the Nascent Private Sector

One can view a reforming socialist economy as comprising two sectors—(1) the newly created private sector and (2) the old state enterprises, or their privatized successors. There is a trade-off between the development of the reforms that are particularly useful to each of these two sectors: An increase in attention to one sector will lead to less progress on reform in the other (Murrell and Wang 1993). Therefore, the relative importance attached to developments in these two sectors is an important ingredient in the evaluation of the progress of reforms. For some, the rise of the new private sector will be crucial (Kornai 1990). In this case, an overly ambitious attempt to transform the old state sector can easily slow the progress of reforms as a whole through its detrimental effects on the nascent private sector.

In Mongolia in 1990, a tiny private sector was showing signs of rapid growth. Paradoxically, given the centralized nature of the rest of the economic system, this private sector was relatively free of state intervention. At the beginning of 1991, with the state sector still under administrative control, the private sector was able to set its own prices and engage in foreign trade, retaining its own foreign exchange earnings. In 1991, 10 percent of the resources in the state distribution system had been set aside to be sold to the new private sector, to encourage its growth. A program of loans to new small businesses began at the same time.

When reforms in the state sector took high priority, the nascent private sector became entangled in the consequences. As the state sector became decentralized and market interventions were used to solve perceived problems, there was a paradoxical increase in the influence of the state on the new private sector. When the state foreign trade system was decentralized, the nascent private sector had to apply for foreign trade licenses. When the shortage of foreign exchange became chronic, new private-sector firms were forced to surrender all their foreign currency earnings. By the beginning of 1992, the nascent private sector had lost the allocation of raw materials that it had previously received from the state distribution system.

The nascent private sector became a focus of the popular protests aimed at the reforms. The old attitudes to the private sector began to be more significant to politicians, and policy toward the new private sector became more punitive. The government even made the distinction between the nascent private sector and the privatized sector, treating the latter more favorably to save the privatized firms from collapse.[33] The ambition embodied in the initial reform program locked politicians into a program of securing the success of the privatized sector at the expense of the nascent private sector.

As reforms proceeded, the old habits and routines of politicians affected the nascent private sector to an increasing degree. One resolution required governmental agencies at both the central and local levels "to control prices for goods set by private shops so that these prices do not exceed the average market level" and "to define procedures for operating ... private shops."[34] Another resolution dictated that "the profit gained solely as a result of a price increase without using the practical possibility of the economic entity and reducing the volume of production should be completely transferred into the state budget."[35] Thus, this measure brought the nascent private sector into the ambit of the revenue-generation mechanism that had always existed in the state sector during the era of centralized socialism, In fact, the Ministry of Finance, under great pressure to increase its revenues, participated eagerly in this program to control prices, which had as its by-product the generation of extra revenues.

Hence, as reform measures brought significant change into the old state sector, the development of the nascent private sector was slowed. This slowing contains many of the elements outlined in the first section of this chapter. Public protest led to a perceived need to react to the economic distress that was befalling the country. That economic distress was interpreted by the populace at large through the prism of the attitudes to the private sector generated under the old system. In reacting, politicians relied upon the stock of knowledge inherited from history. The only measures that were available to mollify the population were those that were familiar from the years of socialism. But they were applied in situations and in sectors to which they had not been applicable under the previous regime.

Conclusion

Mongolia's reforms were characterized initially, and are sometimes still, as the most radical in the reforming socialist world—quick price and trade liberalization and an ambitious scheme for privatization. These characterizations were based on the stated intentions of the top leadership and on the formal measures passed early in the reform process rather than reflecting the reality of policy implementation. Instead, rapid price liberalization came to mean the proliferation of decentralized ad hoc controls, not free market pricing. The establishment of a set of autonomous private actors has not occurred despite the shotgun formal privatization. In trying to pursue these ambitious goals, policymakers were willing to make choices that slowed the establishment of the rule of law and the development of the nascent private sector.

Using the methodology made notorious in the generation of the Laffer curve, one can employ the Mongolian data point to picture reform's rhetoric-realization relationship. I have argued that the reforms of Mongolia, with a rhetoric higher than anywhere in the world, did not advance far. In contrast, many countries in the early 1990s have had much lower levels of ambition and are much more advanced in matters such as the development of the new private sector, the establishment of secure property rights, and the establishment of the rule of law. Any of these countries would provide a second data point. As a third, at the point of origin of our graph, we might place the Kosygin reforms, with little rhetoric and no accomplishments. With these three data points, it is obvious that reform's rhetoric-realization relationship does have a backward-bending portion.

Notes

1. See, for example, Lipton and Sachs 1990.

2. Of course, there is concession to the existing situation in all reform programs. However, the argument here is that reform design must begin with the existing institutional structure, not simply make concession to it.

3. As used here, the term *knowledge* encompasses not only accurate information but also beliefs and understandings that might not be verifiable.

4. The examples cited in this paragraph are all matters that have had an effect on the formulation and implementation of Mongolian reforms.

5. See Oakeshott 1962.

6. Although skepticism about such a claim is at the center of this chapter's argument, this assumption does describe the beliefs of many radical reformers about their situation vis-à-vis their own society.

7. Poznanski has made similar arguments in the case of the Polish privatization program, where ambition was high, creating large uncertainty for enterprises, but progress was actually slow.

8. One academic-politician who deliberated on the relationship between knowledge and policy change believed that "a truth must become not only plain but also commonplace before it will be seen by the people who go to their work very early in the morning" (Wilson 1887, p. 209).

9. In fact, a radical program aims at moving costs forward (Lipton and Sachs, 1990).

10. Two responses to protests by the populace and which led to measures that severely restricted the growth of the private sector were the "Government Commission Responsible for Stopping Any Activity Targeted at Creating a Shadow Economy and for Taking Measures to Prevent Organized Crimes," created in September 1991, and the government's Resolution 279, "Measures to Restrict Producers' Monopoly Power and to Stop Some Negative Phenomena During the Transition to a Market-Based Economy," of October 1, 1991.

11. *Economist*, July 4, 1992.

12. Much of the information given on Mongolia in this chapter is based on personal interviews. In cases where no citations are given, further details on sources of information are available from the author on request.

13. See the *Mongol Messenger* of November 30, 1991, p. 3, reporting on the positions taken by the party newspapers *National Progress* and *Unen*.

14. *Far Eastern Economic Review*, September 19, 1991, p. 70.

15. See *Euromoney*, July 1991, p. 7; *Reuter's*, June 25, 1991; *South China Morning Post*, June 9, 1991; and *Washington Post*, July 24, 1991.

16. Resolution 20, "Some Measures on Shifting the Economy to Market Relations," January 15, 1991.

17. Government of Mongolia, "Summary of Situation," January 1991.

18. Press conference of Deputy Prime Minister Ganbold, Ulaan Baatar, January 16, 1991.

19. Resolution 240, "Additional Measures Toward the Transition to a Free-Price System," September 1, 1991.

20. Ishdorj, Mongol Messenger, November 26, 1991, p. 2.

21. Resolution 35, "Some Measures Regarding Prices," effective March 1, 1992.

22. This is argued at length in Murrell, Dunn, and Korsun 1992.

23. Ministry of Trade and Industry, Order 273, 1991.

24. Resolution 279, "Measures to Restrict Producers' Monopoly Power and to Stop Some Negative Phenomena During the Transition to a Market-Based Economy," October 1, 1991.

25. For example, after social unrest over milk price increases in the capital city of Ulaan Baatar, members of the cabinet pressed the city's price commission to change these prices.

26. Report of the Privatization Commission, Government of Mongolia, August 1992.

27. For example, one measure orders government agencies to "define the size of cultivation of land for each [region and] economic entity not less than that cultivated in 1990 and control implementation of the sowing campaign" for the already privatized agricultural entities. Resolution 18 of February 1991, "On Measures in the Field of Land Cultivation."

28. Report of the Privatization Commission, December 1991.

29. *Independent* June 25, 1991.

30. These observations were obtained during personal interviews.

31. See Enkbaatar, "Why Don't Bills Act?" *Mongol Messenger*, October 14, 1991, p. 2.

32. Aristotle, *Ethics*.

33. Resolution 317, "Measures Concerning the Transfer of Commercial Organizations to the Market System," November 22, 1991.

34. Resolution 317, "Measures Concerning the Transfer of Commercial Organizations to the Market System," November 22, 1991.

35. Resolution 279, "Measures to Restrict Producers' Monopoly Power and to Stop Some Negative Phenomena During the Transition to a Market-Based Economy," October 1, 1991.

References

Hayek, F. A. 1944. *The Road to Serfdom*. Chicago: University of Chicago Press.

Kornai, J. 1990. *The Road to a Free Economy*. New York: Norton.

Lipton, D. and J. Sachs. 1990. *Creating a Market Economy in Eastern Europe: The Case of Poland*, Brookings Papers on Economic Activity, no. 1 (April).

Murrell, P., K. Turner Dunn, and G. Korsun. 1992. "The Culture of Policy Making in the Transition from Socialism: Price Policy in Mongolia," Working paper, IRIS, University of Maryland.

Murrell, P., and Y. Wang. 1993. "When Privatization Should Be Delayed: The Effect of Communist Legacies on Organizational and Institutional Reforms." Mimeo. University of Maryland, College Park.

Nelson, R., and S. Winter. 1982. *An Evolutionary Theory of Economic Change*. Cambridge: Harvard University Press.

North, D. C. 1990. *Institutions: Institutional Change and Economic Performance*. Cambridge: Cambridge University Press.

Oakeshott, M. 1962. *Rationalism in Politics and Other Essays*. New York: Basic Books.

Polanyi, M. 1962. *Personal Knowledge: Towards a Post-Critical Philosophy*. Chicago: University of Chicago Press.

Poznanski, K. 1992. "Reconstituting Property Rights in Poland: A Study in Evolutionary Economics," *East European Politics and Societies* 7, no 3 (Fall).

Wilson, W. 1887. "The Study of Administration," *Political Science Quarterly* 2, no. 2 (June), pp. 197–222.

5

Financial Growth and Macroeconomic Stability in China, 1978–1992: Implications for Russia and Eastern Europe

Ronald I. McKinnon

From 1978, China's liberalization was gradual, with a fairly stable price level and extraordinarily rapid output growth. Since 1989 in Eastern Europe and the former Soviet Union, rapid liberalizations attempted in the face of falling real output have generated much higher inflation. Yet both regions' fiscal policies were surprisingly similar. Like its socialist counterparts in Europe, the Chinese government's revenue share in gross national product (GNP) has fallen sharply; in 1991–1992, its fiscal deficit approached 10 percent of GNP as illustrated below; and it was very high in 1992–1993 as well. How did China manage to avoid inflation when its government was such a heavy borrower from the state banking system?

I begin by identifying four ways in which China avoided resorting to the inflation tax. First, it began by liberalizing in areas like agriculture, where subsequent productivity growth was rapid. Second, it imposed very hard budget constraints on, and gave little bank credit to, the newly liberalized nonstate sectors in industry or agriculture. Third, it did retain intramarginal price controls on, and constrained financial support for, traditional soft-budget state enterprises. Fourth, it set positive real inter-

I would like to thank Mikhail Bernstam, Yingyi Qian, and Christine Wong for generously sharing data and ideas in helping me prepare this chapter.

est rates on savings deposits. The resulting enormous growth in saving and stocks of financial assets allowed the liberalized sector to finance itself, the Chinese government, and the deficits of the slowly reforming state enterprises.

How the Chinese accomplished this remarkable financial feat is analyzed in some statistical detail below. The reader will quickly note similarities with the high financial growth policies followed by Japan in the 1950s and 1960s and by Taiwan in the 1960s and 1970s (McKinnon 1991b, ch. 3). Yet, there is an important difference: the Chinese government's failure to get control over the public finances at the outset of liberalization. Nevertheless, I shall argue that many important aspects of China's dualistic banking and pricing policies could well be adopted by other transitional socialist economies in Europe and Asia. Indeed, China's dualistic system of financial controls are consistent with, and nicely illustrate, the gradualist approach to the transition from centralized controls over prices and output to a more decentralized market economy.

But China's incredibly high real financial growth is not feasible in Russia, and formerly socialist Europe where output growth is low or negative and inflationary expectations are more highly developed. Indeed, such high real financial growth may not be sustainable for much longer in China itself. Thus, to prevent inflation and stem financial decline in the liberalizing European economies, fiscal reforms should come much earlier in their transitions compared to China's. (In more moderate-growth, but less rapidly industrializing, socialist economies such as Laos [Vokes and Fabella 1992] and Vietnam [Fforde de Vylder, 1992], the scope for their governments to rely on deficit finance by borrowing from the liberalized sector is also somewhat more limited than China's—but probably better than Eastern Europe's.)

On the fiscal side, China is an important, if temporary, exception to our preferred order of economic liberalization—as outlined in McKinnon (1991a and 1991b). Nevertheless, China's other financial policies were more or less right. Its interest rate, credit, pricing policies, and step-by-step foreign trade reforms were fully consonant with the crucial need to sustain macroeconomic equilibrium as liberalization proceeds—as we shall see.

This chapter concludes with a brief analysis of the inflationary explosion and sharp output decline in Russia in 1992 arising out of the Yeltsin-Gaidar government's "big-bang" approach to economic liberalization. Did the Russians get the order of economic liberalization wrong or was this unfortunate event the result of adverse exogenous shocks beyond any government's control? Given the great receptiveness of the Russian government to Western advice in 1991 and much of 1992, was this advice lacking in important respects?

Gradual Versus Rapid Liberalization in Socialist Economies

China is often cited as the leading example of a successful gradualist approach to economic liberalization.[1] In 1978, the Chinese began to break up traditional agricultural communes into small farm leases (now ten to fifteen years' duration)—the so-called household responsibility system. From 1979 to 1983, with over three-quarters of the population still in agriculture, farm output surged by 8 to 10 percent per year (Johnson 1990). By 1984, the focus of rapid economic growth had shifted to rural light industry, which began to absorb much of the labor force released by productivity improvements in agriculture. Although small-scale private traders flourished, hundreds of thousands of the new manufacturing enterprises (now simply called TVEs, for township and village enterprises) were owned largely by townships and villages. In this so-called nonstate sector, the TVEs were market-driven and outside the web of official price and output controls that still circumscribed activity in the old heavy-industry state sector.

In this traditional sector, the much larger-scale state-owned enterprises (SOEs) remained under the ownership and control of the central government with no attempt at some form of rapid privatization or price decontrol. The step-by-step, the pricing and financial arrangements facing the old SOEs were also rationalized, but at a more deliberate pace lasting over a decade. Overall price stability in both the state and nonstate sectors was surprisingly well maintained, with retail price inflation averaging 6 to 7 percent per year starting in 1978 (Table 5.1).

The Chinese approach to freeing foreign trade was also gradualist. Instead of a "big bang" that suddenly opened up the whole economy to international competition and world prices, special economic zones somewhat outside the control of the traditional state trading monopolies were started in Guangdong in connection with the Hong Kong trade. These then became progessively more numerous and broader in scope. Inside such a zone, exporters could retain all of their foreign exchange earnings while having freer access to imported materials and foreign capital or trading services.

By the end of the 1980s, an export (and import) boom had become China's new engine of economic growth. Exports had risen from less than 8 percent of GNP in the early 1980s to about 20 percent in 1992. Real GNP growth itself averaged almost 9 percent per year from 1979 to 1992 (Table 5.1). By the early 1990s, however, the distinction between a "special economic zone" and the rest of the economy had eroded. Now, a wide range of SOEs, TVEs, and private enterprises participate with more equal access to foreign trade, and the domestic economy's insulation from world markets has diminished.

TABLE 5.1   China's Main Economic Indicators (percentage rate of growth)

	Real National Income	Real GNP	General Retail Price Index	Urban Cost of Living Index	Free Market Index	Money (M2)	Exports/ GNP	Foreign Reserves[a] (billion $)
1975	8.3		0.2	0.4				
1976	−0.3		0.3	0.3	4.0			
1977	7.8		2.0					
1978	12.3		0.7					
1979	7.0	7.6	2.0			2.7	5.31%	0.84
1980	6.4	7.9	6.0			4.1	6.07%	−1.30
1981	4.9	4.4	2.4			9.7	7.70%	2.71
1982	8.3	8.7	1.9	2.0		13.1	7.97%	6.99
1983	9.8	10.3	1.5	2.0	4.2	19.2	7.55%	8.90
1984	13.4	14.6	2.8	2.7	−0.4	42.4	8.34%	8.22
1985	13.1	12.7	8.8	11.9	17.2	17.0	9.45%	2.64
1986	7.9	8.3	6.0	7.0	8.1	30.2	11.16%	2.07
1987	10.2	11.0	7.3	8.8	16.3	25.3	13.01%	2.92
1988	11.1	11.0	18.5	20.7	30.3	20.7	12.60%	3.37
1989	3.7	4.4	17.8	16.3	10.8	18.7	12.29%	5.55
1990	5.1	5.6	2.1	1.3	−5.7	28.9	16.88%	11.09
1991	7.9	7.3	2.9	5.1	−0.9	26.7	19.30%	21.71
Average 1979–1991	8.4	8.8	6.2	6.9	6.5	22.7		
Preliminary 1992	12.8		5.4	8.6		31.0	20.0%	

[a] foreign exchange reserves are those held by the central bank (the People's Bank of China). Large reserves held by the foreign trade bank (the Bank of China) are excluded.

Sources: Christine Wong, christopher Heady, and W. T. Woo, Economic Reform and Fiscal Management in China (Manila: asian Development Bank, February 1993); Yingyi Qian, "Lessons and Relevance of the Japanese main Bank System for Financial Reform in China," mimeo (Stanford: Stanford University Department of Economics, March 1993). data for M2 are from IMF, International Finance Statistics 1992 Yearbook (Washington, D.C.: IMF, 1992). Other data from China Statistical Yearbook (Chinese Edition) (Bejing: Government of China, 1992).

Although this great economic transformation has been very rapid, it seems fair to characterize the Chinese government's economic policies as gradualist—with the possible exception of the "minimum bang"[2] necessary to get the ball rolling in agriculture in 1978–1979. In 1985, these early Chinese successes encouraged Mikhail Gorbachev to embark on perestroika, and in 1986 smaller Asian economies such as Laos and Vietnam adopted their fairly gradualist "new economic mechanisms," which have been fairly successful.[3] By 1989, the transition from central planning to more market-based economies had become a political imperative throughout Eastern Europe and the former Soviet Union (FSU).

But this poses a paradox. If gradualism in China and smaller Asian economies was successful early on, why did the Eastern Europeans in general, and Russians in particular, later attempt more of a big-bang approach to economic liberalization? Why were the Eastern Europeans so enamored with more sweeping transfers of property rights (including elaborate voucher schemes for transferring state property) and sudden full-scale price and output decontrol in traditional enterprises? This big-bang approach was often coupled with the intention—not always carried out in practice—to swiftly open the whole economy to unrestricted foreign trade with the hard-currency industrial economies.

At least in the initial stages of these rapid liberalizations, abrupt policy changes in Eastern Europe were associated with economic disorganization, sharp falls in output, and, in some cases, inflationary explosions (Aslund 1992). For the much briefer time series on the transition processes in Bulgaria, Czechoslovakia (before its dissolution), Hungary,[4] Poland, Romania, and the Soviet Union (before its dissolution), Tables 5.2 and 5.3 depict the sharp decreases in output experienced by virtually all these economies from 1989 to 1992. This falling output has been accompanied by high, sometimes explosive, inflation—nowhere more evident than in Russia and Ukraine in 1992–1993. In contrast, Chinese output rose sharply after 1978, and throughout the early 1980s price inflation remained very low (Table 5.1).

Were Circumstances in Eastern Europe (Including the FSU) Essentially Different?

Output decline in Eastern Europe can be largely attributed to exogenous political and economic circumstances that differed from those prevailing in China (and in similarly agrarian economies such as Vietnam and Laos) and which were largely beyond the economic control of individual reform governments:

1. Eastern Europe was more industrialized and specialized (too spa-

TABLE 5.2 Gross Domestic Product Growth Rates, 1989–1992

	Percentage Change in Real GDP			
	1989	1990	1991	1992[a]
Bulgaria	−0.5	−10.6	−23.0	−3.0
Czechoslovakia	0.7	−0.4	−15.9	−5.0
Hungary	−0.2	−4.3	−10.2	−5.0
Poland	0.2	−11.6	−7.2	−1.0
Romania	−5.8	−7.4	−13.7	−10.0
Soviet Union	3.0	−2.3	−17.0	N/A

[a]Preliminary estimates.

Sources: Anders Aslund, *Post Communist Revolutions: How Big a Bang?* Washington, D.C.: CSIS, 1992); International Monetary Fund, *Financial Sector Reforms and Exchange Rate Arrangements in Eastern Europe,* Occasional Paper 102, Washington, D.C., (February 1993).

TABLE 5.3 Inflation, Unemployment, and Budget Balance, 1990, 1991, and 1992

	Inflation (% change)			Unemployment (% in December)		General Government Balance (% of GDP)		
	1990	1991	1992[a]	1990	1991	1990	1991	1992
Bulgaria	26	460	49	1.6	10.5	−8.5	−3.7	−3.5
Czechoslovakia	11	59	10	1.0	6.6	0.1	−2.2	−4.4
Hungary	33	32	22	1.7	8.5	0.4	−3.3	−10.6
Poland	586	70	46	6.5	11.4	3.5	−5.6	−7.2
Romania	50	161	203	N/A	4.3	−0.5	−2.6	−1.9
Soviet Union	6	152	N/A	0	0	−8.0	−26.0	N/A

[a]Figures for 1992 are preliminary.

Sources: Anders Aslund, *Post Communist Revolutions: How Big a Bang?* Washington, D.C.: CSIS, 1992); International Monetary Fund, *Financial Sector Reforms and Exchange Rate Arrangements in Eastern Europe,* Occasional Paper 102, Washington, D.C., (February 1993).

cialized) in heavy industry. Because agrarian populations were proportionally smaller than in the Asian socialist economies, the possibility of, and the immediate gains from, returning to smallholder agriculture were more limited.

2. The collapse of the CMEA disrupted trade within the former Soviet Bloc, and then trade among the republics of the former Soviet Union was disrupted.

3. The precipitate decline in the power of the communist party in most of Eastern Europe and the FSU was coupled with the weakening of centralized political control over the economy at large and the weakening of decentralized party monitoring of state-owned enterprises.

Because of the first circumstance typical Eastern European economies, in contrast to the economy of China, were denied a substantial margin on which to liberalize to get immediate increases in output. So pervasive has been this pattern of falling output that many observers suggest that the transition from socialism must naturally have to follow a J- curve: Output must fall before a long-term growth path more characteristic of a liberal economy can be established (Gomulka 1991 and Murrell 1990). On this J-curve view, liberalization must first largely destroy the old order before economic resources can be efficiently redeployed.

Countering this view, many argue that the trade shocks that resulted from the second circumstance were so enormous that some decline in output was inevitable in any event—given the high degree of specialization in the old CMEA trading regime (Brada and King 1991). And in the 1980s, CMEA trade was about half the total foreign trade of Eastern Europe and the FSU. Then in 1991, CMEA trade imploded with 60 to 70 percent of member countries' trade with each other suddenly drying up (Borenstein and Masson 1993). Because this CMEA shock was so enormous, one could argue that a more rapid opening of trade with advanced industrial economies was imperative in Eastern Europe—unlike in the early stages of China's liberalization.

Regarding the third circumstance the ability of the typical European reform government to control resources centrally was so limited that rapid privatization and price decontrol in the industrial sector were more essential in socialist Europe than in socialist Asia. More crudely, rip-offs of the assets of the state-owned enterprises (SOEs) had previously been prevented by the monitoring and oversight of the communist party. With the decline in the party's power, Jeffrey Sachs has argued vehemently for more rapid privatization of both industrial and financial enterprises to stem the tide (Sachs 1992).

Without denying the great importance of the three abovementioned points for what happened in Eastern Europe in general and Russia in particular, I hypothesize that China's longer-running experience with the transition from a planned to a market economy still contains valuable lessons for East Europeans. But rather than trying to cover the whole liberalization landscape at the microeconomic level, this chapter focuses on the problem of macroeconomic control. With China as a benchmark, what are the fiscal and monetary problems that a reform socialist government will typically face, and how can these be best resolved in ways that encourage ouput growth while maintaining price-level stability in the liberalizing economy?

China is by no means a paragon of virtue, however. The sustainability of its own macroeconomic policies, not all of which are transferable to Eastern Europe, is now in doubt. If inflation is to be avoided in the mid 1990s, China must undertake some radical fiscal and monetary restructuring—as we shall see. But first I will review Chinese macroeconomic policies since 1978 to point out what is generally feasible in other transitional economies.

A Chinese Puzzle: Price-Level Stability
in the Face of Fiscal Decline

In the early 1980s, how stable was the "true" Chinese price level in an environment when most prices were still controlled? Figure 5.1 shows that as late as 1981 only about 10 percent of retail sales were free of price controls. By the early 1990s, more than 70 percent of retail prices and 85 percent of the output prices of the collectively owned enterprises (COEs) were market determined. (Even the output and input prices of SOEs were 70 percent decontrolled by 1991.) Consequently, three different consumer prices are presented in Table 5.1. From 1979 to 1991, an urban employee's cost-of-living index rose the most, averaging 6.9 percent per year whereas the more general retail price index averaged 6.2 percent and the "free market" index, made up only of commodities whose prices were decontrolled, rose by 6.5 percent.

Because of this relatively modest growth in the free market and other price indexes, it appears that China began its liberalization between 1979 and 1981 without significantly repressed inflation. At the outset, no major macroeconomic adiustment was needed to work off a monetary overhang by a one-time inflation (as planned in Poland in 1990 or in Russia in 1992), or possibly by a currency reform where outstanding cash balances were cancelled (as in West Germany in June 1948). Thus, for many years after 1978, official price controls in trade among the old state

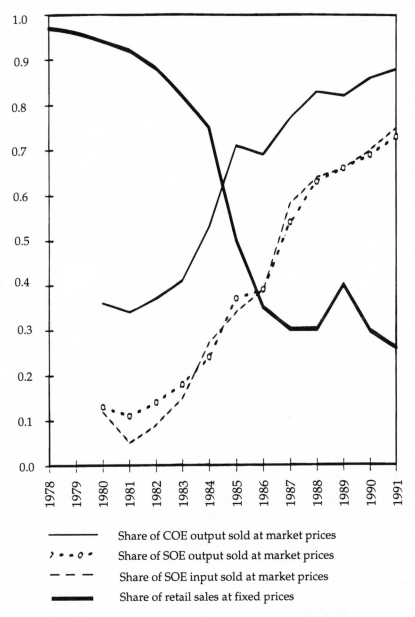

1.0

0.9

0.8

0.7

0.6

0.5

0.4

0.3

0.2

0.1

0.0

1978 1979 1980 1981 1982 1983 1984 1985 1986 1987 1988 1989 1990 1991

—————— Share of COE output sold at market prices

⟩ • ▪ o ◦ Share of SOE output sold at market prices

— — — Share of SOE input sold at market prices

▬▬▬ Share of retail sales at fixed prices

FIGURE 5.1   Price and Market Reform: Output Sold at Free and Fixed Prices

Source: Alan Gelb, Gary Jefferson, and Inderjit Singh, "Can Communist Economies Transform Incrementally? The Experience of China," mimeo (World Bank, February 1993).

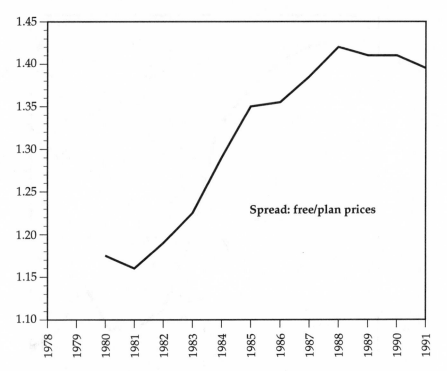

FIGURE 5.2   Premiums Paid in Prices Changed in Free Markets

Source: Alan Gelb, Gary Jefferson, and Inderjit Singh, "Can Communist Economies Transform Incrementally? The Experience of China," mimeo (World Bank,
February 1993).

enterprises could be effectively enforced with centrally determined
deliveries at those prices.

But price liberalization occurred at the margin. In the newly burgeon-
ing nonstate sector, the SOEs could sell their surplus output beyond
what the state contracted for at market prices. Figure 5.2 shows the 20 to
40 percent premium in prices charged in this free market. Fortunately,
the absence of a monetary overhang limited this price gap and thus
limited (but did not eliminate) the tendency for supply diversion—illicit
transfers of scarce goods from the state sector to higher-price nonstate
uses.[5] As general liberalization proceeded alongside rapid industrial
growth in the nonstate sector, the number of price-controlled goods in
the state sector was continually reduced. But even these pegged prices
were rationalized as raw materials prices were increased in stages, and
finished goods prices were sometimes scaled down.

China does not calculate a general producer price index (PPI).

Because a PPI excludes services, it would show lower rates of price inflation—once the effects of price decontrol are removed—than do Table 5.1's retail price indices. Measured productivity growth in services is typically much less than in agricultural and industrial goods, particularly in a rapidly growing economy like China's. The upshot is that since 1979, China has had a very stable price level in comparison to the often explosive price inflation in Eastern Europe.

Even without a monetary overhang at the outset, how was macroeconomic control in China subsequently sustained through 1991? One cannot look to Chinese fiscal policy for an answer. On the contrary, like all communist countries, China depended on price controls and ownership of state enterprises for generating and then collecting huge surpluses from the industrial sector. By world standards, the domestic prices of industrial raw materials and agricultural wage goods were kept down compared to the prices of finished industrial goods. The resulting financial surpluses in most SOEs were then deposited in the state bank in blocked accounts as de facto government revenue.

But in all socialist countries this implicit revenue system begins to unravel naturally as liberalization begins (McKinnon 1991a and 1991b). First, the government-owned share of industrial assets begins to fall. Second, price decontrol and industrial competition from both domestic and foreign sources tends to shrink the profit margins in all industrial enterprises—whether owned by the government or not. Indeed, many once-profitable (though aftificially) SOEs become loss makers. This tendency toward fiscal deterioration was qualitatively the same in China as in Eastern Europe or the FSU.

Table 5.4 shows the very sharp decline in the revenue of the Chinese (consolidated) government from about 34.8 percent of GNP in 1978 to only 18.5 percent in 1991. To be sure, the government also curbed expenditures sharply, but the ambiguous financial position of loss-making SOEs makes the net deficit hard to calculate. Table 5.5 includes "policy loans," that is, "forced" lending to the SOEs by the People's Bank of China. It shows that the "true" consolidated fiscal deficit may have reached 10 percent of China's GNP in 1991.

In summary, China has experienced ongoing fiscal deterioration since 1978. Increasing open and hidden deficits are largely covered by borrowing from the state banking system. Obversely, broad money growth in China has been very high—averaging about 23 percent per year for more than a decade. Thus our puzzle: How did China succeed in containing this inflationary pressure better than the socialist countries in Eastern Europe that were facing similar revenue declines? (To be sure, China suffered significant price increases in 1985 and again in 1988– 1989—but successfully recovered by disinflating.)

TABLE 5.4   China's Fiscal Situation in the Reform Period (percent of GNP)

	Revenue		Expenditure			Budget Deficit	
	Chinese Definition	"Standard" Definition	Chinese Definition	"Standard" Definition	Chinese Definition	Government Borrowing Requirement Definition	Stock Definition
1978	31.24	34.77	30.96	34.49	−0.28	−0.28	−0.28
1979	27.66	31.69	31.94	36.86	4.28	5.16	5.16
1980	24.28	29.10	27.13	32.91	2.85	3.82	3.28
1981	22.83	27.28	23.36	29.35	0.53	2.06	1.17
1982	21.64	27.14	22.21	29.32	0.56	2.18	1.41
1983	21.50	27.66	22.25	29.78	0.75	2.11	1.64
1984	21.57	26.47	21.25	28.22	0.64	1.75	1.51
1985	21.81	26.84	21.56	27.64	0.25	0.80	0.50
1986	23.31	25.23	24.04	27.39	0.73	2.15	1.85
1987	20.96	22.79	21.67	25.00	0.70	2.20	1.75
1988	18.68	19.93	19.24	22.41	0.56	2.48	2.16
1989	18.43	20.41	19.01	22.75	0.58	2.35	1.09
1990	18.50	19.63	19.28	22.51	0.78	2.88	2.15
1991	18.13	18.52	19.30	22.88	1.17	3.36	N/A

Note: "Standard" definition for revenue means subtracting borrowing from Chinese definition and adding the subsidies that vere counted as negative revenue. "Standard" definition for expenditure means adding to the Chinese definition subsidies that were considered negative subsidies.

Government borrowing requirement (GBR) definition is deficit "standard" expenditure minus "standard" revenue.

Stock definition of deficit is GBR definition minus principal repayments.

Source: Christine Wong, Christopher Heady, and W. T. Woo, Economic Reform and Fiscal Management in China (Manila: Asian Development Bank, February 1993).

Self-Finance and Hard-Budget Constraints
for Chinese Farmers

After 1978, China moved swiftly to dissolve the communes in favor of small-holder agriculture, a change in incentive structures that immediately raised farm productivity. Equally important but less well appreciated, state marketing agencies sharply raised—toward world-market levels—procurement prices paid to farmers for compulsory quotas of grains and other foodstuffs (Wong 1992). The remaining surpluses could then be freely sold in private markets. Together with the increase in

TABLE 5.5   Consolidated Deficit of Chinese Government and State-Owned Enterprises, 1988–1991 (percent of GNP)

	Open Deficit[a]	Hidden Deficit[b]	Consolidated Deficit (1)+(2)	A Conservative Re-estimate on Assumption That Hidden Deficit is 70 Percent of Column 2 Deficit
	(1)	(2)	(3)	(4)
1988	2.48	5.14	7.62	6.08
1989	2.35	5.22	7.57	6.01
1990	2.88	7.55	10.43	8.17
1991	3.36	6.76	10.12	8.09

[a]Government borrowing requirement (GBR) definition deficit is "standard" expenditure minus "standard" revenue.
[b]Central Bank financing for the deficits of the state-owned enterprises.

Source: Christine Wong, Christopher Heady, and W. T. Woo, *Economic Reform and Fiscal Management in China* (Manila: Asian Development Bank, February 1993).

output, this big improvement in the newly-independent farmers' terms of trade greatly increased their cash flows. In the early 1980s, this improved cash position meant that farmers could self-finance their on-farm investments, including residential construction, without borrowing significantly from the state banking system or from officially controlled rural credit cooperatives. In effect, very hard budget constraints, but improved terms of trade, were imposed on farmers as they entered the market economy.

As long as the price level remained relatively stable, as it did in the early 1980s (Table 5.1), the newly independent farmers viewed themselves as being undermonetized for purposes of financing on-farm investments. In part because farmers did not have access to bank credit, their desired stock of liquid assets was too small relative to their current income flow. They began building up their cash and savings deposits relative to their rising incomes. More by accident than design, farmers, who were over three-quarters of the population in the early 1980s, became big net lenders to the government through the state banking system.

To show this, farmers' financial position cannot easily be separated from that of the rest of the population. Compared to "urban" household deposits, "rural" household savings deposits, that is, those accruing in rural credit co-ops, initially grew proportionately faster, rising from about 1.5 percent of GNP in 1978 to 6.3 percent in 1984. (See Table 5.6). Nevertheless, the most important part of farm financial assets in the

TABLE 5.6 Household Bank Savings Deposits in China 1978–1991(in billion yuan)

	Total Household Deposits	Increase Over Previous Year	Urban Household Deposits[a]	Increase Over Previous Year	Rural Household Deposits[b]	Increase Over Previous Year	Total Household Deposits/ GNP
1978	21.06		15.49		5.57		5.87%
1979	28.10	33.43%	20.26	30.79%	7.84	40.75%	7.05%
1980	39.95	42.17%	28.25	39.44%	11.70	49.23%	8.94%
1981	52.37	31.09%	35.41	25.35%	16.96	44.96%	10.97%
1982	67.54	28.97%	44.73	26.32%	22.81	34.49%	13.01%
1983	89.25	32.14%	57.26	28.01%	31.99	40.25%	15.36%
1984	121.47	36.10%	77.66	35.63%	43.81	36.95%	17.45%
1985	162.26	33.56%	105.78	36.21%	56.48	28.92%	18.96%
1986	223.76	37.90%	147.15	39.11%	76.61	35.64%	23.08%
1987	307.33	37.35%	206.76	40.51%	100.57	31.28%	27.19%
1988	380.15	23.69%	265.92	28.61%	114.23	13.58%	28.12%
1989	514.69	35.39%	373.48	40.45%	141.21	23.62%	32.34%
1990	703.42	36.67%	519.26	39.03%	184.16	30.42%	39.66%
1991	911.03	29.51%	679.09	30.78%	231.94	25.94%	45.88%

[a] Deposits held by households in the state banking system.
[b] Deposits held by households in rural credit cooperative only.

Sources: Statistical Yearbook of China (Bejing: Government of China, 1992); Yingyi Qian, "Lessons and Relevance of the Japanese Main Bank System for Financial Reform in China," mimeo (Stanford: Stanford University Department of Economics, March 1993).

undermonetized state was probably hand-to-hand currency. Table 5.7 shows currency holdings also rising sharply in the early 1980s from about 6 to 11 percent of GNP, and one suspects that currency is more heavily utilized than savings deposits in agricultural pursuits. (A currency buildup amounts to lending to the government through the central bank.) Finally, in Table 5.6, some unknown fraction of the the urban household savings deposits, that is, those held in regular banks rather than rural credit co-ops, is undoubtedly owned by farm households and smaller-scale rural enterprises. The rapid rate of growth of rural income, combined with the buildup of farmers' financial assets relative to their income, greatly augmented the lending resources of the state banking system.

But also critically important for China's macroeconomic stability at this early stage was the relative absence of direct lending to the newly

TABLE 5.7   China's Monetary Aggregates as Share of GNP

	Savings Household Deposits/GNP	Currency/GNP	M1/GNP	M2/GNP
1978	5.87%	5.91%		28.8%[a]
1979	7.05%			
1980	8.94%			
1981	10.97%			
1982	13.01%			
1983	15.36%			
1984	17.45%			
1985	18.96%	11.5%	39.0%	60.8%
1986	23.08%	12.6%	43.6%	69.3%
1987	27.19%	12.9%	43.8%	73.7%
1988	27.12%	15.2%	42.5%	71.8%
1989	32.34%	14.7%	39.9%	74.7%
1990	39.77%	14.9%	43.0%	86.4%
1991	45.88%	16.0%	47.5%	97.0%

[a] Preliminary estimate.

Notes: M1=currency + enterprise and institution demand deposits.

M2=M1 + enterprise household savings deposits (demand and time) + enterprise and institution time deposits.

In China, household demand deposits are not checkable, but enterprise and institution demand deposits are checkable.

Source: Almanac of China's Finance and Banking (Bejing: Government of China, 1990).

independent farmers. Table 5.8 shows that the total loans of the rural credit co-ops to farm households, to TVEs, and to collective agriculture remained about a third to half of total deposits from 1979 to 1984. (Even by 1991 these loans were still only two-thirds of total deposits.) And farm households borrowed only about half of this reduced total of loans outstanding from the rural credit co-ops. What was not lent out was kept on deposit as an informal reserve requirement with the Agricultural Bank of China (ABC). Because the ABC was a division of the state banking system, these funds were lent back to the government or its designees. Also taking their unrequited currency buildup into account, farmers were big net lenders to the rest of the economy at the critically important outset of liberalization between 1979 and 1984.

TABLE 5.8 China's Rural Credit Cooperative Activities (in billion yuan)

	Total Deposits	Loans to Household	Loans to TVEs	Loans to Collective Agriculture	Total Loans/ Total Deposits (percent)
1979	21.59	1.09	1.42	2.24	22.0%
1980	27.23	1.60	3.11	3.45	30.0%
1981	31.96	2.52	3.55	3.57	30.2%
1982	38.99	4.41	4.23	3.48	31.1%
1983	48.74	7.54	6.01	2.82	33.6%
1984	62.49	18.11	13.50	3.84	56.7%
1985	72.49	19.42	16.44	4.14	55.2%
1986	96.23	25.80	26.59	4.46	59.1%
1987	122.52	34.76	35.93	6.45	63.0%
1988	139.98	37.24	45.61	8.01	64.9%
1989	166.95	41.57	57.19	10.73	65.6%
1990	214.49	51.82	76.07	13.41	65.9%
1991	270.93	63.14	100.73	16.99	66.8%

Sources: Yingyi Qian, "Lessons and Relevance of the Japanese Main Bank System for Financial Reform in China," mimeo (Stanford: Stanford University Department of Economics, March 1993). Data are from *Statistical Yearbook of China* (Bejing: Government of China, 1992).

TABLE 5.9 China: Bank Lending to Nonstate Sector as Proportion of Total Outstanding Bank Loans'

	Urban Collectives	Urban Individuals	TVEs	Agriculture	Total Nonstate Loans
1985	4.95%	0.17%	5.63%	6.85%	17.60%
1986	5.11%	0.13%	6.82%	6.68%	18.94%
1987	5.47%	0.16%	7.25%	7.28%	20.16%
1988	5.58%	0.17%	7.59%	7.19%	20.53%
1989	5.15%	0.11%	7.39%	7.12%	19.97%
1990	4.93%	0.09%	7.42%	7.17%	19.61%
1991	4.74%	0.08%	7.63%	7.39%	19.84%

Sources: Almanac of China's Finance and Banking (Bejing: Government of China, 1990); Yingyi Qian, "Lessons and Relevance of the Japanese Main Bank System for Financial Reform in China," mimeo (Stanford: Stanford University Department of Economics, March 1993).

Financial Deepening and Macroeconomic Balance: The Importance of Positive Real Interest Rates

From the mid-1980s to the present, this dramatic and voluntary buildup of savings by rural households was replicated throughout the rest of the economy as industry succeeded agriculture as China's leading growth sector. Table 5.7 shows the enormous increase in broad money holdings (M2) from about 28 percent of GNP in 1978 to about 97 percent in 1991. Because of the central government's continued ownership and control of the state banking system, it could offset its deteriorating fiscal position by borrowing back these rapidly rising financial surpluses of urban and rural households—or of the nonstate sector generally.

This government borrowing was not inflationary only because the relatively liberalized nonstate sector, including the TVEs, was itself not a major claimant on the state banking system. Table 5.9 shows that in the late 1980s loans to this nonstate sector—whether urban or rural—were generally only about 20 percent of the total outstanding loans of consolidated banking-type financial intermediaries. (And this 20 percent "limit" appears to be holding into the 1990s, as industrial output in the nonstate sector now exceeds that of the traditional SOEs.) Without the government having to resort to a substantial inflation tax, the remaining 80 percent was sufficient to cover the financing needs of the old SOEs and the central government. This noninflationary mobilization of large-scale finance to cover the government's fiscal deficits, both open and hidden, was the precarious keystone of macroeconomic stability in China in the 1980s—and remains so today in the absence of major revenue-raising tax reforms.

But why was the Chinese propensity to save in financial form so remarkably high? Price stability in China was (and is) not perfect. Table 5.1 shows inflationary episodes in 1985 and 1988–1989, and 1993 could be a year of a substantial cyclical upturn in the inflation rate. So China's interest rate policy, particularly on saving deposits, remains very important in preserving the incentives of households and enterprises to build up their financial asset positions. Table 5.10 shows that the authorities have done a pretty good job of keeping savings deposit rates positive in real terms—using annual inflation rates in the national retail price index as the benchmark. (As discussed above, these real rates might look even higher if one used a decontrolled producer price index as the deflator.) A major problem arose in 1988–1989 when inflation soared to 17 to 18 percent per year. This turned the standard fixed interest rates on deposits and loans sharply negative (Table 5.10). But the government responded by fully indexing some interest rates. Nominal rates on three-year household time deposits were increased into the range of 20 to 26 percent in

TABLE 5.10   China: Selected Interest Rates, 1980–1991 (percent per year)

		Nominal Interest Rates				Real Interest Rates	
	National Retail Price Index (% change)	Household 1-year Time Deposit	Household 3-year Time Deposit	Loan to Industry	Loan to Township-Village Enterprise	Household 1-year Time Deposit	Household 3-year Time Deposit
1980	6.0	5.40	6.12	2.52	2.16	−0.60	0.12
1981	2.4	5.40	6.12	2.52	2.16	3.00	3.72
1982	1.9	5.76	6.84	3.60	4.32	3.86	4.94
1983	1.5	5.76	6.84	7.20	4.32	4.26	5.34
1984	2.8	5.76	6.84	7.20	7.92	2.96	4.04
1985	8.8	7.20	8.28	7.92	10.08	−1.60	−0.52
1986	6.0	7.70	8.28	7.92	10.08	1.70	2.28
1987	7.3	7.20	8.28	7.92	10.08	−0.10	−0.98
1988	18.5	8.64	9.72*	9.00	10.08	−9.86	−8.78*
1989	17.8	11.34	13.14*	11.34	11.34	−6.46	−4.66*
1990	2.1	8.64	10.08	9.36	9.36	6.54	7.98
1991	2.9	7.56	8.28	8.64	8.46	4.66	5.38

*Cost of Living adjustment not included. See Table 5.11.
Figures are year-end.
Loan to industry is for circulation capital (one year).
Loan to township-village enterprises is for equipment.

Sources: Statistical Yearbook of China (Bejing: Government of China, 1992); *Almanac of China's Finance and Banking* (Bejing: Government of China, 1990, 1992); Yingyi Qian, "Lessons and Relevance of the Japanese Main Bank System for Financial Reform in China," mimeo (Stanford: Stanford University Department of Economics, March 1993).

1988–1989 (Table 5.11) and so remained strongly positive in real terms. (Once inflation fell back to a very low level in 1990–1991, indexing was discontinued.)

Thus did China preserve the incentives for the nonstate sector in general, and households in particular, to accumulate monetary assets— including, in more recent years, government and industrial bonds. Because potentially excess household purchasing power was soaked up, the supply and demand of "hard" money in the nonstate sector remained more or less in balance.

What about productivity growth in the nonstate sector? Although new industry in the nonstate sector did not get much in the way of bank loans, financial deepening through higher deposit rates could still con-

TABLE 5.11 China: Deposit Interest Rates with Cost of Living Adjustment Allowance, 1988:IV to 1990:IV

	Household 3-year Time Deposit (nominal)	Annual Rate of Cost of Living Adjustment Allowance	Effective Household 3-year Time Deposit (nominal)
1988:IV	9.72%	7.28%	17.00%
1989:I	13.14%	12.71%	25.85%
1989:II	13.14%	12.59%	25.73%
1989:III	13.14%	13.64%	26.78%
1989:IV	13.14%	8.36%	21.50%
1990:1	13.14%	0.89%	14.03%
1990:2	13.14%	1.46%	14.60%
1990:3	13.14%	0.00%	13.14%
1990:4	13.14%	1.42%	14.56%
1990:5	13.14%	1.38%	14.52%
1990:6	13.14%	0.00%	13.14%
1990:III	10.08%	0.00%	10.08%
1990:IV	10.08%	0.00%	10.08%

Sources: Almanac of China's Finance and Banking (Bejing: Government of China, 1990); Yingyi Qian, "Lessons and Relevance of the Japanese Main Bank System for Financial Reform in China," mimeo (Stanford: Stanford University Department of Economics, March 1993).

tribute to the nonstate sector's high productivity growth, observed by Gelb et al (1993). In line with the arguments and evidence put forward in McKinnon (1991b, ch. 2), having access to attractive liquid financial assets inhibits bad physical investments with low or negative yields; at the same time, such access encourages intertemporal arbitrage for making good investments (McKinnon 1973, Burkett and Vogel 1991). In effect, attractive financial assets and productive physical capital are complementary.[6]

Industrial and Financial Dualism in China: The Macroeconomic Role of Price Controls in the State Sector

If there was no hard money overhang in Chinese households in 1978–1979, why then did the Chinese government retain (or only slowly remove) price controls in the old state sector after 1978? Unlike Eastern Europe, China did not attempt any sudden "big-bang" liberalization or privatization of state-owned industry, which had been built up with distorted prices under the umbrella of central planning. Traditional heavy industry—whether in manufacturing, public utilities, or natural resources—remained firmly the responsibility of the central government.

The Chinese government recognized that parts of the old heavy industrial sector would inevitably become unprofitable as prices were decontrolled or "rationalized." State enterprises that became unprofitable with, typically, thousands of workers could not be allowed to collapse just because of a change in economic regime. The social consequences were too dire, and the economic costs would be too great. While slowly raising the prices of raw materials relative to finished manufactured goods into a better alignment with world-market prices, the central government continued to prop up much of state-owned industry by low-cost bank loans and other subsidies. Because this perpetuated the syndrome of the "soft" budget contraint, state enterprises remained on a tight financial leash.

For example, at the outset of the liberalization in the early 1980s, the SOEs were not permitted to bid freely with each other for scarce domestic resources or to bid unrestrictedly in an open market for foreign exchange. Producer prices in transactions among state-owned enterprises remained under centralized control—and were only gradually phased out as the decade progressed. However, the government allowed a two-part pricing system to develop. Once state enterprises had satisfied their delivery commitments to each other at centrally controlled prices, they could sell at the margin any excess production to rapidly growing nonstate enterprises at market-determined—and usually somewhat higher—prices, as we have already seen in Figure 5.1. Similarly, the central government initially allocated all foreign exchange at the official exchange rate and then gradually allowed an interenterprise swap market to develop at a variable but modest premium over the official rate. Only by the early 1990s did this open swap market become dominant for allocating foreign exchange among enterprises.

Contrast this cautious approach with the "big-bang" price decontrol followed by Russia on January 1, 1992. Suddenly state-owned enterprises (with very soft budget constraints) could bid, and negotiate prices freely, for all goods and services or foreign exchange purchased from each other. Russian households, however, remained somewhat wage and cash constrained. The result in 1992 was a price explosion at the producer level (see Figure 5.3). This explosion was led by a tremendous increase in the ruble price of foreign exchange: from about 5 rubles to the dollar at the beginning of the year to about 500 rubles at the end. (This Russian experience is more fully analyzed below.)

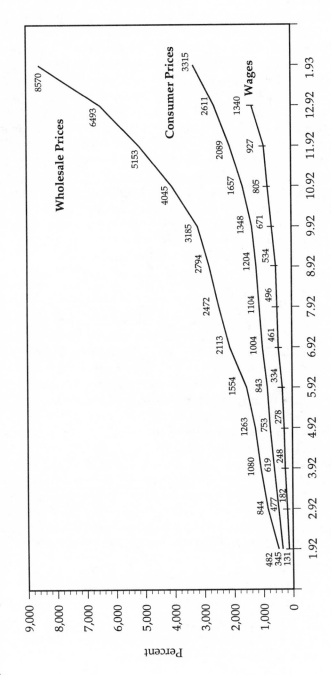

Figure 5.3 Wage and Wholesale and Consumer Price Index, Russia, January 1992–January 1993 (in percent [December 1991=100%])

Sources: Russian State Committee on Statistics data requested by the office of Deputy Prime-Minister G. S. Khizha. Russian State Committee on Statistics data in *Ekonomika i Zhizn*, no. 51 (December 1992), p. 1. Ministry of Labor data in *Izvestia*, February 9, 1993, p. 2. Institute of Economic Policy (Gaidar's) data in *Moscow News Business*, no. 10 (March 1993), p. 11. Data complied by Mikhail Bernstam, Stanford University.

117

Unlike in Russia, the Chinese authorities correctly recognized that price controls are necessary to anchor the producer price level when (1) enterprise budget constraints are still very soft and (2) there was not yet sufficient competition in the provision of individual raw materials or more complex producer goods from a hard-budget nonstate sector. Even if the government succeeded in controlling both wages in SOEs and the stock of "hard" household cash in circulation among households and the nonstate sector, this by itself would be insufficient to peg the producer price level. Although the Chinese authorities slowly adjusted relative producer prices, they still anchored the producers' price level by pegging most of the nominal prices of goods and services traded among state enterprises in the early years of their liberalization.

In positing an optimal order of economic liberalization, I have argued (McKinnon 1991b, ch. 11) that a dualistic set of financial, fiscal, and price controls should apply differentially to the traditional and the liberalized sectors in the early years of the transition. This industrial and financial dualism corresponds loosely to China's distinction between its state and nonstate sectors. An idealized or "model" dualistic control mechanism is further elaborated in Table 5.12.

However, once the cash-constrained nonstate sector becomes big enough to compete vigorously with the old state sector in product markets, the government can relax price controls in the state sector. Together, the TVEs and private industries in the nonstate sector broadly defined now rival in size the aggregate industrial output of the old state sector. In 1973, collective or private industry in China was officially tabulated to be 22 percent of total output but mainly because of the growth of the TVEs, by 1991 this had risen to 53.7 percent (Perkins 1992). Because these new enterprises operating with hard-budget constraints now compete vigorously with the old state sector, in the early 1990s price controls within the latter could be almost entirely eliminated without upsetting the producer price level—providing that the amount of hard cash in circulation in the nonstate sector remains under control. (Even into the 1990s, however, the old SOEs still need to be financially constrained from bidding for scarce resources—such as foreign exchange—insofar as they are also recipients of soft loans from the state banking system.)

Tax Reform and the Optimal Pace of Financial Liberalization: China and Eastern Europe Compared

For the state banking system to be soundly financed and stay profitable, the reform government's high interest rate strategy for household deposits requires even higher average interest rates on loans. China did

TABLE 5.12 Alternative Financial Arrangements for Enterprises in a Model Transitional Economy

	Traditional Enterprises ("State" Sector)[a]	Liberalized Enterprises ("Nonstate" Sector)	
		Collective[b]	Private
Taxation	Expropriation of surpluses[c]	Uniform value-added tax	Uniform value-added tax
Deposit money: domestic commodity convertibility[d]	Restricted	Unrestricted interest-bearing	Unrestricted interest-bearing
Credit eligibility	State Bank	Nonbank capital market	Nonbank capital market
Wages	Government determined	Collectively determined	Market determined
Residual profits	Accrue to government	Dividends to collective—retained earnings for reinvestment	Dividends to owners[e] —retained earnings for reinvestment or lending to other private enterprises
Foreign Exchange Convertibility	Restricted	Current account only (swap market)	Current account only (swap market)
Producer Prices	Pegged with intramarginal delivery quotas[f]	Market determined	Market determined

[a] "Traditional" enterprises are those whose output and pricing decisions are still largely determined by a central government authority or planning bureau with centrally allocated inputs and credits from the state bank to cover (possible), negative cash flows. In China, traditional enterprises would be in the so-called state sector, whereas new entities outside these traditional controls would be in the nonstate sector.

[b] "Collective" can refer to any level of government ownership or sponsorship, as with Chinese TVEs— township and village enterprises. For example, the VAT administered by central government would apply equally to liberalized enterprises owned or registered in different local jurisdictions.

[c] Although residual profits revert to the state, they could include a "shadow" VAT levy to better understand the "true" profitability of traditional enterprises.

[d] "Commodity convertibility" here means the freedom to spend for domestic goods and services or to buy and hold domestic coin and currency—but need not imply convertibility into foreign exchange.

[e] Dividends would be subject to the personal income tax when paid out to private owners, but retained earnings would not be taxed.

[f] After satisfying delivery commitments to other traditional enterprises, marginal output can be sold at free market prices.

not always manage this. Occasionally, an inversion made some loan rates lower than the equivalent deposit rates, particularly during the 1988–1989 period, when nominal deposit rates were indexed (Tables 5.10 and 5.11). Such an inversion adds to the banking system's and the government's "hidden" deficit—beyond simply the deficit associated with the nonrepayment of the bad loans to the SOEs. Nevertheless, Table 5.10 also shows that China did substantially increase real loan rates from the mid-1980s to 1991.

Even without this inversion, this high-interest noninflationary finance implies that the Chinese central government's open and hidden debt, through the state banking system to the nonbank public, is building up fast. But measuring the size of this official debt is complicated and cannot be undertaken here.

Moreover, as long as the government is leaning on the state banking system as a crutch to cover its own fiscal deficits, the scope for liberalizing—let alone privatizing—the banks is limited. At this stage, the government cannot afford a parallel system of independent banks, with unrestricted deposit and lending privileges, to serve the TVEs or the private sector. They would compete away the deposit-taking capabilities of the state banking system. (This may be already happening. The state banks themselves may be hiving off some of their activities to less highly regulated and taxed finance and trust companies [Qian 1993].) If the Chinese government threw away its financial crutch, by, say, permitting unrestricted wildcat banking in the mode of the former Soviet Union (McKinnon 1991b, ch. 11), an inflationary explosion would ensue.

Like East European governments, the Chinese central government failed to set up an effective internal revenue service for collecting revenue in a decentralized market economy. Unlike East Europeans, however, the Chinese resorted more effectively to various "second-best" schemes for revenue collection. After 1978, by retaining control over traditionally profitable industrial enterprises, the central government could continue collecting revenue—turnover taxes and residual profits—directly for itself. Then by the mid-1980s, as revenue from state-owned enterprises fell, the central government began an elaborate system of tax contracting with local governments to remit revenue to the center (Wong, Heady, and Woo 1993).

Still, this left the Chinese central government with a serious revenue shortfall for financing infrastructure investments, subsidies to loss-making old line industrial enterprises, higher agricultural procurement prices, and so on. The salaries of high-level civil servants and educators have declined sharply relative to those paid in the nonstate sector. This decline in the fiscal position of the central government is clearly neither sustainable nor in the best long-run interests of Chinese economic development. Among other problems is that officials become more easily corrupted when their salaries are low.

The Chinese government cannot rely indefinitely on such heavy borrowing because households are no longer "undermonetized"—and the M2-GNP ratio will not rise to infinity. When the ratio of household liquid assets to income peaks out, or even before, there could be a financial crisis if state-sector borrowing continues. The great economic accomplishments of the past several years would then be at risk, and an East European–style inflation cannot be ruled out.

The solution is obvious economically but difficult politically. The Chinese central government must quickly institute an internal revenue service capable of directly taxing all industries—central government, local government, and private—as well as the agricultural sector. Domestic and foreign trade should be covered uniformly so that the rate of business taxation can be kept moderate, as with a uniform value-added tax. At a somewhat later stage, households could be brought systematically under a personal income tax, but that is feasible only as people get wealthier. Aspects of how to implement this new tax regime are analyzed elsewhere(McKinnon 1991a and 1993; Wong, Heady, and Woo 1993).

In the transition in Eastern Europe and the FSU, by contrast, the need for fiscal reform is more immediate than in China. The initial decreases in output (Table 5.2) and unfavorable inflationary expectations (Table 5.3) make it much more difficult for these governments to obtain noninflationary finance by borrowing from their banking systems in the Chinese mode. The growth in the real size of their financial systems is too small— and could even be negative. Thus, if further inflationary explosions are to be avoided, effective fiscal reforms must come much earlier in their transitions.

Russia's Economic Dilemma Before the "Big Bang," January 1992: Partial Price Liberalization and Supply Diversion

It was a major mistake for the Russian Federation, in January 1992, to suddenly decontrol virtually all prices within the state sector and to stop trying to enforce normal patterns of delivery within that sector. As we have seen, this big-bang approach was very different from Chinese gradualism. Yet some conditions in Russia in 1992 were very different from those prevailing in China in 1979. Moreover, the reform government in Moscow was acting in good faith and seemed to be following the advice of international agencies such as the IMF and the World Bank and most Western economists. So a careful review of some of the arguments in favor of the big-bang approach that were presented, prior to that fateful January, seems worthwhile.

Two related arguments in favor of sudden liberalization in Russia can be adduced. The first was mainly macro and, following the Polish precedent of January 1990, was directed toward eliminating a monetary overhang at previously controlled prices by a onetime inflation. The last section of this chapter takes up this influential "monetary overhang" argument.

The second argument was more micro in nature and was concerned with the sieve-like character of the previous system of price controls. In 1990–1991, a substantial fringe of unregulated activities had developed in Russia's nonstate sector, where prices were free and hard moneys circulated. Unlike China, there was more small-scale trade—legal and illegal—and relatively little production in this nonstate sector, if only because Russia had made little progress in liberalizing agriculture. Black-market activities were rampant. This second influential argument emphasizes "supply diversion."

A recent paper, "The Transition to a Market Economy: Pitfalls of Partial Reform" (Murphy et al. 1992), argued that partial reform, where prices are decontrolled in the nonstate sector but not in the state sector, is a mistake. (The authors had been to Russia and had written their paper before January 1992.) If controlled prices in the state sector are set below those in the free market dominated by the nonstate sector, scarce inputs could be diverted from high-value to low-value uses—including diversion into foreign trade. Such massive supply diversion from partial price liberalization, they argued, provoked the fall in output in 1990–1991 in the FSU in general and Russia in particular.

These authors illustrated their important and influential argument with several examples, one of which is worth repeating. Suppose an important industrial input, say, timber, can be used for the production of railway boxcars in the state sector or for the production of family homes in the nonstate sector. The demand for timber to be used for boxcars is relatively inelastic, reflecting a high producer surplus within the railway industry for providing general transportation. In contrast, the demand for timber in the housing industry is relatively elastic, with consumer surplus being relatively low. Like most raw materials in socialist economies, timber traditionally has been underpriced in terms of finished manufactures. Suppose such price controls are retained in the state sector: Users of boxcars cannot bid beyond a set price, say P*, for timber.

In a partial liberalization, suppose now that a nonstate housing industry can bid for timber from forestry enterprises in the state sector at free-market prices. By bidding slightly above P*, the nonstate housing industry could expand very rapidly at the margin. Unrestricted entry by small construction firms could rapidly absorb this key raw material and cause a collapse of the output of vital railway cars in the transportation network. (The same output collapse of railway cars could also happen if the nonstate sector bid away timber products for export.) When output fell in Russia in 1990–1991, there were price controls on what state firms could pay for various inputs in terms of quasi-blocked enterprise money, whereas nonstate firms in the "cash" economy sometimes had a much freer hand in the bidding process—including bidding with more attractive household money.

This provocative paper does not refer to the different financial circumstances—including different monetary circuits—of state and nonstate enterprises. It focuses only on the anomalies of the two-part pricing system. In this narrower context, the authors identified two solutions to this problem of supply diversion: (1) keep the two-part pricing system in place but strengthen the old system of state orders for enforcing minimal deliveries of price-controlled inputs in critical industries within the old state sector or (2) abandon two-part pricing within the state sector and thus eliminate both price controls and bidding restraints on state firms competing with nonstate firms for scarce inputs.

In assessing the first solution, the authors noted that the Chinese government started off its liberalization with an extensive two-part pricing system in the traditional state sector. However, Christine Wong (1992) noted that relative prices within the state sector were also realigned to push them closer to those prevailing internationally.

> During the first period in 1979–1984, in agriculture state procurement prices were raised substantially across the board. … In industry, the prices of 29 producers' goods were raised during 1979–1981, including those for coal, pig iron, coking coal, cement, plate glass, and some steel products. Other prices were reduced: those for machinery, instruments, and tools. The prices of many consumer goods were also reduced from their initially very high levels, including wrist watches, televisions, tape recorders, radios, synthetic fabrics, etc.
>
> At the same time more prices were freed to market determination through two devices. The first was to reduce the scope of planned allocation. In agriculture, the number of products was reduced from 46 to 22 in 1982, and further to 12 in 1984. In industry, the number of producers' goods under plan allocation was reduced from 256 in 1979 to 30 in 1984. By 1984, virtually all "minor" consumer prices had been freed.
>
> The second device was to allow some of the goods in the key sectors that remained under state control to enter into market channels, a development that gave rise to the "dual" price system that emerged in the mid-1980s … whereby the proportion of output under state plans would continue to be traded at plan prices, while extra-plan output would be

traded at (higher) "extra-plan" prices ... to provide better (profit) incentives at the margin. (Wong 1992, p. 72)

However, for the Russian case, Murphy et al. (1992) rejected the Chinese solution of partial liberalization with dual pricing. They claimed that the different political circumstances in China, where the communist party retains centralized power, could force state firms to deliver their assigned quotas at below-market prices—so that private buyers could buy only surplus production at the higher prices. Because of the decline of the communist party in Russia, however, the authors claimed that delivery quotas for state enterprises have already been relaxed—and it would now be impossible to enforce such delivery quotas even if the Russian government wanted to. Therefore, they concluded that the gradualist approach based on partial price reform should be scrapped in favor of full price liberalization: "The most natural implication of the analysis in this paper is that price reform should take the form of a big bang, with all prices being freed at once ... Fortunately, the Russian government moved to an almost complete price liberalization in 1992 " (Murphy, Shleifer, and Vishny 1992, p. 906).

Unfortunately, unrestrained bidding for scarce inputs by Russian state enterprises in 1992 led to an even bigger inflationary explosion and a sharper fall in real output than under the partial price reforms of 1990–1991.

> The Russian economic depression deepened dramatically in 1992 with GDP falling 19% and NMP (net material product) produced down 20%. Since reaching a peak in 1989, the level of NMP produced has fallen by nearly 32%, with GDP falling slightly less. The major change in 1992 compared to 1990–1991 is that consumption had to bear the brunt of the decline in aggregate output—it fell by 15–16% compared to less than 3 percent drop in 1991. The level of net investment ... in 1992 fell to less than one third (!) of its peak 1988 level ...
>
> Russia made no headway in controlling inflation last year. The end-December level of consumer prices was up by a factor of 26.3 relative to December 1991 while the industrial wholesale price index was up a staggering 62.2 times for the same period. These figures imply average monthly inflation rates of 31.3% and 41.1% respectively." (PlanEcon Report 1993. p. 1.)

What went wrong? Was there some major flaw in the three authors' persuasive argument for a big-bang price reform jointly encompassing both the state and non-state (household) sectors? Or did Russian reformers again simply not go far enough—a line of thought to which many influential outsiders[7] still adhere?

Indeterminacy in the Producer Price Level
with Unconstrained Bidding by State Enterprises

The big-bang argument for total price decontrol is flawed if some of the important actors bidding for scarce resources have soft budget constraints. If Russia's state enterprises are not financially constrained, no meaningful equilibrium in producer prices exists. Until their budget constraints are hardened, unconstrained bidding by state enterprises will cause the producer (wholesale) price level to increase indefinitely—and thus also increase relative to retail prices facing cash-constrained households. After presenting some evidence on this point, I shall then discuss the underlying financial mechanisms.

Taking December 1991 as the base month just prior to the massive price increases of January 1992 and using data from the Russian Ministry of the Economy, Mikhail Bernstam of the Hoover Institution plotted Figure 5.3: the course of Russian wholesale and consumer prices and wages on a monthly basis from January through December 1992. The key point to notice is the explosive growth in wholesale prices relative to consumer prices or wages in the initial months after price decontrol. All the increases are astronomical, but by October 1992 wholesale prices had risen almost 2.5 times as much as consumer prices. By the end of the year consumer prices had risen twice as much as wages—so that wholesale or producer prices had actually risen five times as much as wages.

However, in such a financially volatile context, data sources are hard to reconcile. Because of the more or less complete decontrol of prices (but not wages) in January 1992, rates of growth in monthly time series data in 1992 are particularly difficult to interpret. For example, in December 1991, the general retail price index stood at 282.6 (1990 being 100) and then jumped to 941.0 in January 1992: an increase of 230 percent in just one month. But this one-shot outburst of extraordinary inflation was designed to work off the large cash overhang that had been rapidly building in 1991 when retail prices were still (partially) controlled. (Although difficult to measure, the overhang component of household cash holding might have been as high as 50 percent of total wage and salary income in 1991.) But nominal wages remained controlled and rose only about 31 percent in January 1992. So real wages fell very sharply in January 1992, a fall not recouped by subsequent substantial, but controlled, increases in nominal wages relative to retail prices.

Because the Russian government's power to tax the household sector directly is very limited, these imperfect wage controls are the principal means by which the Russian government could restrict the supply of new money—including savings deposits—in the household monetary circuit. And indeed household saving deposits as a share of retail sales turnover fell dramatically, from 60 percent in 1991 to about 25 percent in mid-1992, and virtually vanished by the end of the year. Similarly in this world of imperfect statistics, the currency (in rubles) to GNP ratio was about 10 percent at the beginning of 1992 and had fallen to about 3 percent by the end of the year. This is one reflection of the 1992 "cash shortage" in Russia and other former Soviet republics. (In great contrast to the financial deepening in China with M2/GNP over 90 percent by the end of 1992, the purchasing power of money (in rubles) held by the nonbank public in Russia had become very small—probably of the order of 3 percent of GNP, with the household deposit base of the banking system wiped out.)

Another data source showing the extraordinary pattern of price changes in the Russian economy in early 1992 is in various parts of the *PlanEcon Report* that are collated and rearranged in Table 5.13. Focus initially on just the price movements in the right-hand column. From December 1991 through June 1992, ruble wages increased about 4 times, retail prices between 6 and 7 times, wholesale prices between 18 and 19 times, and the ruble price of dollars about 33 times.

To help interpret this incredible increase in the price of foreign exchange, *PlanEcon Report* (1992) estimated that the purchasing power parity (PPP) exchange rate (using consumer price index [CPI] comparisons) was 6 rubles to the dollar when the "commercial" rate was pegged at 55 rubles to the dollar in June 1992. Subsequently, this commercial rate was further freed to be determined by "market" forces in the Moscow interbank curency exchange (opened in 1991) and rose to 143 rubles to the dollar in July 1992 and to 241 on September 22, 1992: "At the end of trading, [the ruble] had sunk to 241 against the dollar—a loss of 35.5 rubles on last week's level of Rbs 205.5 to the dollar. The volume of dollars traded was also a record, at $68.8m—a sign of the *willingness* of Russian enterprises to use Rbs 15 bn. to buy the US currency as a hedge against inflation" (Italics added; *Financial Times*, September 23, 1992, p. 4). What is going on here? As in the classical centrally planned socialist economy, Russian enterprises are still on a soft money circuit—deposits with, and credits from, the state banks. In contrast, households and the emerging nonstate commercial sector are on the relatively hard money or cash circuit. This softness of financial constraints on the old state enterprises has two related aspects.

First, central government enterprises have traditionally had access to low (nominal) interest rate credits from the state banking system and from other state enterprises. In the face of rapid price inflation, which resulted in almost complete debt forgiveness in real terms (as in 1992), these bank credits become a massive subsidy. In addition, by simply not

TABLE 5.13 Key Russian Inflation Indicators, 1985 to June 1992 (annual change in percent)

	1985	1986	1987	1988	1989	1990	1991	Jan.–June 1992/ Jan.–June 1991	June 1992/ Dec. 1991
Wholesale industrial prices	–	–	–	–	1.2	3.9	138.1	1,360	1,850
Consolidated retail prices	0.6	2.2	1.7	0.3	2.5	5.6	95.0	730	620
Food (excluding alcohol)	0.1	0.6	2.1	0.4	0.7	4.9	118.7		
Alcoholic beverages	6.2	24.7	15.4	0.0	0.0	1.9	26.6	780	600
Nonfood products	–0.9	–0.9	–1.1	0.0	3.1	6.5	100.7		
Prices paid for services	–	–	–	–	–	–	70.6	480	510
Retail prices in									
State and cooperative trade	0.5	2.2	1.6	0.2	2.4	5.2	89.5	790	660
Cooperative trde	1.2	3.4	2.4	0.6	0.5	14.1	111.7		
Collective farms	5.2	1.1	3.7	2.5	7.4	132.1	132.1		
Nominal wages							71.6		397
Commercial exchange rate									3,290

Source: Russian Goskomstat 1992 and *Plan Econ Report*, September 3, 1992.

repaying their trade credits, state enterprises also borrowed heavily from each other. Although ostensibly commercial in nature, this credit is not subject to ordinary commercial restraints and became a prime cause of softness in enterprise budget constraints in 1992.

Second, enterprises had no hard deposit money or interest-bearing assets denominated in rubles that they could hold either for short-term liquidity or as a longer-term store of value. Indeed, in the traditional Soviet monetary system, enterprises were (and are) enjoined from holding household cash balances and had to hold noninterest (or trivially low-interest) deposits with the state bank in several categories of quasi-blocked accounts. In addition to these ruble accounts not being liquid, in the past they have been subject to arbitrary seizure and confiscation by the government as an "informal" method of tax collection. (Residual profits of state enterprises traditionally accrue to the central government anyway.) From the existing explosive inflation, low nominal rates of interest, and the threat of confiscation, enterprises pay very negative real deposit rates on any ruble monetary assets they could not avoid accumulating.

In these circumstances, if state enterprises are given the option of bidding (with their soft money) for foreign exchange assets in virtually any form, they will grossly "overbid" (McKinnon 1991b). Although imported producer and consumer goods are in heavy demand, enterprises are even more desperate to find a nondepreciating liquid financial asset that they can legally hold through time. Apart from excess physical inventories of inputs and outputs, foreign bank accounts or other foreign exchange assets are very attractive inflation hedges at this unfortunate juncture in Russia's financial affairs. Thus, in a market for foreign exchange dominated by state enterprises, the ruble price of dollars is bid up beyond any conceivable level warranted by purchasing power parity.

The Role of Price Controls
on State-Sector Enterprises in the Transition

Before liberalization, price-wage controls in a typical socialist economy have a dual economic function.

First, government revenue depends implicitly on the structure of *relative* prices. The government "distorts" relative prices to generate surplus profits within the state-owned industrial sector (McKinnon, 1991a and 1991b). In comparison to world markets, domestic prices of primary products, industrial materials, and money wages are deliberately kept low relative to the domestic prices of finished manufactures. As described above, the resulting surpluses in enterprise cash flows are then deposited in blocked accounts with the state bank: the government's operative tax revenue.

Second, price controls are also necessary to peg the absolute producer price level, that is, to provide a nominal anchor for prices charged in trade among state enterprises with soft budget constraints. Otherwise, if any open bidding was allowed, producer prices would be indeterminate—as with the 1992 Russian price explosion. (If excess money issue and price inflation existed at the consumer level, continual movement—or indexing—of wholesale prices to ever higher official pegs would become necessary.)

In an optimal order of liberalization for the economy as a whole, both of the above functions constrain the pace at which prices in the state sector can be safely decontrolled. When liberalization begins, the government's revenue position is undermined if competitive pressure undermines monopoly profits in the industrial sector: Finished goods prices fall relative to material inputs and wages. This fall in tax revenue could result in excessive hard-money creation in the household sector and inflationary pressure—first manifest at the consumer level.

Consequently, without a satisfactory internal revenue service for collecting income and commodity taxes on a general basis, liberalizing socialist governments must retain wage controls as a second-best way of taxing personal income. These wage controls maintain the profit position of the state enterprises on the one hand and prevent too much soft enterprise money from being converted into hard household cash—hand-to-hand currency and savings deposits—on the other. For example, to maintain the government's revenue position and a modicum of monetary control, Poland's otherwise big-bang price liberalization at the beginning of 1990 was accompanied by stringent wage controls. Initially, money wages in Poland rose more slowly than the final output prices that consumers had to pay. Similarly, in Russia's big-bang liberalization at the beginning of 1992, wage controls led to a sharp fall in real wages as inflation accelerated.

This draconian, albeit informal, system of personal income taxation may initially succeed in curbing inflation at the retail-household level. Hard cash in circulation may be effectively limited, as was true initially in Russia in 1992. But by themselves, wage controls are not enough to prevent an inflationary explosion in prices prevailing in trade among state enterprises, including the price of foreign exchange. Whence the dramatically unbalanced inflation process observed in Russia in 1992.

Consequently, price and credit controls may have to be retained in the old state sector even after a proper system of general taxation is put in place and the revenue position of the central government appears to be balanced. As long as the money and credit position of the old state enterprises remains soft, direct price controls in this sector will remain necessary until a cash-constrained nonstate sector becomes large enough to be an effective competitor.

Choosing the Right Model of Inflation to Disinflate Efficiently: A Concluding Note

In designing an efficent program for ending price inflation in any economy, it is important to choose the right model of the inflationary process itself. Consider three possibilities.

1. *Open Inflation in Market Economies.* The traditional textbook analysis of open inflation starts with a unified monetary system and market-determined prices. Excessive lending by the central bank to the government or its designees causes cash or "high-powered" money in circulation to rise sharply. With a lag, prices then begin moving upward and eventually catch up with the increased amount of nominal money outstanding. But the money supply is the proximate causal variable for the increase in prices, as in most Latin American inflations.

2. *Repressed Inflation with a Cash Overhang.* In the now-standard analysis of repressed inflation with general price-wage controls, economists (see Barro and Grossman [1976] generally or Lipton and Sachs [1990] for Poland in particular) envisaged a single well-defined monetary "overhang" interchangeably owned by households and enterprises in an essentially unified monetary system. If the economy is to begin functioning properly, however, the overhang must be eliminated by cancelling much of the outstanding nominal money in circulation (as in West Germany in 1948) or by open inflation. By removing price controls and devaluing the currency in the foreign exchanges in January 1990, the Polish government planned (fairly successfully) to inflate away the purchasing power of its monetary overhang. In principle, by limiting new sources of cash injections into the economy, inflation should come to a halt after a once-and-for-all increase in the price level. (Because Poland's fiscal policy remains weak, however, the Poles may not fully succeed in reasserting monetary control.)

These two models—highly simplified—of either open or repressed inflation assume a unified monetary system where households and enterprises are on essentially the same monetary circuit and both have fairly hard budget constraints. Was this a reasonable assumption for Poland on January 1, 1990? In the 1980s, Poland had a history of attempted financial liberalizations and banking reforms (with a lot of missteps) which tended to obliterate the sharp distinction between household cash (and savings accounts) and the deposit or credit money owned by firms. Both could traffic with cash and were subject to restraint in bidding for scarce resources by their cash positions—if the government limited new credits or other subsidies. Then, if the Polish government could get control over the cash base within this unified monetary system, that would be sufficient for bringing inflation under control.

3. *Producer Price Inflation in Enterprises with Soft Budget Constraints.* Russia's financial-monetary system, and that of other Commonwealth of Independent States [CIS] republics, in 1991 to 1993 would seem to be qualitatively different from Poland's at the beginning of 1990. Russia had essentially retained the old socialist distinction between enterprises, which were not cash constrained in their ability to bid for scarce resources, and cash-constrained households. Even so, Russia went ahead and suddenly decontrolled all producer prices with disastrous consequences. Although this Russian model of inflation is not yet in any textbook, it soon will be.

How does Russia get the inflation genie back into the bottle? In the short run, successful macroeconomic stabilization requires a major (re)centralization of the government's control over money and credit—and a reassertion of the primacy of the state-controlled banking system with the elimination of independent "wildcat" banks. Because of the special characteristics of socialist industry, price setting at the producer level, including the exchange rate, may also have to be recentralized as part of the stabilization package. So we have an unfortunate policy dilemma: To secure macroeconomic stabilization in the near term, important banking and commodity pricing policies may have to move counter to what most of us would like to see for the long-run liberalization of the Russian economy.

But this dilemma between short and long run is less acute for fiscal policy. A drastic improvement in the Russian government's ability to collect tax revenue is necessary for macro stabilization on the one hand and for sustaining the longer-term market-oriented and institutional reforms on the other.

Notes

1. Two highly readable overviews of the gradualist Chinese approach are provided by Dwight Perkins (1992) and John McMillan and Barry Naughton (1992).

2. Terminology used by John Williamson (1991).

3. See recent studies done for the Asian Development Bank by Fforde and Vylder (1992) on Vietnam and by Vokes and Fabella (1992) on Laos.

4. Because Hungary has been liberalizing gradually for some time, one could plausibly argue that Hungary does not belong in this group of rapidly liberalizing transitional economies.

5. This problem of supply diversion bedeviled the old Soviet economy in 1990–1991, with price controls in the state sector with very high price premiums in the marginal free or "black" economy (Murphy, Shleifer, and Vishny 1992).

6. In the early 1990s, important new empirical research for the World Bank over a huge eighty-country, thirty-year (1960–1989) sample pooled in cross section and time series provided further strong empirical support for the link between financial depth and high productivity growth. See particularly Levine (1992) and King and Levine (1993).

7. See the commentary "If He Goes" in *Economist*, March 13, 1993, pp. 17–18, which argues for even more sweeping price decontrol in Russia.

Bibliography

Aslund, A. 1992. *Post Communist Revolutions: How Big a Bang?* Washington, D.C.: CSIS.

Barro, R., and H. Grossman. 1976. *Money, Employment, and Inflation.* Cambridge: Cambridge University Press.

Blejer, M., et al. 1991. *China: Economic Reform and Macroeconomic Management,* Occasional Paper no. 76 (January). Washington, D.C.: International Monetary Fund.

Borenstein, E., and P. R. Masson. 1993. *Exchange Rate Arrangements of Previously Centrally Planned Economies,* Occasional Paper no. 102 (February). Washington D.C.: International Monetary Fund.

Brada, J., and A. King. 1992., "Is There a J-Curve in the Economic Transition from Socialism to Capitalism? " *Economics of Planning* 25, no. 1, pp. 37–54.

Burkett, P., and R. Vogel. 1991. "Financial Assets, Inflation Hedges, and Capital Utilization in Developing Countries: An Extension of McKinnon's Complementarity Hypothesis," *Quarterly Journal of Economics* (August).

Fforde, A., and S. de Vylder. 1992. *The Socialist Republic of Vietnam,* Report to the Asian Development Bank, Manila.

Gelb, A., et al. 1993. "Can Communist Countries Transform Incrementally? The Experience of China," *World Bank* (February).

Gomulka, S. 1991. "The Causes of Recession Following Stabilization," *Comparative Economic Studies* 33, no. 2, pp. 71–89.

Johnson, D. G. 1990. *The People's Republic of China, 1978–90.* San Francisco: International Center for Economic Growth, ICS Press.

King, R., and R. Levine. 1993. "Finance, Entrepreneurship, and Growth," paper presented to the conference "How Do National Policies Affect Long-Run Growth?" World Bank, Washington, D.C. (February 8–9).

Levine, R. 1992. "Financial Intermediary Services and Growth," *Journal of the Japanese and International Economies* 6, no. 4 (December), pp. 383–405.

Lipton, D., and J. D. Sachs. 1990, "Creating a Market Economy in Eastern Europe: The Case of Poland," *Brookings Papers on Econonomic Activity* 1, no. 1, pp. 75–147.

McKinnon, R. I. 1973. *Money and Capital in Economic Development.* Washington, D.C.: Brookings Institution.

———. 1991a. "Financial Control in the Transition from Classical Socialism to a Market Economy," *Journal of Economic Perspectives* 5, no. 4 (Fall), pp. 107–122.

———. 1991b. *The Order of Economic Liberalization: Financial Control in the Transition to a Market Economy.* Baltimore and London: Johns Hopkins University Press.

———. 1993. "Macroeconomic Stabilization in Liberalizing Socialist Economies: Asian and European Parallels," in A. Giovannini, ed., *Finance and Development: Issues and Experience.* Cambridge University Press: CEPR.

McMillan, J., and B. Naughton. 1992. "How to Reform a Planned Economy: Lessons from China " Mimeo, University of California, San Diego (November).

Murphy, K., et al. 1992. "The Transition to a Market Economy: Pitfalls of Partial Reform," *Quarterly Journal of Economics* 57, no. 3 (August), pp. 839–906.

Murrell, P. 1990. "Big Bang Versus Evolution: Eastern European Reforms in the Light of Recent Economic History," *PlanEcon Report* (June 29).

Perkins, D. 1992. "China's Gradual Approach to Market Reforms," paper presented to the conference "Comparative Experiences of Economic Reform and Post-Socialist Transformation," El Escorial, Spain (July).

PlanEcon Report. "The Russian Economy During the First Half of 1992" (September 3, 1992). Also published in *Russian Economic Monitor*, (March 10, 1993).

Qian, Y. 1993. "Lessons and Relevance of the Japanese Main Bank System for Financial Reform in China." Mimeo. Stanford: Stanford University.

Sachs, J. 1992. "Privatization in Russia: Some Lessons from Eastern Europe," *American Economic Review* (May), pp. 43–48.

Vokes, R., and A. Fabella. 1992. *Economic Reform in the Lao People's Democratic Republic.* Manila: Asian Development Bank.

Williamson, J. 1991. *The Opening of Eastern Europe.* Policy Analysis 31 (May). Washington, D.C.: Institute for International Economics.

Wong, C. 1992. *Economic Reform in China.* Manila: Asian Development Bank.

Wong, C., C. Heady, and W. T. Woo. 1993. *Economic Reform and Fiscal Management in China.* Manila: Asian Development Bank.

6

China's Economic Success: Effective Reform Policies or Unique Conditions?

Barry Naughton

Over the past two years, the contrast between China's economic performance and that of the former planned economies of the Soviet Union and Eastern Europe has become so large that it is now impossible to ignore. All the European socialist countries and all the former Soviet republics, without exception, have experienced large declines in aggregate output, on the order of 25 percent or more. By contrast, China has experienced GNP growth rates around 8 to 9 percent annually for over a decade. Indeed, of all the former socialist countries, China is the only one that is not currently in a profound economic crisis.

Ordinarily, one might expect that such a contrast would create a boom in comparative studies. After all, China and the European socialist countries are all undergoing fundamental transformations from bureaucratic to market-dominated economies. There has been a vast outpouring of literature about the theoretical requirements of such a transition but precious little empirical work on the different possible approaches. To be sure, a growing, but still small, literature has developed that urges that the Chinese experience be taken seriously (Chen, Jefferson, and Singh 1992; Lardy 1991b; McMillan and Naughton 1992; Singh 1991). And there is a similarly increasing literature on gradualism in Eastern Europe, one that often focuses on the Hungarian experience. But it is perhaps fair to say that there is no existing literature that brings the Chinese and the European experience of transition into focus at the same time—nothing that seriously discusses the alternative policy choices or environmental conditions that shaped the strikingly divergent economic outcomes in the different regions.

Among those who work on problems of transition in general, the Chinese experience is commonly ignored. This is unfortunate, but one can hardly blame specialists in, say, Eastern Europe for this shortcoming. It is not easy to get reliable information on China, and scholars of China are no better in carrying out cross-national comparisons.[1] More disturbing is the tendency to dismiss the Chinese experience as irrelevant or somehow phony. Indeed, this dismissal verges on a kind of psychological denial when carried out by individuals who have themselves been involved in policymaking in European socialist countries with rather mixed results. Thus, one commonly hears a wide range of far-fetched and mutually contradictory reasons why China's experience is irrelevant to other socialist countries.

Some of the various kinds of denial include the argument that China is not really making a transition to a market economy. "Countries in CEE (Central and Eastern Europe) are transforming their economies into market economies ... [while] China's strategy is based essentially on the belief that market elements can be successfully introduced into decision-making processes ... based on continued overall plan coordination" (Hewer 1991). Another point is that China's economic success is based on a few areas in southern China that have received much foreign investment and this has "driven Chinese economic growth." (Thomas 1991). The argument is made that China has adopted only those policies that have already been tried and failed in European countries like Hungary (Csikos-Nagy 1991) or that China's success is possible only because it has an authoritarian government; these policies could not be followed by democracies.

Not one of these objections is correct and not one is based on much knowledge of Chinese experience over the past decade or more. It is the aim of this chapter to begin to describe what is distinctive about China's reform policy, on the one hand, and what is distinctive (and, implicitly, advantageous) about China's initial economic conditions on the other hand. My intention is not to argue that China is a model of economic reform that other countries should emulate. Surely we have seen enough Chinese exceptionalism over the past few decades to keep us satisfied for another decade or two. On the contrary, my objective is to subject China to the same kind of scrutiny to which other transitional economies are subjected. When the differences between China and the European countries are carefully delineated, the differences are in fact great. Nevertheless, a number of policy prescriptions do emerge. These are not of the nature of overall "copy China" recommendations but rather are specific policy insights that may be applicable across countries.

It is crucial to differentiate clearly between two different, conceptually opposite, situations. In the first, China might be thought of as possessing certain advantages that would have made its transition easier regardless of what reform strategy it followed. The second situation, the polar opposite, is that China might have possessed certain initial conditions that made it easier, politically and economically, for it to adopt a particular reform strategy, and then that reform strategy turned out to be the best one, regardless of what initial conditions prevailed. In either case, there is something about China's initial situation, or endowment, that leads to economic success. But in the first case, reform strategy is not an important intervening variable. In the second case, the choice of the reform strategy is the crucial variable that leads to success.

In the real world, the opposition between these extremes of interpretation will not be nearly so neat. There will be aspects of China's initial endowment that will incline it toward a given strategy of economic reform precisely by making it more likely that the strategy will succeed. That is, there will be advantageous conditions that are advantageous both in that they lead to a "correct" reform strategy and that they make the transition process easier, regardless of strategy. In such cases, we will have to make informed judgments about the relative importance of the two factors or aspects of the situation. I argue that China did enjoy certain potential advantages that made the transition process easier and that these advantages inclined the transition process toward a more gradual, fragmented, and piecemeal approach. But that approach also turned out to be the "correct" approach. Both initial conditions and approach to reform policymaking must be evoked to explain the China difference. But this is not surprising. Given the large gap between economic performance in China and Central and East European countries (CEEs), it is natural that we can point to several factors that contribute to that gap.

I will first discuss the difference between the Chinese approach to economic reform and that which characterizes most of the CEEs. I begin by listing five separate features that characterize the Chinese approach but then argue that these separate features in fact interacted in such a way that the reform process as a whole constituted a coherent whole. I then shift ground and discuss the China difference. There are six important factors that differentiate China's initial conditions from those of the CEEs. Most of these are indeed favorable to China's economic growth potential, but only one of the six affects the *choice* of reform strategy. It follows from this that in spite of the difference in initial conditions, it is meaningful to make comparisons between the reform strategies followed in China and the CEEs.

The Chinese Approach to Economic Reform:
Five Features

The key elements are the support given to new entry of firms into hitherto protected sectors (particularly manufacturing) and the introduction of market prices over a broad range of the economy. These elements were sufficient to introduce a new dynamic into the economy, based on the gradual spread of market relations. The key institutional innovation that made this possible was the adoption of a dual price system. The fundamental insight required is that those elements were sufficient to kick off a virtuous cycle of economic transformation.

More broadly we can identify five central features of the Chinese reform strategy that characterize it and clearly differentiate it from other reform strategies. First, macroeconomic stabilization and industrial restructuring were initiated under the old administrative system. A shift of economic priorities toward consumption goods eased macroeconomic imbalances prior to, and during, the early stages of reform. Second, rural reforms took place early and quickly, producing not only a surge of agricultural output but also releasing labor and entrepreneurial energy, which were essential resources during the next stage of reforms. Third, entry was allowed into economic sectors previously reserved for state monopoly control, particularly manufacturing and eventually foreign trade. Fourth, a dual price system was created, under which most goods had both a within-plan price and a market price, with the market price frequently higher than the plan price. Even state-owned firms operated on the market after fulfilling a plan target that was set well below capacity. Fifth, the size of the central plan was fixed in absolute terms, permitting the economy to "grow out of the plan." Government monitoring of state-owned firms continued but was increasingly focused on profitability rather than plan fulfillment.

These characteristics differentiate the Chinese reform process from the "big-bang" experiments in Eastern Europe as well as the partial and half-hearted reforms in Eastern Europe during the 1960s. It is worth noting that some economic features that might appear to be a function of initial conditions are actually the outcome of strategic choices. For example, it might seem that big-bang reforms are compelled by the presence of severe macroeconomic imbalances at the beginning of reform. The reality is more complex. China inherited exceptionally severe macroeconomic balances at the beginning of its reform process. Formal rationing of goods was in place for some twenty commodities. Shortages of even the most basic commodities were common. However, China's more gradual path involved the choice to first address those misallocations primarily through a restructuring of output carried out through the administrative apparatus. By the mid-1980s, the first round of imbalances in the consumption goods markets had been ameliorated, and only then were the next steps in reform taken. Thus, macro imbalances were also a feature of the Chinese reform but were handled in a different fashion.

Ex-Post Coherence of Chinese Reform

The five distinctive features of the Chinese approach to economic reform that are described in the previous section are not in themselves sufficient to delineate an overall coherent reform strategy. It remains to be shown that the particular features interact to produce a coherent whole. In fact, it appears that the elements interact in a way that can produce a virtuous cycle of reform and economic growth. It is possible to combine reform elements such that gradual marketization drives changes in behavior in the initially protected sectors as well. In what way does this process take place? The interaction can be conceptualized in terms of four steps.

1. When the state monopoly over industry and foreign trade is relaxed, entry of new funds proceeds rapidly and has a powerful impact on the overall economy. In China, entry of new firms proceeded at a remarkable pace. Even in the absence of legal protection for independent businesses, entry can be a more powerful force in socialist economies than in comparable market economics. This is so because the very distortions in the price and output structure that are such distinctive characteristics of the socialist system make entry more attractive. First, the socialist price system skews profitability toward the manufacturing sector. The opportunity to share in monopoly profits thus induces rapid entry (Naughton 1992). Second, the size distribution of industrial enterprises is highly skewed toward large firms. Although China was known for the large number of "small" firms in its pre-reform system, even these were relatively large, typically having over fifty employees. By contrast, the size distribution of industrial firms in market economies, both developed and developing, consistently shows small firms (fewer than fifty employees) accounting for at least 25 percent of industrial employment. There are numerous niches in both modern and developing economies that are best filled by small firms, and this is undoubtedly the case in China and other socialist countries as well. Since those niches were initially empty, the potential rewards to entrepreneurs who arrived first were large. Rapid entry ensured high returns and at the same time promised significant efficiency gains for the economy as a whole. In essence, socialist economies create the conditions for the "unbalanced growth strategy" with unbalanced state investment raising returns to independent entrepreneurs in associated sectors.

The numbers in Table 6.1 demonstrate the way that entry has changed the Chinese industrial economy. In 1978, a little over 40 percent of industrial output was produced by large state-run firms; 50 percent by medium and small urban firms (both state-run and "collective"), and less than 10 percent by rural firms. The very small scale sector was insignificant. (These categories differ substantially from the Chinese categories from which they are ultimately derived. See the Appendix.) This is a very unusual size distribution of firms for a developing country, which would typically be expected to have a much larger small-scale sector. The near absence of a very small scale sector in China before reform suggests that there were numerous empty niches, poorly covered by large state firms but appropriate for small competitors. This was also true in the CEEs— indeed, more so given the predominance of very large firms in those economies. A further indication of the significance of these empty niches is the fact that in 1978 the average profitability (profit and sales tax divided by total capital invested) in the rural enterprise sector was 40 percent. That these elevated profit rates were rewards reaped by early entrants into hitherto protected markets is shown by the fact that profit rates on rural industry have declined steadily in the dozen years since, as entry has proceeded, and now range around 15 percent.

By 1991, as Table 6.1 shows, the relative weight of the urban medium and small sector had declined by half and accounted for only 25 percent of total output. The rural medium and small sector had more than doubled in relative size, while the very small scale sector had gone from nothing to 7.7 percent of total output. Entry of new, smaller-scale firms accounted for about 20 percent of China's industrial output by the beginning of the 1990s. Niches had begun to fill in, and the size distribution of China's industry began to display a diversity that resembled that of other developing countries. The economic forces driving entry of new firms are extremely strong in transitional economies.

2. Households respond to the opportunities opened to them. Chinese households responded to new economic opportunity with increased saving and entrepreneurial activity. In China, as in other planned economies, household saving rates were low before the inception of reform. Average annual saving rates were only 2 percent of household income before 1978. But by the late 1980s, households were saving over 15 percent of annual income streams. Household saving not only went into household businesses and construction of housing but it was also deposited in state-run financial institutions, expanding the supply of credit and easing macroeconomic stress (Naughton 1987). Meanwhile, private business employment grew from 330,000 in 1978 to 23 million in 1988. Thus, households responded quickly and vigorously to the new economic reality.

TABLE 6.1 Industrial Output by Size and Ownership Categories (percent of total output).

	1978	1991
Large-scale sector	41.5	43.6
[State]	[41.5]	[40.7]
[Other]	[0.0]	[2.9]
Urban medium and small	49.4	25.1
[State]	[35.8]	[12.1]
[Collective]	[13.6]	[13.0]
Rural medium and small	8.7	20.6
[Township]	[4.8]	[10.3]
[Village]	[3.9]	[10.3]
Other:[a] Medium and small	0.0	2.9
Very small scale	0.4	7.8
Total	100.0	100.0

[a] "Other" output is produced by foreign-invested firms (43 percent) as well as joint ventures between different domestic ownership categories (53 percent). For additional explanation, see the Appendix.

Sources: Chinese Statistical Yearbooks (Bejing, Government of China); Yearbooks of Industrial Economic Statistics; and the 1992 Statistical Abstract, p. 70. The data for 1978 were calculated using the 1970 constant price output data. The 1991 data were calculated from current price output data.

All available evidence indicates that this kind of household response is typical in transitional economies. Hungary's gradual transition has been accompanied by massive formation of private businesses, which have constituted one of the most successful components of the Hungarian reform. Indeed, individuals in Hungary have been shown to stretch their working hours, sacrificing leisure for the pursuit of economic opportunity. Even in Russia, where some have argued that initially weak entrepreneurial traditions have been obliterated by seventy years of central planning, entry of new "cooperatives" (thinly disguised private businesses) has been extremely rapid. The incentives are great, and households do not hesitate to respond to them. The supply of saving and entrepreneurial activity turns out to be highly elastic.

3. Entry drives a realignment of the price system. The early years of Chinese economic reform were marked by a long-running debate over how to reform the price system. Yet the Chinese government ultimately never instituted either a single large-scale price reform or a big-bang–

type deregulation of prices. Nevertheless, after ten years of reform, substantial realignment of prices had occurred. Evidence of this realignment can be easily found. Among industrial sectors, a pronounced trend toward equalization of profit rates marked the 1980s; among consumer prices, a dramatic increase in the relative price of food characterized the same decade (Naughton 1991, 1992). Realignment of prices resulted from the combined effects of administrative adjustments to government-set prices and to the impact of market forces. It is impossible to disentangle the separate contribution of each factor. What seems clear is that the creation of the dual-track price system provided both information to government officials, signaling when state-fixed prices were out of line, and an opportunity for market forces to become manifest directly to producers and consumers.

Government price controls became less effective as market forces grew in importance. Entry into previously high-profit sectors drove down output prices in those sectors while simultaneously bidding up the price of formerly undervalued inputs. Government price controls either followed those trends or else became increasingly ineffective. Simultaneous liberalization of the foreign trade system provided a similar channel for the transmission of world relative prices into the economy (Lardy 1992). By the end of the 1980s, government price controls—persisting alongside market prices—came increasingly to be seen as subsidies or taxes. Price controls remained significant on a portion of energy supplies, and this remains an important distortion in the Chinese economy. But increasingly the character of the distortion is that of a subsidy to energy consumers, whereas the information about the correct price of energy is transmitted relatively clearly by the market prices of key energy commodities (including electricity). With substantial realignment of the price system already in place, China does not need to face the disruption of a sudden drastic realignment of prices subsequent to price deregulation.

4. State firm performance improves. Although the preceding sections have stressed the change in behavior at the household level and the impact of entry of new firms, it is important to stress that the changed economic environment affects the behavior of state-run firms as well. It is important to note that state firms face a radically different environment subsequent to the initiation of substantial reforms.

State firms are faced with the necessity and opportunity to operate on the market. As the Chinese dual-track system developed, nearly all state firms found themselves in the position of buying and selling at market prices. The dual-track system was not a simple state-nonstate dualism but rather included a dual operating environment for state firms as well. This can be exemplified by the evolution of the market for finished steel, the production of which is carried out almost entirely by state-run firms. Official data show that deliveries of finished steel within the central government plan have been stagnant since 1984, even declining somewhat since 1986. Since output has grown steadily, the proportion of output within the central government plan has steadily declined to less than one-third. The situation in steel exemplifies the steady "push to the market" that has affected all state industrial firms.

More important, the movement to the market means that state firms face increasing product market competition. Such competition is much greater in light manufactures than in heavy materials industry (such as steel), but it exists across the board. Profit margins, which were previously protected by entry barriers, have eroded across the board, and state firms thus find themselves facing increasing discipline from product markets. Some of this competitive pressure comes from rural enterprises; other pressure comes from firms sponsored by local governments in other cities and provinces. The cushion of high monopoly profits that used to wrap all state firms has come undone, and the success or failure of individual firms has become increasingly evident. Some firms have, of course, failed to adapt adequately to increased competition and have plunged into the red. Other firms have adapted successfully. Perhaps most significant is that the difference between successful and failed firms is now quite evident from their balance sheets.

Monitoring of firm activity has continued but has increasingly shifted from monitoring of plan compliance to monitoring of profitability. Erosion of monopoly protection has affected government revenues as well as firm profits. As a result, local government officials have essentially been forced to intensify their scrutiny of enterprise profitability. The incentive structure of government as "owner" of state-run firms has shifted. As a result, firms face greater discipline exerted through the managerial hierarchy. In exceptional cases, this discipline may replicate the discipline exerted by capital markets in market economies.

New incentive mechanisms have been created that implement the new objective function of firm overseers. Particularly striking in China has been the use of long-term managerial contracts, in which managerial pay and worker bonus funds are linked to profitability on a three- to five-year term. Moreover, managerial promotion and demotion can be shown to be related to firm performance in a straightforward fashion (Groves et al. 1992).

These changes in state firm behavior have immediate ramifications. Reference to Table 6.1 reveals some interesting facts about state-sector performance over the past decade. Large state firms have maintained their position in the economy. Accounting for slightly over 40 percent of output in 1978, they account for slightly over 40 percent of output in 1991 (and for every year in between). Needless to say, this implies that large state firms also accounted for slightly over 40 percent of total industrial growth during this period—and Chinese industrial growth over the 1980s was extremely rapid. By contrast, a different part of the state sector has been devastated. The state-run medium and small urban firms have dropped sharply from 36 percent of output to only 12 percent of output during the same period. Here is a sector that has been dramatically restructured. There are a few, but only a few, known cases of privatization of these state firms. Thus, in general the shrinkage of the state medium and small sector reflects the impact of competition rather than conversion. Such firms have simply been outcompeted by rural and urban collective and private firms, and their importance in the economy has shrunk dramatically.

Finally, changes in state firm behavior have also been evident in changes in their productivity. Studies of Chinese industrial enterprises have consistently found improvement in total factor productivity since the end of the 1970s (Chen et al. 1988; Jefferson et al. 1991). To a certain extent, such improvement simply represents recovery from the abysmally low productivity of firms following the Cultural Revolution. Nevertheless, productivity growth has been substantial and sustained. Table 6.2 displays the results of total factor productivity (TFP) calculations for six sectors (state firms only). In some ways, these calculations represent an advance on previous figures. The calculations are based on production functions that regress gross output on capital, labor, and material inputs. Output, capital, and inputs have been deflated separately according to price information collected directly from the factories. Thus, these calculations are arguably more accurate than previous aggregate production functions based on broad assumptions about price trends. Productivity trends are shown to differ substantially among sectors. Moderate productivity growth is evident in four sectors; quite dramatic productivity growth characterizes machinery and electronics. These are indeed the sectors where Chinese practice lagged the furthest behind international practice at the onset of reforms and are the sectors in which the scope for productivity improvements was probably the largest.

The factors outlined in this section thus add up to a kind of virtuous cycle of gradual reform. It can be seen that the key initial element is the elimination and relaxation of the state monopoly over industry. Once this occurs, rapid entry driven precisely by the built-in distortions in the planned economy unleashes strong economic forces that push the economy toward marketization. Growth of a market environment in turn pressures the state sector to improve its performance. Continued monitoring of state firms intersects with increased market pressure to produce an improvement in state firm performance. Ex post, it adds up to a

TABLE 6.2 Sector Total Factor Productivity Growth, 1980–1989 (annual percentage growth)

Food Products	Textiles	Chemicals	Building Materials	Machinery	Electronics
2.3%	2.5%	2.7%	3.4%	6.1%	7.9%

Source: CASS/UCSD/Oxford State Enterprise Survey.

coherent strategy of reform. Moreover, there seems no reason to believe that these measures would not be equally coherent in Central and Eastern European countries.

How Different Is China?

The Chinese economy certainly differs significantly from the Central and Eastern European countries. Although all belonged to a common extended family of planned economies derived from the Soviet model, there were important differences in the level of development and the systemic features of these economies. I suggest that there were six important differences between China and the CEEs. In general, these tend to give China greater growth potential than the CEEs. Yet, with perhaps one exception, they do not seriously affect the choice of reform strategy. These factors may indeed have inclined China toward the adoption of a more gradual, evolutionary reform strategy, but they do not seem to have a strong impact on the effectiveness of that strategy, once chosen.

Growth Fundamentals

The Chinese economy appears to have stronger growth potential than the CEEs regardless of system. Even before reforms, China's economy was growing at respectable rates, while the CEEs were verging on absolute stagnation on the eve of the reform process. More generally, China should be seen as an economy with a relatively high human capital endowment (for a developing country) combined with very low wage rates (even for a developing country). Life expectancies and educational levels in China's cities and advanced coastal provinces are not far below those of the CEEs, although living standards are far below those countries. This reflects the success of socialist policies, particularly in the countryside, but also the inefficiency of socialist production. "It is often said that modern China's levels of health and literacy are unusually high for its level of national income, yet the inescapable converse of this observation is that China's level of national income is unusually low for its given level of 'human resources'" (Eberstadt 1989, p. 291).

Moreover, China is adjacent to the East Asian economic region, the most rapidly growing economic region in the world. Technology transfer can be rapid, and international markets are expanding quickly. By contrast, West European eeonomies are prosperous but growing only moderately rapidly so that oppotunities for the CEEs are fewer. Theory and practical experience tell us that the combination of a skilled labor force, low wages, and proximity to large and growing markets should lead to rapid growth. Thus, we would expect China to have more rapid economic growth than the CEEs under a wide range of plausible systemic differences.

Nevertheless, these observations cannot obscure the fact that economic reforms in China led to an acceleration of growth even from relatively robust pre-reform rates, whereas reform in the CEEs led to a reduction in growth even from anemic pre-reform rates. It is this contrast that is really at the heart of the contrasting performance. The CEEs have nearly all consciously followed reform policies that were expected—even to some extent intended—to produce a contraction of output in the short run. The contrast in growth experiences cannot be dismissed as the accidental result of a series of external factors, all of which happen to disfavor the CEEs by comparison with China. Quite the contrary, the contrasting growth experience is a fundamental and probably inevitable outcome of the choice of reform strategies. By focusing on rapid reform programs with a high degree of simultaneity, CEE reformers have purposely adopted strategies designed to produce maximum change in price structures in a short time, sharply increase international competition, and greatly increase short-run uncertainty. Indeed, in a number of cases they have done so explicitly to shatter the former economic system and make the process of change irreversible.

A Comparatively Heterogeneous Production Structure

In the Soviet Union, production was concentrated in a small and declining number of factories, totaling just over 40,000 by 1979. Moreover, factories with over 1,000 workers accounted for 74 percent of Soviet industrial output and 75 percent of the industrial work force. By contrast, China never established the degree of centralized control over industry that prevailed in the Soviet Union. Local governments at all levels established and managed industrial enterprises, and production was dispersed over many factories. This feature was reinforced by economic reform. By 1987, China had 98,000 state-run factories; 164,000 urban collective factories; 1.59 million rural collective factories, and 5.6 million individual and private entrepreneurs engaged in industrial production (Ferris 1984 p. 9). Thus, whereas the organizational form of Chinese state-run enterprises reflects its Soviet antecedents, Chinese industry is more diverse than Soviet industry, in terms of both production scale and ownership form.

A Fragmented Planning System

China had a fragmented planning system with de facto local government property rights even before reform. Chinese central planning, unlike Soviet planning, did not cover the totality of output. Central and local governments divided the responsibility for administrative allocation. Thus, although the market was excluded in either case, the Chinese system had permitted the de facto development of local government property rights. Local governments had not only a presumptive claim on the allocation of output of locally run factories but also first claim on the profit stream generated locally.

Clearly the fragmented planning system and the heterogeneous production structure were related. Alongside the cluster of huge, Soviet-style firms, predominantly controlled by the central government, were smaller firms run by local governments. It seems clear that such a structure helped the Chinese muddle toward an effective economic reform model. Local governments, acting as owners and investors, competed to enter profitable industrial sectors.

Thus, new state-owned entry was as important to the overall process described above, as was entry by private or rural collective firms. Moreover, local governments in China range from the large (Chinese provinces with the population of European countries) to the fairly small (county-, township-, or even village-level governments). Arguably, these smaller governments have something like hard budget constraints. Possessing limited access to concessionary credits, and none to the monetary mechanism, these local governments may act more like diversified corporations, competing with other locales, than with sovereign entities. They may be a type of corporate body. With relatively hard budget constraints, and direct supervision of firms, these local governments had a strong interest in profit maximization. Although their objectives were no doubt diluted—maintenance of employment probably ranked high as well—an interest in profitability is certainly a strong characteristic of these governments.

Thus, the heterogeneous planning and output structure encouraged a decentralized, experimental approach to reform that tended to convert local governments into corporate bodies. The more centralized, homogeneous structure of the former Soviet Union might make it more difficult for the post–Soviet Union to muddle toward such a model of reform. However, once such a model is recognized, it could easily be emulated. Decentralization of authority of industry to local government could quickly, and without difficulty, replicate at least some of the Chinese conditions. Moreover, the homogeneity of the Soviet production structure should imply that there are even more profitable niches available for exploitation in the Soviet case. In that sense, the forces driving entry would be even stronger.

Foreign Trade

China's foreign trade—unlike that of most of the CEE countries— was conducted primarily with market economics before reform. In 1978, 86 percent of China's trade was conducted with predominantly market economies, and only 14 percent with other planned economics. Even before reform, Hong Kong played a major role as an intermediary in facilitating China's exports to market economics, taking 27 percent of China's exports in 1978 (MOFERT 1984). This trade orientation—which dates back to the Sino-Soviet split of the early 1960s—provided China with some opportunities to learn about world markets. Moreover, a significant part of China's early exports to market economies were light manufactures, particularly textiles and food products. These were precisely the commodities in which China was likely to have a long-run comparative advantage, so that the limited learning about world markets was concentrated in the most important industrial sectors.

More important, the orientation of China's foreign trade spared it the massive disruption caused in the CEEs by the collapse of the CMEA trading system. On balance, trade was a stabilizing force in China's economy. Domestic economic fluctuations—which were considerable— were dampened by the ability to run large short-run trade deficits. Both in 1985 and for several months at the end of 1988 and in early 1989, China allowed a temporary flood of imports to abate inflationary pressures. And each time, the trade balance shifted back toward balance (or surplus) after the reestablishment of domestic economic balance.

An additional critical characteristic of China's foreign economic transactions is the relative marginality to the national economy of the most open regions. Here again, the relatively low level of economic development—in this case the relatively low level of national economic integration—proved to be a short-term advantage in reform strategy. In particular, it allowed the early adoption of the remarkably radical policy of adopting export processing zones (or "special economic zones"—SEZs in Chinese parlance). At the start of reforms in 1978, the South Coastal provinces of Guangdong and Fujian, sites of the first SEZs, were marked by two distinguishing characteristics. First, they had historic links to several different overseas Chinese communities and to Taiwan. The early establishment of the SEZs was an attempt to take advantage of these links in very specific forms. Each SEZ was oriented toward a specific overseas Chinese community with which it shared a local dialect and family and residual economic ties. Second, the South Coastal region had been systematically neglected over thirty years of industrial development in the People's Republic. Because of early fears of an invasion from Kuomintang forces on Taiwan, as well as suspicion of southern commercial traditions, only a tiny handful of the hundreds of large factories built since 1949 were in these South Coastal regions.

These two characteristics implied that allowing Guangdong and Fujian to pursue the open-door strategy was virtually costless. There was little existing state-planned industrial economy to be disrupted. Overseas Chinese could be expected to play fundamental intermediary roles. Questions of national sovereignty would not arise because most of the "foreign" investors were actually Chinese. It was an enclave strategy in which the enclaves were triply protected. First, because the early SEZs were themselves enclaves; second, because the foreign element was Chinese; and third, because the larger regional economy in which they were surrounded was easily partitionable from the main national economy. After the enclave strategy proved successful, it was gradually expanded to other areas within the South Coast region, such as Zhejiang and Jiangsu provinces.

Elevated Household Saving Rates

China appears to have been rapidly characterized by the kind of elevated household saving rates that also mark the other East Asian economies. Since growth is impossible without investment, and investment impossible without ample domestic savings, a predisposition to high household saving rates (if they exist) must certainly be an advantage to both the reform and the growth processes.

Yet why should such high saving rates be a purely East Asian phenomenon? A number of European countries have very high saving rates. Moreover, there is substantial reason to believe that high household saving rates in China are a response to abundant economic opportunity (high real rates of return) rather than cultural factors. As we have seen, there are reasons to believe that similar rates of return might prevail at least initially and in the CEEs as well.

More generally, the question should be expanded: What kind of savings and investment mechanism should be used during the transition? It seems foolish to sacrifice a large amount of potential investment by tumbling the economy into a deep recession compounded by extensive uncertainty. Moreover, saving is strongly influenced by the dynamics of the economy. Even if it were possible to create overnight an economy in which all the available resources had the "right" prices, the crucial saving-investment balance would depend on short-term growth of income. In turn, many prices would be dependent on rates of investment. Thus, there seems to be an insoluble interdependence between saving rates and price structure. If it is possible to maintain a high-investment, high-growth path, it will certainly be easier to converge to a new, more efficient dynamic equilibrium than if it is necessary to first establish equilibrium in a static or shrinking economy.

A Large Rural Population.

Here we come finally to a factor that appears to favor the Chinese reform strategy. A little over two-thirds of the Chinese population is rural. This portion of the population has never had the same income guarantees that were implicitly extended to urban populations in both China and the CEEs and it correspondingly was not subject to the same intensity of social and economic controls. As a result, the rural population has come to be a more fertile soil for entrepreneurship and economic innovation than has the urban population.

This is particularly evident around the periphery of large cities. Suburban areas—considered "rural" in the Chinese classification and subject to lesser degrees of social and economic control—have emerged as the most prosperous and rapidly growing parts of the economy. Much of the "rural industry" that has been so dynamic in China is in fact "suburban industry." In suburban areas, economic opportunity, often linked to nearby cities, intersects with looser economic controls. The rural areas provide a kind of space in which economic innovation can proceed and within which individual entrepreneurs can prosper. Conversely, urban populations are often quite cautious about economic reform. Aware of their privileged positions and income security, urban residents are far less willing to plunge into the dangerous waters of independent entrepreneurship. In this case, China's larger rural population seems to give an advantage to the Chinese strategy. Economies like that of the Czech Republic, with a small rural population and very large state employment, may be forced to move toward privatization and structural reform within the state sector earlier rather than rely on gradually accumulating market pressure from outside that sector.

Of these six factors, then, only one unambiguously affects the choice of an economic reform strategy. We must conclude that China's reform experience is potentially applicable to Central and Eastern Europe as well.

Conclusion

The large differential in economic performance between China and the CEEs can be at least partially explained. It is overly simple to argue that the performance differential resulted solely or primarily from differing reform strategies. In fact, there are substantial reasons, rooted in China's initial conditions, to expect that China would experience both a higher overall growth rate and a smoother transition to a market economy than the countries of Central and Eastern Europe. Yet it is unlikely that these factors explain the entire performance differential. Instead, when one examines the key features of reform strategy, it appears inescapable that China's reform strategy produced substantial benefits in terms of economic growth over a period of more than a decade while also turning out to be a coherent strategy of economic transition. As such, that reform strategy appears to merit wider consideration, and comparative studies that include China and the CEEs are urgently needed.

Appendix:
Industrial Output by Size and Ownership Categories.

Table 6.1 reclassifies Chinese data in two important ways. First, two Chinese categories of industrial enterprise, large and medium, are here combined into a single category labeled "large-scale sector." The original Chinese categories are quite misleading. According to the 1985 Industrial Census, 98 percent of the enterprises classified as medium-sized by the Chinese employed over 500 workers. In international classifications, firms with over 500 employees are generally considered very large. Thus, the combination of the Chinese large and medium-sized enterprises is roughly comparable to the very large sector in other economies.

Second, the Chinese publish data on output produced by size categories, but there are no cross-classifications with ownership data. For 1978 this presents no problems, since aside from a handful of large urban collective firms, all large-scale output came from the state sector. The "very small" sector in Table 6.1 is assumed coterminous with the Chinese category of "individually run enterprises" (an ownership category). By the late 1980s, however, the category of "other" enterprises has begun to be significant, accounting for 5.8 percent of total output by 1991. The "other" category consists of both foreign-invested firms and joint ventures between domestic ownership firms. On average, this type of firm is of intermediate size, with about 200 workers per enterprise in 1990. Nevertheless, some of these firms are large. I have assumed that, at a maximum, 50 percent of the output from this sector could come from large (by my definition) enterprises. This is a generous assumption that almost certainly overstates the "other" share of the large-scale sector. This assumption is then used to compute the state share of large-scale production and then by subtraction the share of state output in the urban medium and small sector. Since the share of output allocated to "other" ownership tends toward overstatement, the large-scale state share may be slightly understated and the state medium and small share overstated. Thus, from the standpoint of the arguments being made in this chapter, the assumptions are all conservative, and more precise figures would strengthen the argument.

Notes

1. Indeed, much of the problem lies with the underdeveloped state of Chinese studies in the West and Japan. Chinese data are copious but are marked by definitional inconsistencies and conceptual problems. Although they can be used, they must be used with care and often after adjustment. Study of China has not been sufficiently developed to provide the necessary data base to scholars outside the China field, and as a result, data about China have sometimes been greeted with justifiable suspicion. Unfortunately, problems of miscomprehension are sometimes more serious among specialists in the European socialist countries because they encounter in China concepts and statistical categories that are familiar from their world in the Central and East European context but have been altered in the Chinese environment in substantial ways that may not be apparent.

References

Chen, K., et al. 1988. "Productivity Change in Chinese Industry: 1953–1985," *Journal of Comparative Economics* 12, no. 4 (December), pp. 570–591.

Chen, Y., G. Jefferson, and I. Singh. 1992. "Lessons from China's Economic Reform," *Journal of Comparative Economics* 16 (June), pp. 201–225.

Csikos-Nagy, B. 1991. "Letter to the Editor," *Transition* 2, no. 9 (October), pp. 7–8.

Eberstadt, N. 1986. "Material Poverty in the People's Republic of China in International Perspective," in U.S. Congress Joint Economic Committee, ed., *China's Economy Looks Toward the Year 2000*, vol. 1, Washington, D.C.: Government Printing Office, pp. 263–322.

Ferris, A. 1984. *The Soviet Industrial Enterprise*. London: Croom Helm.

Groves, T., et al., 1992, *China's Evolving Managerial Labor Market*, University of California San Diego Discussion Paper 92–36 (September).

Hewer, U. 1991. "Reform vs. Replacement" (Letter to the editor), *Transition* 2, no. 10 (November), pp. 6–7.

Jefferson, G., et al. 1991. "Growth, Efficiency and Convergence in China's State and Collective Industry," *Economic Development and Cultural Change*.

Lardy, N. 1991a, *Foreign Trade and Economic Reform in China, 1978–1990*, New York: Cambridge University Press.

———. 1991b. "Is China Different? The Fate of Its Economic Reform," in D. Chirot, ed., *The Crisis of Leninism and the Decline of the Left: The Revolutions of 1989*. Seattle: University of Washington Press.

McMillan, J., and B. Naughton. 1992. "How to Reform a Planned Economy: Lessons from China," *Oxford Review of Economic Policy* 8, no. 1 (Spring).

MOFERT. 1984. *Zhongguo Duiwai Jingji Maoyi Nianjian 1984* [Yearbook of China's Foreign Trade and Economics]. Beijing: Duiwai Jingji.

Naughton, B. 1987. "Macroeconomic Policy and Response in the Chinese Economy: The Impact of the Reform Process," *Journal of Comparative Economics* 11, no. 3.

———. 1991. "Inflation: Patterns, Causes and Cures," in *China's Economic Dilemmas in the 1990s: The Problems of Reforms, Modernization, and Interdependence*, vol. 1, pp. 135–159. Study Papers submitted to the Joint Economic Committee, Congress of the United States. Washington, D.C.: U.S. Government Printing Office.

———. 1992. "Implications of the State Monopoly over Industry and Its Relaxation," *Modern China* 18, no. 1.

Singh, I. J. 1991. "Is There Schizophrenia About Socialist Economic Reform Theory?" *Transition* 2, no. 7 (July–August).

Thomas, S. 1991. "Apples and Oranges," (Letter to the editor) *Transition* 2, no. 10 (November), p. 7.

PART THREE

The Evolutionary Paradigm: Theoretical Debate

7

Governance, Evolution, and the Transformation of Eastern Europe

Jozef M. van Brabant

The core of the debate between radicals and gradualists is not really about the comprehensiveness of remaking the economies of the eastern part of Europe. The notion that many aspects of their societies must be overhauled in a number of different dimensions is generally accepted. There is, however, much less of a consensus about the speed and intensity with which an orderly sequenced transition strategy can realistically be implemented throughout the economy, subject to the overriding sociopolitical constraint that I specify below. This chapter first examines the practice of applying the label "shock therapy" for the policies that must be, and have partly been, implemented in economies in transition that now hope to transform themselves quickly into viable economies. Further on, the chapter discusses the dichotomy between shock therapy and gradualism as the allegedly sole dualistic choice in which transition policies can logically and realistically be cast, this leads us to a brief discussion of the market as an evolving societal institution. The chapter then illustrates these propositions with reference to the call for rapid divestment, through organized sales or giveaways, of the vast bulk of state assets as the core of the transition strategy. (This has largely been a passive industrial policy in disguise and as such has been ill-advised.) Finally, the chapter looks at the five pillars of proper and improper transition strategies in four domains in light of the alternative evolutionary strategies on transforming the economies in transition that are realistically available.

The opinions expressed here are my own and do not necessarily reflect those that my employer may hold.

"Shock Therapy": A Misnomer of Sorts

Before I proceed the notion of transformation policies deserves to be clarified. Inasmuch as this concept suggests incisiveness of actions over a fairly protracted period of time, I much prefer this term over "transition policies," which suggests temporizing and a fairly short-term horizon. The designation "transformation policies" is used guardedly to refer to a strategy aiming at taking advantage of, and when necessary maintaining, a sociopolitical consensus on the material and other costs inflicted by far-reaching societal mutations. These are essentially away from a one-party–dominated political system with a largely degenerate administratively planned economy toward a pluralistic political system with over-whelmingly market-based decisionmaking. In other words, I exclude from my purview the countries that still lack a basic consensus on transformation or whose aims differ fundamentally from those specified here.

As a point of convenience, countries such as Bulgaria, the former Czechoslovakia, Mongolia, Poland, Russia, and the former Yugoslavia (until 1990) are considered to have adopted shock therapy. Most other countries, notably Hungary, are reckoned to have embraced gradualism, or temporizing, in tackling the issues at hand, namely, regaining a modicum of economic stability and forging ahead with the long process of the multiple structural reforms that will, in the end, determine whether these economies will discover a new growth path. Almost by definition that will have to be in the endogenous mode, featuring sustainability over a protracted period of time (say, one to two decades) with substantial growth rates (say, 5 to 8 percent as an annual average).

The critical distinction among postcommunist economies that allegedly embraced shock therapy and gradualists does not lie in the policies embraced but rather in the initial conditions that led up to the policy stance actually taken. It is only once the initial conditions are clear that one can logically and realistically prescribe a potential cure for the disorder(s) to be dealt with. A thorough assessment of these conditions, hence the issuance of recommendations for assistance, cannot be obtained as a result of a superficial examination of elementary statistics by newcomers to the study of the legacies of communist-style central planning.

The phrase "shock therapy" is technical terminology usually applied by psychiatry departments in hospitals and related mental institutions as a last resort to treat patients suffering from certain types of severe mental depression and catatonic schizophrenia. The electrical shock propelling current through the body with the goal of stimulating nerve cells, notably in and thus altering the chemistry of the brain, to resume more normal functions is designed as a therapy.[1] As such, it aims to achieve a certain end, namely, relieving the symptoms enumerated through the electroconvulsive shock. The curing agent is in any case not the shock but the convulsion. In some cases, this may lead to curing the patient. But the cure comes through the relief brought on by the convulsion, not through the application of the electrical shock. Furthermore, following the convulsion, the cure is likely to become evident only gradually, if at all, over a protracted period of time. If no cure is in sight, and the symptoms of severe mental disorder persist or return, another application of shock therapy, literally in the sense of electroconvulsive therapy, may be ordered in an attempt, once again, to induce relief and possibly a cure for the diagnosed disease following a protracted period of time.

Shock therapy is in the first place a therapy. The notion "shock" can be utilized also in different senses, such as in the case of a violent collision, concussion, or impact (say, the cavalry charging into the masses) or a body of workers selected or volunteering for some especially arduous task (say, Stakhanovite shock troops). It can also connote a sudden and disturbing physical or mental impression, such as the debilitating impact of learning about somebody's untimely passing. In the latter case, it could not possibly be associated with therapy, as the shock is the registered act of some interaction between persons or on the part of one or more persons reacting to a certain disturbing event.

It is ironically this latter sense of shock that has become associated with economic policies in the shock therapy mode in some economies in transition. Indeed, the purpose of these economic policies is not to administer the shock to treat the symptoms of the underlying disease but to apply a curative therapy that unfortunately involves a shock. In other words, in contrast to the medical use of the term where the shock is the intended therapy, shock in these economies is the consequence (perhaps unintended) of the therapy, possibly because of misdiagnosis of the disease that shockers may have earnestly felt they were attempting to cure.

Application of the term "shock therapy" is not appropriate in attempts to clarify the policies pursued in some economies in transition. The metaphor, as used by economists, implies a short, sharp shock with immediate effects. In that sense, it should be not too far removed from the textbook, neoclassical abstraction of instantaneous and costly adjustment to a new equilibrium. Although "instantaneous" should be handled elastically, one must wonder whether a three- to four-year economic depression can still meaningfully qualify as a shock, let alone a therapy. The language of the shockers, however inappropriate from a clinical perspective, promises unambiguously a more rapid adjustment than is possible in practice. As a result, shockers must bear some responsibility for the current disappointment, fatigue, and disillusion, bordering in some cases on sheer despair, in many economies in transition.

If the metaphor of shock therapy is taken literally, namely, as an application of scientific (or medical) wisdom that provides quick and lasting relief from a severe disorder, then one must come to grips with two strands of problems. One is that the notion itself is simply inapplicable since such a strategy in reality cannot be implemented. Certain things can be done quickly, some other things must be done quickly, and there is a range of tasks of transition policies that cannot be done quickly. For the market economy to function properly, there is a need for near-simultaneous completion rather than a simultaneous start of the various strands of transformations. Second, it should not, then, come as a surprise that the record of transition policies allegedly pursued in the mode of shock therapy in the East has not been successful. But this is a topic that has been vigorously argued about by both advocates and detractors of shock therapy. Neither selective memory and statistical manipulation nor elastic use of the notion 'success' has been very helpful in this debate, though.

Shock Therapy Versus Gradualism: An Aberrant Dichotomy

It is an irony of sorts that most of the neoclassical dissenters involved in advising the economies in transition in one mode or another have paid little heed to the more philosophical and historical preconditions for some of the foundations that prop up their analyses. This is arguably nowhere more marked than with the Hayekian argument on the market as a source of information and the real requirements for entrepreneurship to take off. Indeed, Friedrich von Hayek never failed to emphasize the importance of learning in becoming entrepreneurial and he also recognized that there is a legitimate need for a social agenda, including guaranteeing a minimum wage; assisting individuals in providing for some common hazards; or cushioning the other excesses of market rivalry (Gray 1989). Beyond such a welfare net, however, entrepreneurs should be left alone to exploit proprietary information to their own benefit.

Much similar comments can be made with respect to the Ordoliberalismus, the broad ideology that underpins the original version of the social market economy. It argues for a powerful state to restrict itself to setting up and controlling a competitive market order (this embodies a concept of the state that is as unrealistic as Plato's philosopher king or the benevolent-despot model [Leipold 1990, p. 60]). The key point, however, is the need to empower the state, something on the order of the Kantian ordo constitutionalis (or a constitutionally anchored order), to forge such a competitive market order as soon as feasible. This suggests that the constitution of the state and related collective agents deserves as much attention as the constitution of the market process to which so many have paid attention and shock therapists have taken exception as a fait accompli.

It is one of the great ironies of our age that those counseling the policy-makers of economies in transition into proceeding rapidly and holistically have, perhaps unintentionally, presented their arguments in a thoroughly autocratic and often arrogant fashion, suggesting demagogically that there is no alternative. This is odd, to say the least. Shockers fail to appreciate that big-bang policies are not really the stuff of how societies at peace operate. They may be embraced during a war or revolution. But they are decidedly exceptional events in societal decisionmaking otherwise. The very essence of the market economy and truly democratic politics is precisely that there is nearly always an alternative. The general tendency there is to gradualize as many adjustment problems as possible. Notably in open societies the nature and distribution of adjustment costs are a legitimate concern of consensual politics.

Hence, there is truly no other way to well-punctuated and modulated gradualism. This need for genuine discussion and for assuaging the electorate's fears and interests by listening to them and taking them into account is especially relevant to economies in transition. Indeed, here the issues on which a consensus must be crafted and maintained are not simply banalistic economic details. Rather, they are fundamental questions about the structure of society and the nature of changes in the political and ethical values presently still associated with collectivism and in some cases the Mitteleuropa or the earlier eastern Slavic autocratic syndrome with all of its historical legacies. It is now precisely the job of the economic adviser to estimate the costs of the various alternatives and compare them with the expected advantages so that responsible choices can be made by those who must either bear the costs directly or face the political consequences of misjudging them.

Shock therapy in contrast to presumed gradualism typically implies the simultaneous and rapid deployment on all fronts of all relevant categories associated with the transition. These include sequencing, speed, comprehensiveness, intensity, and sectoralism with at least four broad ranges of issues: macroeconomic stabilization in both the stock and the flow senses; liberalization of domestic and foreign markets, including fostering a rapidly expanding private sector based largely on new savings from domestic and foreign origin; privatization of state-owned assets, including forms other than sheer divestment through sales or giveaways, notably commercialization and corporatization and possibly restructuring, of the assets controlled by the state and its various interlocking interest groups; and institution building or erecting the framework within which market-based economic decisions can be taken and political choices voiced in a transparent, predictable, reliable, and comparatively inexpensive manner.

By contrast, gradualism connotes an approach involving a good deal of attention to appropriate sequencing of the various components and subcomponents of the policy package of stabilization, liberalization, privatization, and institution building. Sequencing inevitably affects other attributes of the policy package; it is impossible to conceptualize the entire range of issues pertaining to the transformation of a degenerated, administratively planned economic system with plenty of legacies from communism. Shockers frequently demagogically portray the gradualists as aiming at restoring the status quo ante or preferring another form of collective conservatism, but the truth is virtually always much more nuanced.

Given the four interlocking aspects of the transition strategy (stabilization, liberalization, privatization, and institution building) and the five qualifiers attached to the strategy (speed, sequencing, comprehensiveness, sectoralism, and intensity), one could set forth a four-by-five matrix in which the various options available to policymakers are laid out. Some cells will have only one option. Thus, stabilization must be done quickly, with great intensity, without sequencing or sectoralism, and with comprehensiveness in the monetary variables.[2] However, stabilization cannot be ensured without looking at the fiscal side as well. Whereas policymakers may commit to a marked reduction in expenditures and/or a sharp rise in fiscal revenues to reach budget balance relatively quickly, realities in the economies in transition are likely to quickly defeat any attempt to adhere to any such declamatory stance.

There are also policies that could be introduced quickly but might be ushered in over a more protracted period of time. This includes price and foreign-exchange liberalization. The argument frequently invoked by those advocating shock therapy that, for example, trade and price liberalization cannot be introduced gradually is simply not true. Even a casual reading of postwar history of developed countries quickly demonstrates the lack of rigor of this argument. The point that these commentators should have made is that in their view these postwar policies could and should have been introduced more rapidly than policymakers felt they had a sustainable mandate for. That is to say, the truly important requirement of such policies is not so much that they be gradual but that they be credible.

Credibility is not simply a matter of providing information or making propaganda about the ultimate benefits of the intentions of the transition. What is needed is a coherent program with credible sequencing that policymakers and the population at large can support, if only tacitly. But there is no magic, let alone simple, formula of how government can best secure that goal. Policies are credible when most actors are confident that the government's course is feasible and will be adhered to, barring untoward circumstances. Once the policy is firmly put in train, confidence will be associated with quickly emerging signals for changing economic behavior, including in resource allocation.

Finally, there are things that cannot be done quickly, among them privatization, restructuring the state-owned enterprises, or laying other foundations of a pluralistic system for largely market-based decisions. When done rapidly, such changes are not able to withstand strains in the social and political arenas, in part under impact of the adversities of the multiple transformations. But even in these domains some aspects, such as small-scale privatization, can be carried out much faster than others, such as divestment of large state-owned enterprises (SOEs).[3] Most advocates of shock therapy appear to believe that it is conceivable that a radical transformation in attitudes, expectations, and behavior in economic agents can be brought about in a comparatively brief period of time. Neither logic nor history yields hard evidence thereof, however.

This only goes to show that, in practice, the distinction among the issues that can be done quickly, those that must be done quickly, and those that cannot be done quickly will, at best, remain artificial. For example, calling for restructuring government revenues and expenditures as part of stabilization policies in practice is not as easy as it may sound. Raising revenue will depend on reforming the fiscal infrastructure. On the expenditure side, the entire range of contingent commitments, such as interenterprise debts, and the sociocultural functions of state-owned enterprises will need to be rethought. All this will in part be a function of privatization, enterprise restructuring, the social safety net, and the stimulus provided for the emergence of new small and medium-sized-firms.

In sum, the argument between shockers and gradualists diverts attention from the paramount issues of policymaking for the transformation of the Eastern societies. At their core, they are twofold: to establish a credible program for transformation policies and to elicit and maintain popular support for the program's implementation, including for correcting for adversities if and when they occur rather than letting them fracture an already fragile sociopolitical support base.

The Market as an Evolving Institution

Before we look at the essential role of markets, the potentially important conceptual problem of the most useful meaning of the word "market" must be made clear. As Jan A. Kregel (1990, p. 45) put it, most economists have mistaken the force of competition for the human-created institution called a "market" when they argue the virtues of the free-market mechanism that is supposed to coordinate self-interested individual actions. Indeed, as Lionel Robbins (1952, p. 56) observed, the pursuit of self-interest unrestrained by suitable institutions carries no guarantee of anything except chaos. A market is essentially a set of institutions set up by humans rather than an immutable part of the natural environment. For that reason, there are various market configurations composed of specific institutions that let the forces of competition unfold. The latter provide a constraint on self-interested behavior of individual agents, channeling it into a confined range of mutually compatible outcomes. Those that do not enjoy this attribute as per the evaluation of participants will induce some agents to change the institutions that form the market and allow the forces of competition to resume operating. This action will be initiated either by those benefiting from or by those disadvantaged by the outcomes that do not conform to the established market institutions.

In addition, most advocates of free markets have generally also tended to assume that, as an organizational and coordinating mechanism, markets are cost-free and that private transaction costs are zero or negligible. This is simply not true (Dunning 1992, pp. 16–17). In practice, even to create and sustain reasonably functioning (though not perfect) markets, some burdens will have to be borne by society at large over a considerable stretch of time. These include the creation of a legal framework for the identification, protection, and enforcement of contracts regarding all kinds of market-based transactions. At times, as in societies that have a particular proclivity for litigation, reliance on explicitly detailed, ostensibly market-based, contracts with spelled-out pecuniary costs and benefits leads to increased dependence on laws, lawyers, litigation, and codified procedures for ostensibly market-based contracts that in other societies are handled with a greater degree of trust in partnerships. It also involves the creation of an entire industry that insures against risk. Both are quite costly indeed.

The stylized facts of neoclassical economics, or the tyranny of this impeccably objective paradigm, in Alice Amsden's (1993, p. A21) words, posit that, when available, properly functioning markets for production factors (capital, labor, land, and other natural resources) as well as for all kinds of goods and related services must aim at efficient resource allocation; efficiency is here understood as the maximization of the sum of the discounted values of consumer and producer surpluses (Hay 1993, p. 2). This outcome is almost trivial. The key operands of this statement are "properly" and "when available." One or more markets may not be available or function only poorly because either no equilibrium exists or economic agents do not behave competitively, thus leading to market failure. This may be deliberate through bounded rationality or opportunistic behavior. If so, another question is how quickly functioning markets can be erected and what should be done in the interim to mitigate market failures.

In what follows, then, the notion "market" means a particular set of institutions in which chiefly competition guides self-interested behavior of economic agents in such a way as to produce a limited set of acceptable outcomes, which are thus classed as coherent or mutually compatible (Kregel 1990, p. 47). This excludes the possibility of adhering all but exclusively to the basic tenets of the neoclassical approach, for it presumes that the market produces order out of chaos at no cost by providing perfect information about self-interested actions on the part of economic agents. Just like perfect planning is an impossibility, the operation of markets for which information is perfect is of trivial interest. The real world is riddled with imperfect and asymmetric information. Moreover, gathering and processing this information is costly. As a result, cases in which the neoclassical paradigm might even approximately hold are at best rare (Stiglitz 1991).

The market approach assumes that all economic agents have their own interest at heart and, on the whole, can proceed to maximize it without directly influencing the outcome of other economic agents (Leipold 1990). In other words, market failures are presumed to be absent. But this is frequently not so. A real world without market failures is rather implausible, as endowments over which agents have property rights and the specifics of marketing and production technologies are hardly such that atomistic competition among economic agents solely bent on maximizing their profit or utility can be presumed to emerge. Furthermore, there are scale economies and externalities that, if not corrected for, will distort market outcomes. Also, monopolies, and oligopolies exist. Some are natural monopolies or oligopolies. Others are subject to corrective action. Both will need to be regulated through other than pure market channels (Willig 1993). Questions may arise even with respect to the trade-offs between efficiency and equity that the market, left to itself, would at best inadequately address.

This has profound implications for the formulation, evaluation, and implementation of alternative public policies. Given the legacies of communism and the East's historic achievements, issues of distributional equity simply cannot be ignored by those involved in managing the transitions, even though precepts on distributional equity have been changing rapidly and incisively under impact of the transition. Markets do not function properly in the above sense when it comes to public and semi-public goods, externalities, increasing returns, market imperfections of various kinds (which define whether price, information, and mobility features of perfect markets depart from prevailing ones), and the possible social inequity of even efficient market outcomes. These realities are found in all markets some of the time and in some markets all the time.

Basic precepts of competitive market allocation are most certainly not fulfilled in the economies in transition. This will remain so for some time to come. As a result, an adequate framework must be put in place with a view toward seeking to mitigate market failures through a host of devices. In the extreme, markets fail altogether and government may find itself entrusted with ensuring the more efficient production of truly public goods. These are activities whose consequences consist of nonappropriable benefits (such as national security) or noncollectible costs (such as crime). Government may even be asked to deliver semipublic goods if it can do so more efficiently than the regulated private sector. Note that this assignment with all its attributes need not be indelibly etched in granite forever; nor need it be the public sector as such that actually produces the goods and services, such as through state-owned enterprises. Regulation in various forms can provide a useful intermediate format when imperfect information prevents the emergence of perfect competition (Stiglitz 1993, Willig 1993). This too may be required only on a temporary basis until new market-based mechanisms can be innovated.

Although the prospects for a steady transition to genuine market-oriented systems in the East are at this juncture quite promising, their crystallization cannot reasonably be expected within a brief time span. Indeed, any existing market, however congruent with the neoclassical paradigm it may be, cannot be transplanted lock, stock, and barrel in record time without causing severe dislocations that in time will lead to the endogenization of the market; in some cases, the transplant may be rejected altogether. In approaching the core issues, technical economic affairs should be separated from sociopolitical precepts on wealth and income distribution, unless the latter are still the basic elements of ongoing, unsettled political rivalry, as in most successor states of the former Soviet Union.

One of the main purposes of such a new environment is to improve the efficiency of resource allocation and, at the same time, fulfill tasks that the market will not take care of under normal circumstances or will do so only inadequately. In view of the considerable constraints on perfect competition, asymmetries of information, restrictions on the ability to contract, limits to designing comprehensive incentive rules, and other real-life features, there are many markets that simply do not function properly. If only for that reason, one may seek relief through non-market intervention, provided the latter is not itself subject to failure that exceeds the dimension of the market distortion to begin with.

If some market functions poorly or is absent, optimal resource allocation can at best be obtained for goods and services that neither on the output side nor on the input side require transactions that would have taken place if the existing market had been better organized to begin with. There are probably few goods and services, let alone production factors, for which this is likely to hold at all in the real world, particularly in the East. In the presence of incomplete risk or futures' markets and imperfect information, markets are in general never constrained Pareto-efficient, assuming that government is subjected to the same kinds of informational and/or incomplete-market constraints facing the private sector (Stiglitz 1989). Once that is verified, there is a potential for government intervention. Whether this should be realized depends very much on how government can discharge those tasks, given the severe limits on information at its disposal.

A market economy cannot function well without there being properly functioning markets for goods and services as well as production factors, notably capital and labor, hence the importance of completing the transformation processes simultaneously. Wide layers of individuals in the economies in transition like to entrust the entire gamut of wholesale and retail trading for goods and services to agents other than those embodying the old material-technical supply system. Wholesale trading will of necessity have to be entrusted to firms interacting chiefly on the basis of their own economic interests within a macroeconomic framework set and maintained by the state. Similarly in the case of retail trade: It will increasingly be undertaken by private and cooperative small and medium enterprises which will be seeking to maximize returns on their assets.

Effective competition in contemporary trading of goods and related services can be ensured relatively easily. Liberalizing market access to foreign competitors would be one avenue. Competition can also be enhanced by encouraging the creation of new small and medium enterprises for which elementary capital markets must be in place. Also the separation of economic from other functions of state-owned enterprises and deconcentration of economic activity, especially in huge conglomerates, can help foster competition. All this can be achieved without running the risk of generating the diseconomies of scale associated with deliberately nurturing a mom-and-pop trade network. That serious obstacles inhibit funneling adequate information to individuals to bolster the growth of small and medium enterprises is rarely fully appreciated in economies bent on leapfrogging the natural evolution of economic forces.

The real challenge for policymakers, then, is not that some markets function poorly. Rather, because the entire infrastructure for market-based decisionmaking is being laid almost from the ground up, decision-making can for now be efficient only in a restricted sense. Furthermore, it is as yet highly uncertain how quickly functioning markets can realistically be innovated. In the meantime, emerging markets are bound to exhibit shortcomings. Moreover, some are likely to become operational much sooner than others. As in the mature market economy, some will continue to transgress on the conditions for optimal allocation, notably in the case of capital markets. The latter's principal functions should be ensuring the efficient allocation of existing capital so as to obtain the maximum contribution to newly created national wealth, the most effective mobilization of new capital to enlarge the reproduction process, and the disposition of capital owned by the state or privately to ensure exit and entry and thus raise capital's net worth through competition.

The key question that thus arises is whether another means of coordinating diffuse decisions can be imagined either as a substitute for or as a complement to the missing or poorly functioning markets. Should markets, then, be complemented with other instruments, policies, and institutions? One can hardly avoid a positive answer if it is recognized that there are market failures that do not necessarily coincide with government failures provided a minimum of governance capabilities can be mustered. Both the combinations of policy options through market and plan as well as governance capabilities will shift over time, thus calling for governance dynamism in tune with pragmatic subsidiarity (Brabant 1993a, b).

Also this feature of the uncertainty and unwarranted expectations of more desirable alternatives whose real implications will become visible only over time form part of the initial conditions in economies in transition. That is to say, the choice of policy package in the four dimensions indicated here and with respect to the five attributes invoked will depend not on choosing shock therapy over gradualism or the other way around. Rather, the ability of a country to pursue credible changes depends crucially on the nature and strength of its economic, political, and legal institutions; on its social cohesiveness and traditions; and on the conditions prevailing at the start of the transformation process. These factors will obviously differ among countries and will thus determine the speed at which economic forces and institutions can realistically be transformed.

Note that credibility in the sense invoked signals not solely policies that are credible but policies that can also be implemented and sustained in a credible way. In other words, a good deal of the feasibility of trans-formation processes depends on the imagination, and indeed cunning, of the political leadership, not only to project confidence in economic programs but also to create and sustain a popular consensus behind a positive vision of the society at which it is aiming (UNECE 1993, p. 7). Although it may not be very politic to come up front with an estimate of the costs of the transition (their scale, duration, and distribution), policymakers cannot avoid preparing measures for attenuating their impact on the more vulnerable segments of the population. Moreover, since the costs of the transition will appear much more quickly than the benefits, the degree of social support, with given safety nets, will determine the scale of the shock that can be sustained without derailing the entire transformation program.

From these broad observations it follows that the market economy is an abstract notion, regardless of what may eventually crystallize. Whatever variant may be aimed at, it can in real life be introduced only gradually. The speed of doing so is, of course, a function of the prevailing disarray and the acceptable cost of adjustment. That is to say, some changes in the development strategy and in the economic model that economies in transition inherit can be introduced rapidly. These shifts may also be sought more gradually. In either case, unanticipated developments may call for fine-tuning the transition strategy or perhaps even temporarily reversing it for tactical reasons. In contrast to the diversity in pace of reform envisaged, there is greater uniformity about the particular coordination mechanism to be designed. But various of its components must be introduced at different phases of the transformation. This ushers into the debate about the four transformation pillars (stabilization, liberalization, privatization, and institution building) once again the five qualifiers of the economic transition (sequencing, comprehensiveness, speed, intensity, and sectoralism).

Whereas the construction of a market economy and its proper management cannot be altogether devoid of politics, the ambition to establish a functioning pluralistic, market-based economy sets an agenda for transformation that encompasses modifications in basic institutions in the broad sense, socioeconomic policies, and a large variety of policy instruments. These economies must re-create markets almost from the ground up, in the process remilling their most essential nuts and bolts. Indeed, these economies cannot gloss over the need to innovate or resuscitate the basic institutions of the market economy, including setting private property rights; creating a solid financial infrastructure, perhaps even stock exchanges and other securities markets; establishing private enterprises and commercializing State-owned enterprises and eventually divesting most of them; erecting the constitutional infrastructure for property rights and for how best to legally protect them; establishing the rule of law and enforcing it; embracing the principle of profit-oriented activities; motivating human attitudes and behavior into accepting a marked degree of open income and wealth differentiation; and so on.

None of these features was present at the time of the political revolutions, at least in the degree to which they condition a well-functioning market economy. In many respects, little progress has since been made. Many of these aspects will not sprout spontaneously. Rather, they require an activist state, particularly during the earlier phases of the transition. This complements the role of the state in tackling the type of market failures familiar from mature market economies (provided government failure will not exacerbate matters) as well as coming to grips with the allocative failures attributable to the absence or poorly functioning markets for some considerable time to come. Moreover, the natural order of things is based on interdependence. There will hence be hysteresis effects associated with what is now done well or badly (Pickel 1992).

In delineating the role of the state, it does not suffice to be concerned about the gestation of functioning markets and how, at least in the interim, market failures could be remedied. The real task of the transformations is indeed that these countries need to identify a new, self-sustainable growth path that over a protracted period of time will generate sufficient economic wealth to persuade the electorate at large that key planks of the transformation agenda are being delivered upon. It is unlikely that such a new endogenous growth mechanism will become available in a wholly spontaneous matter once macroeconomic stabilization will have been regained and the basics of privatization and liberalization will have been put in place along with the building of institutions.

The pivotal question, then, is whether another mechanism, such as industrial policy as part and parcel of economic governance, might usefully be embraced. In any case, sustainable development requires broader guidance mechanisms and incentives than either the market or the central plan, regardless of the degree of government interference designed to correct market failures, can impel upon individual agents. At the same time, market institutions need to be maintained and upgraded, including through proper governance; hence the critical role of how the state can best discharge its responsibilities. Likewise, a crucial role may accrue to government in helping identify, and at times foster, the foundations of a growth path that is sustainable over the long haul.

Privatization as Passive Industrial Policy

The advocacy of what ought to be done to establish unfettered markets frequently confounds the virtue of the market with ownership functions under capitalism, but the two may well be completely unrelated. It also ignores overwhelming evidence that pure markets are fictive and that moving closely towards the ideal can be rather stultifying. Two focal points of the transition toward market-based decision-making have been whittling the role of the state in economic policymaking in general and fostering rapid privatization in particular. Both have continued to be emphasized in the debates on transformation policies, in spite of the fact that for now markets are at best available in a highly truncated form; this will remain the case for some time to come.

From the very inception of transition policies, the clear delineation of private property rights and the fast reestablishment of private property from the inherited all-but-exclusive state ownership have been core tenets in the political debates on how best to forge ahead. One obvious reason has been the felt need to gain a counterweight to the pervasively engrained, badly monitored state-owned property under communist rule. Another has been fundamental claims to reverse, and in some cases to restitute for, the long denial of private property in a wide range of real and financial assets under communist rule. Since then different efforts have been launched in the particular economies to foster private property, notably on the basis of reassigning property rights and indeed divesting state-owned assets. The experience to date cannot be regarded as an overwhelming success anywhere among the economies in transition, however. In some cases, the efforts have tended to divert much scarce time and human and financial resources from other critical issues deserving urgent, in some cases even priority, attention in sculpting transformation policies and implementing them. In recent months, this emphasis on the primacy of privatization in the transition has been repeated with somewhat less authority, fervor, urgency, self-conscious assertiveness, and preconceived convictions (see IMF 1993).

I contend that privatization has on the whole been a surrogate industrial policy by default, that is, a policy pursued in lieu of an industrial policy (see Brabant 1993a, b). At best it has been a passive stance in how best to administer society's assets. If only for that reason, privatization as tackled cannot but have a range of dysfunctional implications. At the very least, these implications detract from the salutary features inhering in a more positive, consciously designed and implemented, industrial policy. The urgency of formulating such an approach cannot be fully understood without a fairly rounded grasp of the deleterious features of helter-skelter privatization with various sociopolitical brakes (see Brabant 1992a).

Among the many critical aspects of the transformation's agenda, something that will be pivotal in determining how successful the process can possibly be and how quickly the scenario can be enacted, is the selection of which existing SOEs should survive, in whole or in part, and which should not. Of perhaps greater importance is the need for clarity about the means by which private initiative should be bolstered, if at all. But the starting points other than sheer political rhetoric or outright demagoguery need to be recalled. Technically speaking, the human and physical capital stock inherited from communist planning depreciates abruptly with (1) opening up these economies to international competition; (2) the forced disintegration of the former carefully nurtured trading links within the context of the Council for Mutual Economic Assistance or the former unified dinar, koruna, and ruble markets (which could have been smoothed to some degree had a more objective policy stance ruled the formulation and implementation of the transition's agenda [Brabant 1991, 1992b]); (3) the radically changed precepts on how economic affairs should henceforth be conducted; and (4) the economic recession, possibly depression, that has been accompanying the first years of transformation policies. At the same time, the structure of the economy is to be changed rather rapidly through new productive investments.

There is, then, a dual problem. As mentioned, one is the critical role of encouraging savings and fostering private initiative in establishing new small and medium enterprises and mobilizing this resource for carrying the transformation process forward as rapidly as circumstances permit, possibly in conjunction with petty privatization (Murrell 1992a, b, c). The other concerns state-owned assets, particularly those held in the form of SOEs. They are a problem for a variety of reasons. Prior to the political revolutions, vast areas of economic activity were organized in state-owned enterprises. These were not run as orthodox enterprises. Rather, they were akin to loosely conceived departments of an enormously sprawling, ill-fitting, and badly managed economic bureaucracy in which rent seeking was the norm. Managing assets with a view to maximizing net asset values certainly was never the principal, let alone sole, task of state-owned enterprises. Supervision of these enterprises with a view to ensuring efficiency was not really viewed as a task incumbent upon those entrusted with ownership functions.

To bolster the movement towards market-based economic relations in a constructive manner, all state enterprises must at least be incisively modified. This is necessary to alter the ways in which traditional state enterprises can be managed in the interim until they can be privatized or, for those that will remain in the public sector because of the need for state control, until they can be transferred to a new agency entrusted with governing public firms. Managing the process by which the survival and health of SOEs will be determined must perforce remain an activity in which the government will have to involve itself not only as owner but also as custodian of the framework within which some semblance of economic, political, and social order is preserved.

One of the greatest follies of the transition has been the commitment to divest state assets quickly, in some cases with a strident cry for the replacement of management in place. The first could not be accomplished mainly for economic, financial, legal, political, and administrative reasons. The second ran afoul of the political process, socioeconomic expectations on the part of wide layers of the population, and the fact that policymakers have had to learn the hard way to work with the resources at hand. As a result, the reaction of state-owned enterprise management to transformation policies, frequently in collusion with labor, has generally been defensive. Privatization was initially conceived in several economies as a rapid process in which the cadres in place, workers as well as management, were not invited to take an active part and in which the outcome as regards job security was at least uncertain.

The rational reaction of workers and management faced with these multiple threats, the rational reaction of workers and management has been short-termist protection, when necessary, and to alienate state property, where feasible in some form, usually by management or the nomenklatura. The end result has in any case been a marked decapitalization of productive assets, thus undermining the long-term viability of firms. This process has been possible because the state, even the new one, has not been a good owner. It has exercised at best haphazard control over the assets that it ultimately owned or for which it acted as societal custodian.

More important has been the fact that governments have willy-nilly embraced policy measures to assuage the destabilizing effects of widespread and protracted unemployment. Explicit decisions regarding the fate of many state enterprises, apart from the early rhetoric, particularly when they could aggravate already rapidly rising unemployment levels, have been reluctantly deferred by finding ways to keep firms afloat. The means used have been a variety of outright subsidies, additional credits at below-market rates that are at least implicitly guaranteed by the government, various kinds of tax relief, and tariff and other types of protection against foreign competition. All this has stifled legal private initiative and significantly muted the contribution to market-based decisionmaking that the privatization process began to put into effect. It has dysfunctionally fostered arbitrage and short-termism in the way in which savings can be productively mobilized in these economies.

The expected bolstering of factor productivity has, as a result of this widespread uncertainty and pessimism, not yet taken place. This is a pity, because this bolstering should be the real objective of the economics of transition, tempered with concerns about large-scale unemployment via an affordable social safety net. Instead, neither have the old regimes been removed from micromanaging essential parts of the economy nor have the new regimes managed to distance themselves from commitments to supporting these enterprises without having any thought-out strategy on what should be done. These failures can be ascribed to the inexperience of the new policymakers. But they also derive from the misguided advice of the international community in general and the multilateral economic organizations in particular (Brabant 1993b).

In other words, the transition has in many cases proceeded with a de facto industrial policy in which privatization has become a surrogate for positive state action in restructuring the microeconomic sphere, which became a taboo. The existence of an implicit industrial policy is often not even acknowledged as such, whereas public stances remain in favor of a thorough hands-off policy. This has been regrettable. Perhaps most cogent is that, by the very nature of the transition, the economies in transition will have to embrace measures to drastically change their economic makeup. This involves not only altering the relative weight of branches: It also calls for ensuring that remaining firms will be or will be deemed soon to become competitive, thus profitable in their own right. It is rather unlikely that this structural change can be engineered with minimal delays while relying chiefly on poorly profiled market forces.

Firms that are not now profitable, largely because of the profound economic recession and the unsettled state of the transitions, deserve to be supported in the interim through state activism, if only because valuable assets can thus be rescued from abrupt extinction or alienation to private owners, literally for a pittance in some cases. Likewise, good firms deserve to be catered to, for example, by facilitating commercial borrowing and smoother access to foreign markets, such as through export guarantees. Such activism and related interventions to cushion the adverse impact of privatization sloganeering should really have been cast within the framework of an explicit industrial policy (Brabant 1993b) rather than letting it develop in an entirely ad hoc manner, provided elementary governance capability could be mustered.

Admittedly, the preceding only scratches the surface of the complexities of privatization (Brabant 1992a). I trust, however, that even this truncated discussion has clarified the daunting nature and overwhelming range of obstacles inhibiting the multiple tasks of fostering a market economy, largely on the basis of private property. Even a pragmatic, nonideologically motivated medley of privatization methods will require some order in which to proceed. One is by fostering the private sector. Once the these economies have clear property rights and adequate institutions of the market, the role of the private sector in fostering the emergence of a fully-fledged market economy will be very important indeed. Private capital formation should be encouraged for as long as it remains within the remit set by law and the economic environment traced by macroeconomic policies and institutions more generally. This is particularly important in the case of small and medium enterprises. Some initial stimulus may be required to offset the most egregious negative externalities during the initial phases of the transition.

Matters are vastly different when it comes to the utilization of existing capital assets, the bulk of which are in the hands of the state or subject to ill-defined surrogates. This is an area of concern that the transition per se has to come to grips with in order to prop up genuine economic transformation. The crucial questions at this juncture, then, should not only encompass rapid divestment through outright sales or free distributions but also must ensure that existing capital assets owned by the state can be and are utilized more productively than under administrative planning. Even in that respect alternative paths have been confusing policymakers and confounding the transition agenda (Brabant 1992a, 1993b). This option is being increasingly heeded particularly in these economies where the disappointment about privatization as an economic instrument, as opposed to its political dimensions, has been considerable.

Part and parcel of the agenda should be the questions concerning which assets to privatize, how quickly the ultimate divestment should occur, who should adjudicate the selection of assets to be privatized, who should supervise state assets until they become private property, what criteria should be enacted to ensure that such assets in the interim are managed properly, and many others. In all this it cannot be ignored that most existing SOEs are going operations, even though they are beset by a severe economic depression. This may be insurmountable for some sectors. But the bulk of state-owned enterprises continue to operate and generate some gross profit. Furthermore, state enterprises that are making losses because of the environment for transition but which stand a good chance of making it with minimal support from public authorities should not be ignored in this effort. In some cases, the transfer of these assets to private agents may be arranged by eliciting new investment for restructuring purposes even when the state retains a property stake for perfectly sensible reasons (Demougin and Sinn 1992).

I trust that the above discussion has at least brought home the point that rapid movement with divestment by its nature is bound to be relative. Short of war, revolution, or profound civil disorder, there can only be various degrees of speedy divestment, regardless of how expedient reaching that goal is judged to be. Policymakers would be well advised to conceive and implement the campaign according to a clear strategy rather than by simply deserting the state sector altogether. They should also recognize early on during the transition that frequent modifications, apart from steady fine-tuning, will be an obligation for good economic governance throughout the entire process as new capabilities are gained in private, nonprofit, as well as state sectors.

The Fundamentals of Transition Policies

Whereas sequencing (a euphemism for orderly gradualism in some versions of transformation policies) was the fashionable topic for economic debate in 1990 and early 1991, soon thereafter it was rejected as superfluous by those adhering to economic mechanics in favor of comprehensiveness and speed.[4] In response to the pervasive contraction in the economic fortunes of the group, however, the issue of sequencing has resurfaced as a policy topic whose resolution is paramount for designing, implementing, monitoring, assessing, and fine-tuning transition policies. If only for their own interests, it is incumbent upon policymakers to minimize the duration and depth of the economic slump, hence to care about the magnitude of the changes in policies and the order in which they are introduced. In any case, mutations in economic structures and behavior can materialize only over time. Sequencing is hence still very much an essential feature of the transition to be debated and refined as experience is gained.[5] There simply is no alternative to adhering to some sequencing.

A certain order has to be brought to the various transformation components to ensure that the unavoidable adjustment costs are contained to a workable minimum, spread over wide layers of society and some period of time, and sanctioned through some consensual decisionmaking. Perhaps even more important, sequencing with a capability of swift fine-tuning is a prerequisite in order to avoid chaos. How fast should the transformation be accomplished? Given that so many of the critical features of a market economy, let alone a pluralistic democracy, are available in these economies at best in a very rudimentary, at times only embryonic form, one must doubt the ability of these countries to transform themselves quickly into fully functioning market economies. Most transition policies, both those contemplated in the confused constellation of forces in countries that still lack a sociopolitical consensus as well as those introduced notably in Central Europe, cannot be pursued without provoking a severe recession. Reversing this depends crucially on the success of new small and medium enterprises.

One of the most banal platitudes of the rapidly expanding inventory of discourses on the East's economic transformations has been that economists and perhaps others know how market and planned economies function and how the transition from a market to a planned economy was accomplished. But they know next to nothing about undoing the planning environment and the wide-ranging legacies of the communist dominance in societal affairs. It is sheer rhetoric to contend that we know how to transform a market into a command economy when at the same time the experiences then incurred are being flagrantly ignored. Advocates of rapid, technically smooth transition policies are mostly ignorant of recent history. At the very least, a thorough knowledge of the hindrances encountered in creating planned economies, after the revolution in Russia and World War II elsewhere in the East, should have made it clear that virtually all countries had to contend with disastrous attempts to build new institutions from scratch and radical changes in the forms of ownership (Hussain and Stern 1993).

Even as concerns the re-creation of market economies in the East, pleading complete ignorance is neither helpful nor strictly true. Certainly, there are no hard-and-fast rules about the nature, composition, and speed of real-life transformations. Indeed, thus far no single Eastern economy has succeeded in overcoming even the basic legacies of administrative planning. Admitting this is not quite the same as baldly asserting complete darkness in the toolbox of what needs to be done during the transition; what could be done and how it could best be accomplished; how the various components could most usefully be sequenced; and at what speed and with what intensity they could be introduced, monitored, and fine-tuned, possibly staggered for various economic sectors. At least we do know that these economies do not possess markets, competition, an adequate regulatory framework, or the macroeconomic and legal arenas within which economic agents can pursue their own interests in an orderly manner. However, at the transition's inception these economies embody a vast set of policies, institutions, and policy instruments that have no place in a market economy. Policies, such as price liberalization, can be reformulated relatively easily. But to do so with the institutions and instruments at hand is inviting failure. Both are in urgent need of thorough change.

Moreover, there can be little doubt that markets will remain incomplete for a long time to come. Even when they will become available, policymakers must attempt to come to grips with standard market imperfections and failures and prevent government failures from aggravating them or from providing the wrong responses to the socioeconomic consensus regarding precisely what it is that the state should accomplish. Furthermore, all these economies must undergo measurable changes in the sectoral composition of output and, within each broad type of activity, in the range of enterprises that can with some degree of confidence be expected (in the true probabilistic sense) to survive the rigors of competition in a highly convoluted reality. This can be accomplished in a number of distinct ways. The cleanest may arguably be through the trial and error of spontaneously emerging markets. Its costs may be frightfully high, if not altogether insuperable, however.

The enabling environment calls not only for markets for all kinds of intermediate and final products and services but also for all kinds of primary inputs, including capital and labor with their distinct characteristics. It furthermore requires markets that allocate different kinds of resources over time. Moreover, markets can function more or less smoothly only when there is an adequate institutional and legal framework for economic activity, ownership, enterprise formation, entrepreneurial decisionmaking, and other essential features of reasonably mature economies. These rules and regulations, and their institutional infrastructure, need not be overly complex. Indeed, simplicity and clarity are beneficial features of the legal and institutional frameworks. But that does not necessarily facilitate their speedy gestation. Finally, activities of microeconomic agents must be coordinated through macroeconomic policies that in part mirror the consensual preferences held by society's agents. This reflection should preferably be accommodated in such a way that economic agents can express their sociopolitical aspirations in a reasonably unhindered manner.

Rather than aiming primarily at maximizing static resource allocation and ensuring some minimum pace of reproduction, the overarching economic task should be the identification of a more dynamic growth path and the application of policies within established institutions and requisite policy instruments that are likely to facilitate reaching this growth path and advancing along it. At that stage, purely allocative decisions can temporarily be left to the market. However, maintaining dynamism in economic development is not something that can be reached by a once-and-for-all change in economic structure. It must be a fairly continuous process of identifying and exploiting temporary advantages or conditions that promise to yield such advantages provided the proper preliminary measures to seize the opportunity are indeed grasped. Seen in this perspective, the task of ensuring functioning markets should not be viewed out of proportion with the wider obligation incumbent upon good economic governance to ensure sustainable long-term modernization and development (Brabant 1993a,b).

From these broad observations, it follows that, regardless of what may eventually crystallize, the market economy is an abstract notion, as discussed. Whatever real-life variant may be aimed at, it can be introduced only gradually. The speed of doing so is, of course, a function of the prevailing disarray and the acceptable cost of adjustment. That is to say, some changes in the development strategy and, more important, in the economic model can be introduced rapidly. These shifts may also be sought more gradually. In either case, unanticipated developments may call for fine-tuning the transformation strategy, perhaps even temporarily reversing it for tactical reasons. In contrast to the diversity in pace of reform envisaged, there is greater uniformity about the particular coordination mechanism to be designed. But various of its components must be introduced at different phases of the transformation, thus ushering into the debate once again how best to structure the five qualitative features of the four principal transformation domains discussed earlier.

Conclusions

The analysis presented here indicates that the debate between advocates of shock therapy and gradualism has to some degree been a waste of energy, a pointless exercise in semantics that has unfortunately had calamitous consequences for policymaking in economies in transition. Many reasons can be adduced in justification. For one thing, shock therapy is an inappropriate term for the policies targeted in some of these economies. Also, the content of the alleged therapy and its time dimension have been so ill-defined that shock is hardly an appropriate term. What has really been surprising is the shocking nature of the counseled policy agenda and recipes introduced. Dramatic first steps may be necessary but will hardly suffice to succeed. Finally, the urgency that the shockers suggest is required to forge ahead with the transformation of the Eastern societies has largely been demagoguery. The very essence of democracy and working toward its firm implantation, short of war or revolution, is precisely the careful exploration of alternatives and the introduction of painful changes over time with the costs being spread over various layers in society.

Short of sociopolitical circumstances being such that a leap in the dark is the only promising way of divesting these economies from the shackles of the legacies of communism, the arguments advanced here suggest that order in the transformation processes is critical although there may be few experiences upon which managers of such a mutation can draw for guidance and inspiration. Even so, the strategy to overcome the many roadblocks to erecting a market-based economy and pluralistic political decisionmaking of economies in transition is implicit in the analyses developed. The proper order must set the pace and depth of feasible transformations, subject to social constraints on implied adjustment burdens. Initial conditions, capabilities, path dependency, and related features of the transition should be fully factored into any realistic transformation strategy.

Because there is no alternative to an evolutionary approach to the transformation of these societies, barring utter chaos, the real core of the debate should hence be twofold. It should first of all carefully identify the initial conditions for changing these societies. At the same time, it should assess the kind of institution building, in the economic as well as in the political arenas, that is of paramount importance in successfully forging ahead with a well-defined transformation strategy. This qualifier can apply only when the program formulated by policymakers enjoys a minimum of sociopolitical consensus not only at the time the strategy is being formulated but, arguably even more important, when policymakers must face up to and counter unexpected setbacks with the transformation.

Notes

1. "Therapy" literally means the treatment of physical or mental disorders by nonsurgical means.

2. It is surprising that shockers have preferred inflating away monetary overhangs over more instantaneous forms of confiscating excess money in circulation, something that is resorted to when shock therapy fails.

3. In what follows, I use the notion "SOEs" as a shorthand to designate all assets that presently belong to the state, at least nominally, or over whose use the state may traditionally have exerted a determining influence. This includes the cooperatives as well as private property over which property rights were fuzzy (such as rural and urban real estate in many Eastern countries).

4. For some of the arguments, see Blanchard et al. 1991; Calvo and Frenkel 1991; Sachs 1991.

5. For details, see Brabant 1991; Bruno 1992; Carlin and Mayer 1992; Newbery 1991; Nolan 1992; Nuti 1992; Nuti and Portes 1993; Pickel 1992; Portes 1991.

References

Amsden, A. H. 1993. "From P.C. to E.C.," *New York Times*, (January), 12 pp. A21.

Blanchard, O., et al. 1991. *Reform in Eastern Europe*. Cambridge and London: MIT Press.

Brabant, J. M. van 1991. *Integrating Eastern Europe into the Global Economy: Convertibility Through a Payments Union*. Dordrecht, Boston, and London: Kluwer Academic Publishers.

———. 1992a. *Privatizing Eastern Europe: The Role of Markets and Ownership in the Transition*. Dordrecht, Boston, and London: Kluwer Academic Publishers.

———. 1992b. *Unravelling the Ruble Rregime*. London: European Policy Forum.

———. 1993b. Industrial Policy in Eastern Europe: Governing the Transition. Dordrecht, Boston, and London: Kluwer Academic Publishers.

———. 1993b. "Governance, the State, and Industrial Policy in Eastern Europe," paper prepared for the American-Polish Round Table, Charleston, S.C., September 15–16.

Bruno, M. 1992. "Stabilization and Reform in Eastern Europe: A Preliminary Evaluation," *IMF Staff Papers*, no. 4, pp. 741–777.

Calvo, G., and J. A. Frenkel. 1991. "From Centrally Planned to Market Economy: The Road from CPE to PCPE," *IMF Staff Papers*, no. 2, 268–299.

Carlin, W., and C. Mayer. 1992. "Enterprise Restructuring," *Economic Policy*, no. 15, pp. 311–352.

Demougin, D., and H.-W. Sinn. 1992. *Privatization, Risk-Taking, and the Communist Firm*, NBER Working Paper Series No. 4205 (November), Cambridge.

Dunning, J. H. 1992. "The Global Economy, Domestic Governance, Strategies and Transnational Corporations: Interactions and Policy Implications." Mimeo, Rutgers University, Newark.

Gray, J. 1989. "Hayek on the Market Economy and the Limits of State Action," pp. 127–143 in Dieter Helm, ed., *The Economic Borders of the State*. Oxford: Oxford University Press.

Hay, D. 1993. "The Assessment: Competition Policy," *Oxford Review of Economic Policy* 2, pp. 1–26.

Hussain, A., and N. Stern. 1993. "The Role of the State, Ownership and Taxation in Transitional Economies," *Economics of Transition* 1, pp. 61–87.

IMF (international Monetary Fund). 1993. "Seminar Explores Sequencing of Reforms in Former Socialist Economies," *IMF Survey* 1 (January 11), pp. 10–12.

Kregel, J. A. 1990. "Market Design and Competition as Constraint to Self-Interested Behaviour," pp. 45–57 in K. Groenveld, J. A. H. Maks, et al., eds., *Economic Policy and the Market Process: Austrian and Mainstream Economics*. Amsterdam: North-Holland.

Leipold, H. 1990. "Neoliberal Ordnungstheorie and Constitutional Economics," *Constitutional Political Economy*, no. 1, pp. 46–65.

Murrell, P. 1992a. "Evolution in Economics and in the Economic Reform of the Centrally Planned Economies," pp. 35–53 in C. Clague and G. C. Rausser, eds., *The Emergence of Market Economies in Eastern Europe*. Cambridge, Mass.: Blackwell.

———. 1992b. "Evolutionary and Radical Approaches to Economic Reform," *Economics of Planning* 1, pp. 79–95.

———. 1992c. "Privatization Complicates the Fresh Start," *Orbis* (Summer), pp. 323-332.

Newbery, D. M. 1991. *Sequencing the Transition*, CEPR Discussion Paper Series No. 575 (August), London.

Nolan, P. 1992. *Transforming Stalinist Systems: China's Reforms in the Light of Russian and East European Experience*, Discussion Papers on Economic Transition DPET 9203 (August), Cambridge: Department of Applied Economics, University of Cambridge.

Nuti, M. D. 1992. "Economic Inertia in the Transitional Economies of Eastern Europe." Mimeo, Commission of the European Communities, Brussels.

Nuti, M. D., and R. Portes. 1993. "Central Europe: The Way Forward" pp. 1–20 in Richard Portes, ed., in *Economic Transformation Central Europe: A Progress Report*. London: CEPR; Brussels: Commission of the European Communities.

Pickel, A. 1992. "Jump-Starting a Market Economy: A Critique of a Radical Strategy for Economic Reform in Light of the East German Experience," *Studies in Comparative Communism* 2, pp. 177–191.

Portes, R. 1991. "Introduction," *European Economy*, Special Edition No. 2, pp. 1–15.

Robbins, L. 1952. *The Theory of Economic Policy*. London: Macmillan.

Sachs, J. D. 1991. "Accelerating Privatization in Eastern Europe," Paper prepared for World Bank Annual Conference on Development Economics, April 25–26, Washington, D.C.

Stiglitz, J. E. 1989. "On the Economic Role of the State," pp. 11–85 in Joseph E. Stiglitz et al., *The Economic Role of the State*. Oxford: Basil Blackwell in association with Bank Insinger de Beaufort.

————. 1991. "Whither Socialism? Perspectives from the Economics of Information." Mimeo. Revised draft of Wicksell lectures (August). Department of Economics Stanford University, Stanford.

————. 1993. "The Role of the State in Financial Markets," Paper presented to the World Bank Annual Conference on Development Economics, May 3–4, Washington, D.C.

UNECE. 1993. "Economic Survey of Europe in 1992–1993, United Nations publication, sales No. E.93.II.E.1, New York.

Willig, R. D. 1993, "Public Versus Regulated Private Enterprise," Paper presented to the World Bank Annual Conference on Development Economics, May 3–4, Washington, D.C.

8

A Critique of the Evolutionary Approach to the Economic Transition from Communism to Capitalism

Josef C. Brada

Our interpretation of the existing system suggests that there is no other way of improving it than by an evolutionary approach. We do not pretend to know all of the solutions, [but] we are afraid of the unrestrained reform romanticism of some of our colleagues. ...We try to be led by pragmatic flexibility rather than by moralistic or ideological fundamentalism. Sound reform measures should be guided by properly understood and well-articulated national interests, not by abstract ideas. ...
—Vaclav Klaus and Tomas Jezek (1991, pp. 37–39)

[T]he economic transformations envisaged (in Eastern Europe) ironically mirror the communist project. They implement an intellectual blueprint... drawn up within the walls of American academia and shaped by international financial institutions. These transformations are meant to have radical effects, to turn all existing social relations upside down. They offer a panacea, a magic elixir which, once taken, will cure all ills.
—Adam Przeworski (1992, p. 45)

Rhetoric and Reality

Surprisingly, given the totality of communism's collapse, its rival economic system, capitalism, has made little progress in filling the void. Although the successful creation of a viable capitalist system on the ruins

This chapter is an expanded and revised version of Brada 1993b. I am indebted to George Breslauer, Alan Gelb, Peter Murrell, Inderjit Singh, and Ben Slay for comments on previous drafts, although, of course, I alone take responsibility for all views expressed herein.

of the planned economy is a novel effort, the difficulties encountered even in those countries that have made relatively successful efforts to do so and the seeming failure of transition efforts in most of the countries of the region have stirred a debate between those who favor a rapid and broad effort to introduce markets, private property, and other elements of the capitalist system and those who favor a more gradual program of dismantling the old economic system and the evolution of capitalism, possibly of a uniquely indigenous variety, in response to the political and economic forces in the region.

Those who support rapid and broad measures for the transition to capitalism point to the success of such measures in combatting open or repressed inflation, in creating functioning markets, in introducing private ownership and capitalist institutions, in laying the foundation for future economic growth, and in the integration into the world economy that such programs have produced in the Central European countries that have pursued them with the requisite resolution. They also point to the chaos and dysfunctional economic behavior that characterize those countries that have failed to eradicate communist-era economic institutions, enterprises, and methods of economic management.

Critics of rapid reform policies fall into several groups (Kiss 1993). One, which includes scholars such as Murrell (1991, 1992, 1993a) and Poznanski (1992a, 1992b, 1993), bases its analysis on the paradigm of evolutionary economics. Numerous other critics employ different paradigms, including neo-Marxism (e.g., Przeworski) and Keynesianism. In this chapter, even though I focus as much as possible on the writings of the self-described advocates of the evolutionary approach, I at times touch on arguments raised by those who operate in other intellectual frameworks. The justification for this is that both the criticisms of rapid change and the policy alternatives put forward by these critics, such as expansionary monetary and fiscal policies, state intervention, and the continued existence of a large state sector, are often, though not always, the same as those raised by the "strict" evolutionists.

Critics of rapid change argue that too-extreme transition measures have caused grave dislocations in economic activity, as are evident in the production declines suffered by countries that have adopted policies of rapid system change and orthodox macroeconomic stabilization. They argue that a less radical and sweeping approach to transformation, one that temporarily retains many of the institutions of central planning and allows markets, the private sector, and capitalist institutions to emerge gradually, would be less costly in terms of foregone production and human dislocation. The gradual reform of the People's Republic of China, which has been characterized by increases in output and relative price stability, is often cited as an exemplar of an evolutionary path of transition from socialism to capitalism.[1]

Unfortunately, although real choices remain open to the peoples of Eastern Europe and the former USSR, and although real evidence is increasingly available on the effects of various transition strategies, the debate between advocates of rapid change and the evolutionary approach has taken on an increasingly ideological and philosophical tone. This increasingly ideological nature of the debate has led to a number of curious intellectual reversals of terminology and ideology, as is amply illustrated by the quotations that open this chapter. The first, written by the finance minister, and later prime minister, of Czechoslovakia and his adviser, argues strongly against ideologically based reforms introduced by "unrestrained romantics." The authors, who engineered the radical Czechoslovak price liberalization of 1991 and the mass voucher privatization of 1993, the most extreme and wide-ranging one-two punch of East European transition programs, were warning against grandiose schemes to "optimally" combine market and plan or post-plan socialist institutions and mechanisms. To them, it was precisely the evolutionary approach of attempting to devise a means for the two systems to coexist while leading to a successful transition that smacked of the academic intellectual blueprint for experiment and social engineering that Przeworski in the neo-Marxist tradition attributes to those who advocate the big bang.

Not only has the idea of what constitutes social engineering been stood on its head by some proponents of evolutionary transition but they have also sought to capture for their own use the philosophical basis of liberal economics in which rapid transition strategies were rooted. Thus, in 1991, in the article from which I draw the opening quotation, Klaus and Jezek describe themselves with some self-consciousness as liberals of the Friedmanite and Hayekian type respectively. Evolutionists at that time tended to base their analysis on the intellectual legacy of Schumpeter, but now, as is evident from Murrell (1993a) and Poznanski (1919), they have sought to capture Hayek for themselves. They are, of course, right to try to do so, for at least Hayek got it right regarding the long-run viability of capitalism and socialism and Schumpeter got it wrong, but one must bear in mind that disputes based on rival interpretations of the same sacred texts are always the most bitter and least enlightening, particularly to outsiders.

As Slay (1993) points out, much of the controversy stems from a confusion of ends and means. That is, preferences about transition measures are often confused with preferences about, or conceptions of, the end state of the economy. Thus, even if the freeing of all prices and the total disengagement of the state from the economy were the best means of beginning the transition from communism to capitalism, scholars like Murrell and Przeworski seem suspicious that the end product would have to be a Reaganite-Thatcherite economic system. Similarly, even if some measure of price controls and state ownership could be shown to be the optimal transition strategy, advocates of rapid change would view these with suspicion as necessarily leading to a Scandinavian-type welfare state or, worse, some form of "third way." Although the end state is to some extent path-dependent, it should be the merits of transition policies within the period of transition and not in some final steady state that should be the basis for their evaluation.

A second source of confusion comes from the failure of proponents of both transition strategies to come to grips with key concepts. One of these concepts is time. At the outset of the debate on transition policies, the sequencing of transition measures received considerable attention, and the focus on sequencing implicitly provided a temporal element. It was understood that drafting and enacting laws, privatizing firms, creating institutions, and so on took time and that, even when put into effect, there would be a time lag until these new elements could benefit the economy. There was, of course, disagreement on the order and pace at which measures ought to be introduced, but even noteworthy advocates of rapid sequencing such as Lipton and Sachs (1990a, 1990b) sought stabilization and the freeing of prices before privatization.

The concern for the temporal element has largely disappeared from the debate. Many proponents of the "big bang" seem to preach a policy of "the faster the better." Evolutionists, in contrast, speak of gradual change, but phrases such as "many years" or "when conditions are appropriate" in their writings give less the impression of a well-thought out dynamics and more of a disregard for how long the process may take or when the transition is to reach its end.

A second concept that has fallen victim to the escalation of rhetoric is the clear definition of what is meant by evolutionary and "big-bang" policies. Stabilization, market liberalization, and privatization are all somehow lumped into the same category even if the means of implementing them, the effects they are intended to have, and the need for them in various countries vary tremendously. Thus, to some observers, any country that has undertaken any decisive action in any area of price liberalization, stabilization, or privatization, no matter how uncoordinated to other elements of a coherent economic strategy such measures may be, is seen as an example of a big bang strategy. Thus, van Brabant in his contribution to this volume observes that "countries such as Bulgaria, the former Czechoslovakia, Mongolia, Poland, Russia and the former Yugoslovia are considered to have adopted shock therapy."

However common such a view may be, these countries cover such a broad range of actual policy experiences that the notion of shock therapy would have to be so broad to encompass them as to make the term useless as an analytical category.

For example, what is the common element in the stabilization policies of the former Czechoslovakia, which were based on successfully achieving a balanced budget for the first three years of the reform program and those of the Russian Republic, whose government's budget deficit for the same period may well have averaged 15 percent of gross domestic product (GDP)? Similarly, what is the common element in the foreign trade liberalization program of Poland, where the currency became freely convertible and trade was legalized for all economic agents and Russia or Bulgaria, where much of the old communist trade practices and apparatus continues in place? If indeed shock therapy is to be defined as any economic policy or combination of policies adopted in this group of countries in the past few years, then shock therapy or the big bang must surely stand discredited on the evidence. But obviously what is discredited is not really a radical approach to stabilization and liberalization of economies but rather simply bad policymaking. Evolutionists face a less daunting problem of definition, since no country has expressly adopted an evolutionary strategy. Hungary perhaps comes the closest, but even there how much of policy is driven by an appreciation of the evolutionist argument and how much is temporization is unclear.

Prices and Markets: Economic Efficiency
and Macroeconomic Stabilization

One of the key elements of the big-bang approach is the rapid elimination of controls over domestic prices, including the price of foreign exchange and thus of imports and exportables. The arguments for rapid price liberalization rest on two conceptually separate, but often conflated, bases. One of these is that the instant introduction of market prices will lead to increased economic efficiency and higher levels of consumer welfare. The second reason for rapid freeing of prices is to effect a program of macrostabilization by eliminating repressed or open inflation. Many critics of the big-bang approach have argued that the former goal is unimportant and that the latter goal has imposed costs far beyond the benefits that it offers.

The Price System and Microeconomic Efficiency

The liberalization of prices, assuming a relatively stable level of aggregate prices such as would exist if there were no repressed or open inflation, should lead to a more rational allocation of resources. Queues for rationed goods would be eliminated (Lipton and Sachs 1990a) and consumers would no longer be forced to expend their money for unwanted goods through a process of forced substitution (Kornai 1980). In this way consumer welfare would increase. In fact, in Poland and Czechoslovakia this clearly occurred; queues disappeared, and efforts devoted to providing better service and a wider assortment of goods to consumers were evident even to casual visitors from the West and had a profound impact on the psychology and welfare of domestic consumers (Glikman 1993, pp. 8–13).

The equilibration of the consumer market, the reassertion of consumer sovereignty, and the better assortment of goods available to the population are gains that are often ignored or dismissed by critics of the big bang. Such a dismissal of benefits to consumers of any policy measure may be surprising to noneconomists, but it comes as no surprise to practitioners of the science. Gains to consumers in the form of more rational prices, better service, and a wider assortment of goods count for little in the policy proscriptions and in the calculations of the evolutionists. This is in part because such gains are thought to be hard to measure, in part because they are seen as subjective and thus somehow less real than changes in firms' profits or in households' income. Thus, against the consumer gains brought about by the rapid liberalization of prices are arrayed charges of monopoly pricing, the emergence of consumerism, conspicuous consumption by the wealthy, maldistribution of purchasing power, and so on.[2]

Although economists are somewhat better at measuring the efficiency with which resources are allocated to production than in measuring gains to consumers, this has not led the critics of rapid price liberalization to produce more coherent critiques of the argument that such price liberalization would lead to a more efficient utilization of resources in the productive sector. In fact, the criticisms raised are self-contradictory. One line of argument, to be found in Whitesell (1990) and Murrell (1991), is that the planned economies in fact allocated productive resources quite efficiently. The obvious implication is that getting market prices "right" will yield few benefits since the static allocation of resources is already quite good.[3]

The evidence for the efficiency of resource allocation under communism is based largely on econometric studies, which have to be interpreted with great caution. For example, evidence that socialist firms tend to be close to the frontier of a stochastic production function is taken as evidence that technical efficiency in socialist economies is as high there as in market economies. Since the "frontier," which represents best observed practice, is based only on observations of firms in one or other of the two types of economic systems, there is no way of judging whether the frontier, or level of technical efficiency, of firms in socialist economies approaches that of firms in market economies. The finding that socialist economies trade according to the dictates of their comparative advantage as dictated by their factor endowments is taken by Whitesell (1990) to mean that such trade is optimal, whereas in fact it only proves that such trade does not reduce social welfare relative to a situation characterized by autarky.[4]

A second argument against rapid marketization is that the freeing of prices will lead to large losses among firms, causing widespread bankruptcy and unemployment. Some argue that such losses would occur because large, inefficient state firms need time to make themselves efficient. If this argument is to be accepted, then, of course, the preceding one, that productive resources are efficiently allocated, must be wrong. But if socialist firms have, in fact, misallocated resources in the past, we are then left with the question of whether and how effectively they will respond to strong price signals emanating from the market. On this point I present some evidence below.

Alternatively, it can be argued that productive resources were efficiently allocated given the pattern of demand that existed in the planned economy but that this allocation differs radically from that which would obtain in a market economy. Thus even efficient firms in those sectors that experience declines in demand would suffer losses. This, however, suggests a rather limited, if not false, notion of efficiency since it implies that resources are deployed efficiently to produce an inefficient output assortment, such as tanks, vast amounts of steel, and so on. The efficient production of unwanted goods hardly makes sense. Moreover, keeping entire sectors afloat despite a lack of demand for their output is a costly exercise.

Price Liberalization and Economic Stabilization

The liberalization of prices in Eastern Europe and the former USSR has not, of course, led solely to changes in relative prices. Rather, the liberalization of prices has also led to sharp bursts of inflation, followed in some countries such as Poland and Czechoslovakia by a decline in the rate of inflation and in most others by continuing, if not accelerating, price increases. Moreover, in all these countries, price liberalization was accompanied by sharp declines in output. Critics of rapid price liberalization have made much of these macroeconomic developments. Among the alleged policy errors were excessive deflation resulting from a too-precipitous decline in aggregate demand, a credit crunch caused by the destruction of enterprise-sector liquidity (Calvo and Coricelli 1993), and even the possibility that open and repressed inflation in Poland were containable without resort to drastic measures and thus that the reduction of aggregate demand by means of the big bang was unnecessary (Kolodko 1991).

Unfortunately, although the evolutionists have been quick to criticize alleged policy errors in the implementation of big-bang policies, it is noteworthy that none of the criticism has sought to present a gradual or evolutionary program for stabilizing an economy characterized by serious inflationary pressures. Indeed, the policy proscriptions of the gradualists have been either of an ex post character, arguing for expansionary monetary and fiscal policies and for "industrial policies" (see Brabant 1993) to help ailing sectors in economies that have adopted big-bang policies, or utopian, putting forward the Chinese experience as appropriate for Eastern Europe and the USSR. We will examine the evidence regarding China's macroeconomic experience below.

Absent a viable gradualist stabilization program, one must assume that the gradualists would prefer either high levels of open inflation or price controls and repressed inflation to stable prices accompanied by a temporary decline in output. Such a choice is, of course, problematic, as the gradualists seldom admit to any economic costs arising from continued high rates of inflation.[5]

More to the point, economists are beginning to obtain a better understanding of how stabilization through price liberalization works in postcommunist economies, and thus much of the post hoc, *propter hoc* criticism of big-bang stabilizations is being replaced by a clearer appreciation of both their advantages and shortcomings. The first point, which evidently needs some emphasis because of the belief that, for example, the Russian Republic has undertaken a big-bang approach to stabilization via price liberalization, is that price liberalization is insufficient to stabilize an economy suffering from inflationary pressures. Without a simultaneous hardening of the budget of enterprises and a reduction or elimination of the state's budget deficit, price liberalization will merely lead to further inflation as enterprises expend unlimited funds for real assets and foreign exchange.[6]

Of course, fiscal and monetary restraint was always part of the orthodox big-bang package, and thus claims that the big bang did not work in countries such as Russia make little sense because neither firms nor the government were able to fulfill their part of the big-bang strategy. Indeed, in Europe only Poland in 1990 and Czechoslovakia in 1991 were able to implement what can be viewed as orthodox versions of the big-bang strategy. Hungary, though implementing a variety of liberalizing measures, especially in the realm of foreign trade, did not resort to a drastic freeing up of prices because of past price liberalization.

Our understanding is also growing of the effects of exogenous events on the outcome of stabilization efforts. Although it was understood that the collapse of Eastern Europe's trade with the USSR in 1991 had a severe impact on output in Eastern Europe, recent work by Rodrik (1992a,b), Berg and Sachs (1992), Brada and King (1992), and Bofinger (1993) has begun to separate out the effects of this shock from other, domestic, developments. Although the estimates vary, they do suggest that changes in the level of output in the region were dominated by the effects of the trade shock in 1991. A telling example of the predominance of the trade shock over any dislocations caused by price liberalization can be seen from a comparison of the dynamics of Czechoslovak and Hungarian industrial production in 1991, a year in which Czechoslovakia carried out its sweeping price liberalization. Industrial production in Czechoslovakia declined by 24.7 percent, in Hungary by 21.5 percent. Given Czechoslovakia's greater trade dependence on the CMEA, the similarity of output responses to the trade shock leaves little scope for lost output from the disruptive effects of price liberalization in Czechoslovakia.[7]

The interaction between macroeconomic developments and policies is also becoming better understood. The essence of shock therapy is to turn the economy from a state of excess demand, where the purchase of whatever is produced is always financed by consumers, enterprises, or the state to one where aggregate demand determines the level of output. Shock therapy reduces consumer demand by reducing the real value of consumers' cash holdings and incomes by reducing enterprise investment and by forcing the state to bring its budget into balance. Of course, without a precise measure of the degree of excess demand, and with no means of calibrating the effects of monetary and fiscal policy, it is possible that policymakers will reduce demand by more than is necessary to wipe out excess demand and inflation. This problem has been set out elegantly by Gomulka (1991) and analyzed at length by the Vienna Institute for Comparative Economic Studies (1993).

The upshot of this research is that policymakers may have set government spending and revenues at the wrong levels and that monetary targets were not always appropriate. However, economics is not an exact science, and the ability of policymakers in developed market economies to predict with any precision the effects of tax or spending changes, interest rate movements, and so on, is notoriously poor despite a long history of policy interventions that should enable them to calibrate their models of the economy. Consequently, it is not surprising that East European policymakers, working with no historical basis by which to calibrate their models, may have erred. Surprisingly, evolutionists, though eager to point to macroeconomic policy errors of authorities in countries that have implemented big-bang policies, seem surprisingly sanguine about the ability of policymakers to carry out the greater requirements for government *dirigisme* required by evolutionary policies.

Recent work is also beginning to uncover sources of policy surprises. Schaffer (1992) showed that a large part of the surplus in the Polish budget in 1990 was the result of inflated enterprise profits caused by the fact that profits were calculated by valuing the consumption of inventories in production at historical prices. As prices increased in 1990, profits did also because material inputs were valued at unrealistically low, pre-liberalization prices. Since the government's revenue depended heavily on profit taxes, the budget was in surplus in 1990, imparting a deflationary impulse to the economy. In 1991, as inventory prices began to reflect the new price level, profits and tax receipts declined, leading to a budget deficit. Schaffer also demonstrated that cash flow in the enterprise sector was hard hit in 1990, but recovered in 1991, explaining the movement of wages in the Polish economy as well.

Schaffer's work also points out the importance of starting conditions. Poland's fiscal situation was dictated by the effect of the interaction of historical cost accounting and the post–price liberalization surge in prices followed by much lower price increases on enterprise profits. Czechoslovakia, which undertook its price liberalization in the face of much more moderate inflationary pressures, experienced a much smaller postliberalization price surge and consequently has managed to maintain a balanced budget through 1994.

Despite inevitable policy errors, the two East European countries that introduced comprehensive stabilization and price liberalization packages have fared much better than the others in the region. In Poland, inflation has fallen to only 40 percent per year, which is nonetheless better than inflation in countries that have not introduced a big-bang stabilization, but in 1992 its GDP increased despite the negative effects of a severe drought on agricultural output, and industrial output and construction activity were both up sharply in the first quarter of 1993. In Czechoslovakia, core inflation in 1991 and 1992 was 10 to 11 percent per year, and unemployment in the country peaked at 6 percent.[8] Although there is uncertainty regarding the effects of the Czech-Slovak split on GDP in 1993, an increase in aggregate output in the Czech Republic is possible. Indeed, Czechoslovakia's record on output, inflation, and unemployment in 1991–1993 may well prove superior to that of Hungary despite the latter country's more moderate reform policies over this period. In any case, the output declines in Czechoslovakia and Poland are no worse than those to be found in those East European countries and ex-USSR republics that have not introduced coherent stabilization programs, and their prospects for growth are clearly better. Thus, although the implementation of orthodox stabilization and price liberalization policies in Czechoslovakia and Poland may have been attended by inevitable mistakes in policymaking, it requires no great effort to demonstrate that in terms of inflation, consumer welfare, and growth potential these economies are much better off than countries that have not attempted, or have attempted only partially, similar orthodox stabilization measures.

One of the glaring weaknesses of the gradualist critiques of orthodox stabilization is that they imagine a rather idealized stable equilibrium as the counterfactual that would exist if orthodox stabilization were not introduced. Thus they are unable to account for the uncontrolled explosion of real wages in pre-1990 Poland or in Gorbachev's USSR; the declines in output that were already taking place in these and other countries under the traditional economic system that they believe would sustain production and living standards if only it could be retained for the indefinite future; and the monetary imbalances that were being generated by the planned economy throughout the region. No doubt orthodox stabilization programs are more painful than some evolutionary scenarios, but the comparison needs to be against real-life alternatives, and the gradualists have yet to explain how the planned economies of Eastern Europe and the USSR were to be reequilibrated to yield acceptable macroeconomic outcomes.

China: The Dog That Did Not Bark

Rather than develop practical alternatives to orthodox stabilization that would apply to the circumstances of Eastern Europe and the former USSR, proponents of evolutionary transition prefer to point to the People's Republic of China as a ready-made model. China has indeed combined gradual systemic change in industry with rapid economic growth and macroeconomic stability for over a decade (Chen, Jefferson, and Singh 1992). Although Chinese economic performance is indeed impressive, a closer analysis suggests that applying the Chinese lesson to Eastern Europe or Russia may be neither as desirable nor as feasible as it seems.

First of all, contrary to evolutionists' emphasis on gradual changes in ownership and on maintaining a degree of control over prices, the Chinese reform in agriculture involved both a rapid and massive expansion of private property rights, something akin to the "giveaways" of productive assets that evolutionists argue should be avoided in Eastern Europe, and an extensive freeing of agricultural prices. Not surprisingly, evolutionists point to China's economic growth, which comes largely from the radically privatized agricultural sector, while at the same time emphasizing the gradual changes in state-owned industry, disregarding the fact that the latter's performance continues to be a major drag on the economy.

The Chinese reform also operated under rather unique starting conditions. The extent of macroeconomic disequilibrium was much less than existed in the USSR, for example, and a much larger share of the work force was employed in agriculture, and in particular in an agricultural sector that was less dependent on machinery and intermediate inputs from industry than are the agricultural sectors of the East European countries.[9] Thus, gains in productivity were quite easy to achieve, helping to improve the living conditions of the majority of the Chinese population. In Eastern Europe such gains were less likely, as agriculture depended on industrial, often imported, inputs, and even if productivity had risen, it would have helped only a small fraction of the population.

Moreover, according to a recent analysis by McKinnon (presented in this volume), China can hardly be taken as a useful model of macroeconomic stabilization. Although China has had a relatively good record on inflation over the past decade, McKinnon noted that this record masks the existence of large government deficits.[10] That China has been able to avoid inflation despite these deficits is because of a sharp increase in private saving, from 2 percent of incomes at the start of the reforms to a level of 15 percent, and it is only this increase in the public's demand for money that has prevented the outbreak of serious inflation. McKinnon concluded his analysis by suggesting that this Chinese model of macroeconomic policy may not be sustainable for much longer in China and that it is not applicable in Russia, where a much more drastic fiscal reform would be necessary.[11] Moreover, saving rates are much higher in Eastern Europe and Russia than they were in China, thus making an increase in private saving much more difficult to achieve.

Finally, there are political obstacles to the use of the Chinese model in Eastern Europe in that it is not obvious that the sort of control exercised by the party in China in the functioning of the economy and implementation of the reforms is consistent with the type of pluralistic democracies that the revolutions of 1989 are trying to bring into existence in Eastern Europe and the former USSR. I deal with this connection between the economic and the political transformation of society in a subsequent section of this chapter.

Privatization and Building the Institutions of Capitalism

Although the evolutionary critique of rapid price liberalization and macroeconomic stabilization fails to deliver any useful alternatives, in the area of system change, meaning the replacement of communist-era institutions, firms, and economic mechanisms by privately owned firms and capitalist institutions and policy instruments, the evolutionists have produced a comprehensive and rich set of proposals. This is not surprising because the evolutionary approach is based on a literature that concerns itself with the design and evolution of economic and social institutions.[12] The evolutionary argument, put simply, is that the physical system of production, distribution, and economic control that existed in Eastern Europe and the former USSR was supported or sustained by a set of formal and informal institutions. These institutions had evolved during the communist era in such a way as to sustain the physical system in a reasonably effective way. Thus, to radically change the nature of the physical system by, say, privatizing and breaking up enterprises or by marketizing relations among them must lead to large declines in output because the new physical relations cannot be mediated by the old socialist institutions and therefore transactions costs will be very high.[13] Likewise, economies that keep in place the physical relations that existed under socialism, say, by retaining the existing state ownership of enterprises or by allocating a large proportion of products and inputs by administrative means, but destroy the old institutions of administrative control such as industrial ministries and planning bureaus, will also dissolve into chaos and suffer output declines.[14]

Using a formal two-sector model of the economy, Murrell and Wang (1993) set out the policy implications of this line of reasoning. Socialist firms and institutions cannot adapt to new conditions, and attempting to make them adapt through privatization entails large social losses. Thus they should be carried over into the future with their existing modes of operation and supporting institutions. Privatization must take the form of a limited but growing private sector consisting of small entrepreneurial units whose emergence will then lead to the slow evolution of capitalist institutions. Thus only gradually will the economy be privatized, marketized, and, finally, capitalist.

Evolutionists also express great doubts about the readiness of individuals in the region to act effectively in a genuine market setting, and they argue that without a proper market ethos, institutions of the market will be defective. Thus Poznanski (1992b, pp. 60–61) wrote that the region generally lacks a developed market ethos, that is, work discipline, self-reliance, respect for property, understanding of law, and honoring of commercial contracts (less applicable to the most advanced Eastern European countries such as Czechoslovakia, Hungary, and Poland). Although there is no doubt that education about the market system is needed in transitioning economies, that people in the region cannot act in their own self-interest in accord with existing legal norms belies the upsurge in entrepreneurship that has characterized Eastern Europe in the post-1989 period and which now accounts for even 50 percent of output in Poland and 20 percent in the Czech Republic.

Unfortunately, this pessimism regarding the ability of people to manage their economic fortunes leaves a gap in evolutionary models, since they are unable to explain when state assets can be turned over to private individuals. Poznanski (1993, p. 31) simply proposed that "the pace at which privatization proceeds is determined by the speed at which the supply of market agents is expanded in these economies, or ... the pace at which the market ethos will spread out." Murrell and Wang are hardly more precise, leaving the reader to wonder how, absent a market test where entrepreneurs are free to fail and succeed, one is to determine when the public's ethos is sufficiently advanced to free it from the petty tutelage of the paternalistic state.[16]

The evolutionary argument finds its analogies in the emergence of capitalism from feudalism, where the institutions of capitalism are alleged to have emerged slowly in response to the needs of the nascent capitalist mode of production through a slow process of evolutionary selection that gradually weeded out the inefficient organizations and nurtured the efficient.[17] At some level of generalization, this is a line of argument for which I have some sympathy, but in its particular historical analogies as well as in the way in which it is applied to Eastern Europe it has fatal flaws. The first of these is a definitional one. Although evolutionists posit the critical need for capitalist institutions and the dangers to the economy from their absence or inappropriateness, they never set out precisely what capitalist institutions they consider as vital to the East European economies or explain why these institutions are critical. Thus the reader of their tracts is left with the task of reifying this abstract concept of "institution" and therefore the assertion that certain institutions are indispensable is incapable of falsification because the concept of institution has no conceptual or empirical correlates.[17]

If, however, one could agree on a minimal set of institutions, such as banks, stock exchanges, laws on corporate governance, contractual obligations, and property rights, and so on, that the evolutionists might have in mind, then their argument that these particular institutions must evolve over time in a slow process of social Darwinism and cannot be created in some reasonably suitable form by conscious human action is demonstrably false. One need only to refer to the work of Alexander Gerschenkron (1962) to see that much of the industrial revolution that swept Western Europe in the eighteenth and nineteenth centuries was underpinned by institutions that were consciously designed and put into operation by individuals and governments in rapid spurts of institutional innovation. Indeed, Gerschenkron extended this process of institution innovation to the Soviet period, and Spulber (1966) carried the argument over to the case of Eastern Europe.[18]

Gerschenkron viewed industrialization in Continental Europe as an effort of latecomers to catch up with England, which was the first country to pass through the industrial revolution. Latecomers felt a tension between their own economic situation and that of countries that had successfully industrialized. Lacking in the latecomers were precisely the institutional prerequisites or preconditions for the development of a modern industrial society. Gerschenkron demonstrated that the absence of these prerequisites was overcome by the creation of institutional substitutes through private or state initiatives. Thus in France and then in Germany the state supported new private institutions, such as large universal banks, that served to overcome the existing lack of more traditional institutions to promote capital formation, financial intermediation, and the application of entrepreneurial activity. Farther to the East, where preconditions for industrialization were ever less favorable, the state itself had to assume the tasks of organizing and maintaining such institutions.

This is not to deny that, once founded, such institutions were subject to both internal evolution and a Darwinian competition with alternative institutions. What is important, however, is that institutional innovation was breathtakingly rapid, surprisingly often successful, and, even more surprising, frequently the result of government initiative or support for nascent private initiatives. Also important for today's Eastern Europe is Gerschenkron's finding that the focus of these innovations was on institutions oriented toward activity in heavy industry, banking and the other "commanding heights of the economy" and not the small business and service sector that the evolutionists see as the means of introducing capitalism in Eastern Europe.

This historical experience should not be surprising. No doubt good institutions make for better outcomes than bad institutions, but the great difference in institutional arrangements, even among developed market economies, suggests that the Darwinian selection of institutions does not converge to some unique and optimal set of organizations. Indeed, Williamson himself cautioned against an interpretation of his work that would claim that "the institutions emerging from the competitive process will be efficient or 'transaction cost minimizing'" (Bowles and Gintis 1993, p. 95). Williamson warned "that is too strong. I hold only that the institutions emerging from the competitive process will be comparatively efficient; and I eschew reference to minimizing and maximizing" (Williamson 1993, p. 107). Consequently, if the institutions observed in market economies after some period of selection are not optimal but only better than rival alternatives then the conscious design of institutions in economies that lack them can in fact lead to relatively satisfactory outcomes.

A second problem with the gradualist program is that it rests on several unstated assumptions whose validity is doubtful at best. The first of these is that a capitalist and a state-owned and managed system can coexist in a way that will enable each to exploit its comparative advantage to the utmost. It has long been understood that "one needs to perceive the Soviet-type economy as a coherent whole—a true system—with its own inherent logic, necessary components, and natural interaction of these components. It, like any other economic system, is as much an organism as a mechanism, tending to counteract forces impinging from the outside" (Ericson 1991, p. 11). Thus, there is no guarantee that the evolutionary approach, which requires the long-run coexistence of a large Soviet-type system with a small, nascent, and fragile capitalist system in a single economy, will eventually result in a triumph of capitalism over socialism.[19] Indeed, just the opposite is to be expected, as the economically and politically powerful state sector will act to marginalize or wipe out small capitalists.

Perhaps one might be willing to take such a risk if it were indeed the case that maintaining a mixed economy, one part state owned and planned and the other private, would yield high levels of output and welfare by preserving the production of the socialist sector. However, recent theoretical work (Zhou 1993) as well as past experience with partial reform in socialist economies suggests that such arrangements are likely to reduce rather than improve social welfare and the functioning of the economy. In the end, as with the discussion of price liberalization, the desirability of rapid privatization and institutional change in transitioning economies depends to a large extent on the response of state-owned or formerly state-owned firms to such reform measures, and it is to the evidence on this point that I now turn.[21]

Enterprise Behavior in the Transition

It has been something of an article of faith that socialist enterprises and managers were too sclerotic and unresponsive to the radical introduction of market forces, hard budget constraints and new, private owners. This belief owes much to Kornai's (1990, p. 62) influential view that "the manager of a state-owned firm ... wants to invest more, obtain an even greater amount of hard currency, import more machinery and equipment from hard currency markets, travel more and let his colleagues do the same; and, of course, he wants to pay more wages, since this can boost his popularity among employees and ease the tensions around him. It is time to abandon hope that the budget constraint can be hardened."

This view is echoed by Murrell (1991, p. 41), who wrote that "given that [the communist] system survived from a number of decades in a number of countries, it is reasonable to suppose that organizational routines were selected according to the needs of the unreformed environment. ... Moreover, the allocation of personnel to positions has occurred within that bureaucratic system. Thus, the centrally planned systems will have an allocation of human capital and of management styles that matches the dictates of a non-market environment."[21] Murrell then added that "because the ... organizational structure ... is suited to the existing environment, it is unlikely to be suitable for a new market environment."

Early evidence seemed to confirm these views. State-owned enterprises in Poland reacted to the liberalization of January 1990 with paralysis. Production continued at levels well in excess of sales, and firms passively accumulated losses that they financed by dissipating their assets, borrowing from banks, and finally by simply failing to pay their bills. This behavior, however, was largely the result of the failure of the Polish government to introduce an effective privatization program and by the resulting lack of clear property rights in the state enterprise sector. This ambiguity regarding property rights was exacerbated by the fact that workers' councils and a form of worker ownership had been introduced prior to the 1990 price liberalization.

Bienkowski (1992) has shown that much of the dysfunctional behavior of Polish firms resulted from this lack of clear property rights, with both managers and workers making operating decisions that served their own interests at the expense of rational responses to market signals. Bienkowski concluded that "ways must be found to stop the current actors, who represent the old power structures and interests of the state enterprises, from destroying these enterprises before privatization can be realized" (p. 750). Of course, the recognition that a lack of clear property rights was at the root of the poor market-responsiveness of many Polish state-owned enterprises could argue either for rapid privatization or a "re-nationalization" by the state in order to restore clear property rights. Whether to reestablish state ownership rights or to privatize thus depends on whether privatization, or even the prospects of privatization, can induce managers to respond to market signals in a rational and socially desirable way.

Evidence on the effects of privatization, or, at this early stage of the transition process, the credible prospect of systematic privatization, on the behavior of state-owned enterprises is beginning to accumulate.[22] Given the short time since the beginning of the transitions and the delays in collecting data, much of the evidence so far on enterprise behavior comes from case studies. Although cases always have something of the nature of anecdotes, if the anecdotes tell a consistent story then it may be possible to draw generalizations from them.[23] In this chapter, I rely primarily on Estrin's (1993) summary of, and conclusions drawn from, a set of forty-three enterprise studies carried out in Czechoslovakia, Hungary, and Poland in 1992. I will supplement these with Trk's (1993) summary of twelve case studies of Hungarian firms and with six case studies of Hungarian firms carried out by Brada, Singh, and Trk (forthcoming).

The conclusions that can be drawn from these cases are best summed up by Estrin (1993, p. 5) who wrote that "in all three countries, but especially in CSFR (Czech and Slovak Federated Republic), most state owned enterprises are making major adjustments in the light of their new circumstances, and these responses ... appear to represent the bulk of industry-level adjustment." Estrin and the authors of the cases from which he drew his conclusions examined the short- and-long term adjustments of the firms to external shocks and the viability of these firms, and they related these to the behavior of managers and workers. In the case of short-term responses, the behavior of enterprises with respect to output, employment, product assortment, pricing, and market orientation were evaluated. Unresponsive firms failed to make adjustments in these areas, continuing to produce a relatively unchanged volume of output at past levels of employment, accumulating debts and losses along the way.

Estrin concluded that three-fourths of all firms had made significant adjustments. There were few systematic differences between sectors but significant intercountry differences. Despite the fact that both Poland and Czechoslovakia had adopted big-bang stabilization policies, one-third of Polish firms had made no effective production response in the more than two and one-half years since January 1990. In contrast, all Czechoslovak firms were judged as having made significant responses, and almost one half of them were categorized as "very active" in their responses. The Hungarian sample fell between these two extremes, as is confirmed by Trk (1993) and Brada, Singh, and Trk (forthcoming), who also reported cases of firms that were acting responsively and others that were, in Trk's words, "drifting," again in a way that reflected their prospects for privatization.

Similar results emerged in the case of long-run responsiveness, which judged firms on the basis of their ability to develop and implement a long-term strategic plan for dealing with the new market environment. The majority of firms had engaged in a long-term response to the rapidly changing environment, but significant cross-country differences emerged. In Hungary, many firms had been engaged in strategic planning for some time, whereas others continued a hand-to-mouth existence.[24] In Czechoslovakia, "there were major changes in enterprises' attitude towards their long run strategy ... during the period of study due to the impact of the first wave of mass privatization on managerial thinking. ... [A] majority of firms had developed a long run strategy... [and] management thinking was intimately [tied] to their proposals to restructure and privatize" (Estrin, 1993, p. 23). Estrin's findings regarding Polish firms confirm those of Bienkowski: that most Polish firms are rudderless.

In terms of enterprise viability, Czechoslovak firms also fared best and Polish firms worst, despite that both countries had undergone big-bang privatization. Estrin attributed these differences between the three countries to managerial autonomy, motivation, and responsiveness. In Czechoslovakia and Hungary all firms were rated in the highest category for managerial motivation, and the majority received high ratings for managerial autonomy. In contrast, only one-fifth of Polish firms received the highest rating for managerial motivation and in one-third of them managers were either poorly motivated or lacked authority. Correspondingly, in Poland workers dominated enterprise decisionmaking at one-third of the enterprises in the sample. In Hungary and Czechoslovakia, worker power was minor. These differences in managerial autonomy and motivation are directly connected to actual or prospective privatization and the consequent establishment of clear property rights. Thus, Estrin concluded, the "emphasis on privatization ... seems to explain much of the considerable progress towards enterprise adjustment observed in the CSFR and [Hungary]... This confirms the view that progress in privatization is pivotal ... to the process of restructuring and reorienting to the market environment" (Estrin 1993, pp. 38, 39).

The weight of available evidence suggests that rapid marketization and progress with privatization can in fact change attitudes in, and the behavior of, formerly state-owned firms. This means that big-bang policies, if implemented systematically, can in fact yield benefits in terms of improved utilization of resources and greater managerial effort, and East European societies do not need to bear the costs of a slow dismantling of old socialist structures and the dysfunctional economic behavior such structures imply.

Politics, Big and Little

The decision to pursue a course of rapid change from a socialist to a capitalist economic system does not depend on economic considerations alone; indeed, economic considerations may be secondary. Even if the case for a big-bang privatization and price liberalization were not as compelling as the forgoing discussion suggests it is, people may opt for a faster pace if it is likely to promote their political objectives. This possibility, of course, stands on its head the conventional wisdom that the populations of Eastern Europe would turn from democracy and capitalism if the economic costs of transition were too high or of too long a duration.[25] That this loss of support for democracy, if not always for individual leaders, has not occurred in those countries where big bang transitions took place, but may be happening in countries where the economic transformation has been much less rapid, suggests that the revolutions of 1989 were not about economics alone or perhaps even not about economics primarily.[26]

To the extent that a relationship does exist between democracy and capitalism, the costs of transition from socialism to capitalism cannot be measured in economic terms alone. Political objectives, however difficult to quantify, must also play a role in our evaluation of the outcomes. The most telling example of the need for this sort of broader calculus is evident in the case of China. Those who argue for a slow transition to capitalism, if that is where the Chinese leadership is headed, point to that country's successful economic performance over the past decade under a program of limited and gradual economic reform. Thus, they argue, such an evolutionary transition entails much lower economic costs than were borne by Poles in the course of the big bang. Even if one accepts the economic causality implicit in the above argument, the welfare calculus ignores the fact that the process of slow reform adopted by the Chinese Communist Party not only allowed the Party to remain in power but, indeed, by its very politico-economic logic, required it to do so.[27] Thus the superior economic outcomes enjoyed by the Chinese population must be weighed against the costs of the Tiananmen Square tragedy and the subsequent political repression. Given a similar choice, East Europeans would not have been willing to accept the bargain forced on the Chinese people because democracy and political self-determination were as much, if not more, the real goals of the 1989 revolutions, as was improved economic performance.

The prevailing view of pretransition politics in Eastern Europe was based on the concept of the social contract, whereby the Party guaranteed workers a tolerable economic existence and equality. In return, workers conceded to the Party a monopoly over political power. When the centrally planned economy could no longer deliver the goods to enable the Party to keep its side of the bargain, this theory argues, the workers overthrew the Party. This social contract view of East European politics was at best a bad generalization. People knew that the regimes under which they lived were corrupt and cruel. Society was offended so much more by the moral failings and vacuity of communism, the terrible doublespeak of its propaganda and cultural apparatuses, not to mention the murders, incarcerations, and disruption of careers in the name of socialist legality than the drab and underpowered Trabants and Skodas that communism stingily doled out to the workers.

Nor was it a system characterized by equity; rather it was rent-seeking, at the level of the individual as well as at more aggregate levels, and opportunism distributed income in ways that reflected political power and not economic justice. It is striking, for example, that in the works of dissident writers such as Havel or Kundera there is very little, if any, description of economic conditions under communism but a great emphasis on the spiritual and moral vacuum that communism created. That dissidence in the GDR and Poland centered on churches and other social movements is also no accident; indeed even Solidarity's program was at first more a call for the dignity of the working class than a union-ist call for higher wages and shorter hours.

There are, as well, more historically deterministic explanations for the East European demand for democracy. These largely involve turning on its head Schumpeter's (1950) prediction that capitalism's economic successes would lead to its replacement by socialism with the argument that it is socialism's successes that have led to its demise in favor of capital-ism and, by extension, to democracy. That socialism was a system of mobilizing resources of rapid industrialization in the USSR and Eastern Europe was a generally accepted fact. However effective socialism may have been in mobilizing resources for creating a nineteenth century industrial economy, it was an utter failure in the postindustrial period, in large part because of its organizational shortcomings.[28]

If, then, the peoples of the former Soviet empire desire democracy rather than bread, are there implications in this for the choice between evolutionary and rapid transition strategies? The answer is yes on two counts. The first rests on the empirical observation that "there has been no case of political democracy that has *not* been a market economy" (Berger 1992, p. 9). There are, of course, arguments why this empirical regularity should hold, but this is not the place to develop them. The second reason for opting for a rapid transformation if a functioning democracy is the desired end state rests on public choice arguments. These arguments suggest that leaving the entrenched bureaucrats and Party members in power to run the state-owned sector will provide them with both the incentives and the economic wherewithal to form powerful lobbies and interest groups that will undermine the creation of a true democratic system. Developments in those former Soviet republics where neither privatization nor price liberalization has taken place, and where the old guard continues to cling to its economic powers, make these dangers amply clear.[29]

Notes

1. See Poznanski 1992b.

2. Ironically, "inconspicuous" consumption by the nomenklatura was amply evident under the old system and the state's control over the production of consumer goods and over trade was a form of monopoly that any market-based system of industrial concentration would find virtually impossible to match.

3. To be fair, both Whitesell and Murrell have denied this implication in private correspondence. Nevertheless, I believe that the implication flows rather naturally from the purported evidence.

4. For an elaboration of these arguments see Nove 1991 and Brada 1992.

5. Thus Przeworski (1992, pp. 48–49) discussed the adverse effects of austerity programs on future growth but was surprisingly silent about the adverse effects of inflation on saving, investment and human capital formation.

6. For an excellent analysis of this point, see McKinnon 1993.

7. Of course, some have argued that the CMEA trade shock was the result of the dismantling of the CMEA, another mistaken measure of big-bang iconoclasm (Murrell, 1993a, pp. 217–218). Unfortunately this charge does not stand up to close scrutiny. It was the trade policies and subsequently the economic collapse of the USSR that led to trade declines in the region. Finland, also heavily dependent on Soviet trade, tried to balance trade with the Soviet Union in 1991. As a consequence, Finnish exports to the USSR, and along with them the Finnish economy, collapsed, with a fall in output that was not dissimilar to those experienced by Poland and Czechoslovakia (Kajaste 1992). Of course, the East European countries could have followed the lead of another of the USSR's non-CMEA trading partners, India, which continued to export to the USSR in 1991. When reciprocal Soviet deliveries failed to materialize, India was stuck with Soviet debts of doubtful value, something that the CMEA mechanism also could have produced for Eastern Europe in 1991 (Brada 1993). It is also worth noting in this regard that post-1991 trade among former CMEA countries held up the best among Poland, Hungary, and Czechoslovakia, the countries that had the most liberalized domestic economies and foreign trade regimes, but fell sharply among those countries that continued to rely on state-mediated trade.

8. It is important to bear in mind that the measured falls in output doubtless overstated the actual declines (Osband 1992) and also understated the recent upturn, in part because statistics on output tended to miss the emerging private sector. Moreover, under conditions of transition, the connection between official measures of output and changes in social welfare are likely to be tenuous, (Chang 1991, Winiecki 1991).

9. Woo (1994) provides a perceptive analysis of this.

10. Although China's long-term record on inflation has been fairly good, it has been achieved at the cost of a series of boom-bust cycles that are largely the result of the unwillingness to liberalize capital markets.

11. Those who believe that there is, indeed, some form of gradual reform approach that is applicable to, at least, Asian economies should read Drabek's (1990) analysis of the gradual Vietnamese reform for a cautionary lesson.

12. The essence of this literature is that economic relations among agents are subject to a variety of costs stemming from imperfect information, opportunistic behavior, uncertainty, and so on. To reduce these costs, institutions appear. These benefit society if their ability to reduce transaction costs exceeds their resource costs. Examples of this literature include Nelson and Winter 1982;, Williamson 1975, 1985; and North 1981.

13. By physical relations, I mean flows of goods, services, capital, factors of production, and information.

14. As Murrell (1993a, p. 217) put it: "The organizations that were expected to change their behavior in response to the new conditions have failed to do so. This is particularly the case for large state enterprises. ... It is now clear that the hope for Eastern Europe lies primarily in the new organizations that are created in the private sector and then selected and shaped by market forces.... . The phasing out of old institutions must be smooth and gradual, in companion with the rise of the new institutions of the private sector."

15. These evolutionist recommendations remind me of a discussion with Czechoslovak reformers in early 1989. Someone proposed that small business should be encouraged and that a law be passed that anyone could start a small business as long as he or she possessed a certificate that would attest to the fact that the individual had taken and passed a test in entrepreneurship. Presumably the test would be drawn up by a committee of government officials.

16. Thus, "the evolutionary approach emphasizes the importance of selection processes, or entry and exit, in accomplishing change. Changes within organizations are de-emphasized in favor of a focus on shifts in economic resources from inefficient (or technologically obsolete) to efficient (technologically progressive) organizations or to new organizations better suited to the new economic environment. *It is a given that these institutions will take many years to create*" (Murrell, 1992, pp. 40, 50, emphasis added).

17. I do not agree that capitalism in Eastern Europe would not benefit from the presence of the capitalist institutions that are to be found in modern industrial societies. Nevertheless, one cannot posit that the absence of such institutions in Eastern Europe would preclude the existence of broad-scale capitalist production for two reasons. The first is that institutions reduce costs of certain transactions; they are not, however, indispensable for such transactions. Second, there may well be relatively effective second-best solutions to the absence of certain institutions. Unless proponents of the evolutionary view identify specific institutions and the costs imposed by their absence, debate on this issue is impossible.

18. These findings regarding the invention and rapid introduction of socialist institutions are also problematic for the evolutionists' claim that socialist institutions are now valuable because they have evolved to be suitable for a system of state-owned enterprises. Indeed, the opposite is true; these institutions were created and put into operation en masse, and it seems clear, given the downward spiral of economic performance in the region, that bureaucratic tinkering with the economic mechanism never increased its capacity for managing an economy consisting of large state-owned firms. That bureaucracies always evolve toward increasingly greater efficiency is an easily disproven hypothesis; see Murrell and Olson 1991 for just such evidence for East Europe.

19. To carry the evolutionary analogy further, would one have bet on the mammals over the dinosaurs if there had not been a cataclysmic event (what paleontologists might call a big bang) that made the dinosaurs extinct?

20. The reader may be surprised that I have not touched directly on the feasibility or desirability of large-scale privatization. In part this is because much of the debate on this topic is not even worth reading, much less writing about, although I must admit to having done both in the past. Moreover, with the conclusion of the first wave of voucher privatization in Czechoslovakia, it is evident that large-scale privatization is feasible; whether it is desirable should be left for history to judge, as there has been too much ex ante pontificating on this topic.

21. Behind such neutral economic terms as "human capital" and "management styles" lurks a fantastic human reality. What Murrell really proposes is not only retaining socialist economic institutions but also keeping existing communist planners, party secretaries, ministers, union leaders, and industrial officials in their positions of power for the indefinite future. What the political feasibility and economic consequences of such a strategy would be I leave to the reader's imagination.

22. By systematic privatization I mean a process with clearly established rules and procedures, not casual "nomenklatura privatizations" and the extralegal appropriation of state assets by individuals or groups.

23. The reader should recall Peter Wiles's dictum that economic data are nothing more than aggregated anecdotes.

24. For more on this, see the Taurus and Budaprint cases in Brada, Singh, and Trk (forthcoming).

25. Critics of big-bang policies often claim this. For example, Przeworski (1992, pp. 45–46) wrote that East European leaders are "exhorted to plunge into reforms about which only one thing can be known with certainty: they will make most people worse off for some time to come. They are urged to short-circuit the democratic process by introducing reforms so swiftly that citizens will have no time to mobilize effectively against them." Unfortunately, such a view of East European politics is at a loss to explain the fact that Vaclav Klaus, the architect of the Czechoslovak big bang, was the largest vote-getter in the 1992 elections. Nor can it explain why the Antall regime in Hungary is so unpopular despite its gradualist transition strategy.

26. Public opinion polls carried out in Eastern Europe show that the preference for democracy is, in fact, even stronger than the preference for capitalism, although both are greatly preferred by more than 50 percent of all respondents.

27. Thus, Li (1993) wrote: "Economic reform should be carried out according to a general plan and step by step under the leadership of the Communist Party and through the organizations of the Communist Party and the existing organs of state power."

28. The most popular exponent of this revision of Schumpeter's prophecy is Fukuyama (1992). A related argument based on factor proportions is that of Rogowski (1989).

29. For an overview, see Hillman 1992.

References

Berg, A., and J. Sachs. 1992. "Structural Adjustment and International Trade in Eastern Europe: The Case of Poland," *Economic Policy* 14, no. 2 (April) pp. 37–49.

Berger, P. 1992 "The Uncertain Triumph of Democratic Capitalism," *Journal of Democracy* no. 2, (June), pp. 7–16.

Bienkowski, W. 1992. "The Bermuda Triangle: Why Self-Governed Firms Work for Their Own Destruction," *Journal of Comparative Economics* 16, no. 4, (December), pp. 750–762.

Bofinger, P. 1993. *Output Decline in Central and Eastern Europe: A Classical Explanation*, CEPR Discussion Paper No. 784.

Bowles, S., and H. Gintis 1993. "The Revenge of Homo Economics: Contested Exchange and the Revival of Political Economy," *Journal of Economic Perspectives* 7, no. 1, (Winter), pp. 83–102.

Brabant, J. M. van. 1993. *Industrial Policy in Eastern Europe: Governing the Transition*. Boston and Dodrecht: Kulwer Academic Publishers.

Brada, J. 1992. "Allocative Efficiency: It Isn't So," *Soviet Studies* 44, no. 2, (Summer), pp. 343–347.

Brada, J., and A. King. 1992. "Is There a J-Curve for the Economic Transition from Socialism to Capitalism?" *Economics of Planning* 25, no. 1, pp. 37–53.

Brada, J., I. Singh, and A. Trk. *Firms Afloat and Firms Adrift: Hungarian Industry in the Transition*. Armonk, NY: M. E. Sharpe (forthcoming).

Calvo, G., and F. Coricelli. 1993 "Output Collapse in Eastern Europe: The Role of Credit," in M. Blejer, G. Calvo, F. Coricelli, and A. Gelb, eds., *Eastern Europe in Transition: From Recession to Growth*, World Bank Discussion Paper No. 196, Washington, D.C.

Chang, G. 1991. "Immiserizing Growth in Centrally Planned Economies," *Journal of Comparative Economics* 15, no. 4, (December), pp. 711–717.

Chen, K., G. Jefferson, and I. Singh. 1992. "Lessons from China's Economic Reform," *Journal of Comparative Economics*, 16, no. 4, (June), pp. 201–225.

Drabek, Z. 1990. *A Case Study of a Gradual Approach to Economic Reform: The Viet Nam Experience of 1985–88*, World Bank Report No. 1DP74, Washington, D.C.

Ericson, R. 1991. "The Classical Soviet-Type Economy: Nature of the System and Implications for Reform," *Journal of Economic Perspectives* 5, no. 4, (Fall) pp. 11–28.

Estrin, S. 1993. "Restructuring, Viability and Privatisation: A Comparative Study of Enterprise Adjustment in Transition." Mimeo, London Business School, London. Revised version forthcoming in *Journal of Comparative Economics*.

Fukuyama, F. 1992. *The End of History and the Last Man*. New York: Free Press.

Gerschenkron, A. 1962. *Economic Backwardness in Historical Perspective*, New York: Praeger.

Glikman, P. 1993. "Recession, Stagnation, and Ways Out," *Eastern European Economics* 31, no. 3, (Spring), pp. 4–77.

Gomulka, S. 1991. "The Causes of Recession Following Stabilization," *Comparative Economic Studies* 33, no. 2, (Summer) pp. 71–89.

Hillman, A. 1992. "Progress with Privatization," *Journal of Comparative Economics* 16, no. 4, (December), pp. 733–749.

Kajaste, I. 1992. "Finland's Trade with the Soviet Union: Its Impact on the Finnish Economy," *Economic Bulletin for Europe* 44.

Kiss, K. 1993. *Western Prescriptions for Eastern Transition*, Working Paper No. 18 (June), Institute for World Economics of the Hungarian Academy of Scienes .

Klaus, V., and T. Jezek. 1991. "Social Criticism, False Liberalism, and Recent Changes in Czechoslovakia," East European Politics and Societies. 5, no. 1, (Winter), pp. 26–40.

Kolodko, G. 1991. "Inflation Stabilization in Poland: A Year After," Working Paper M17, Institute of Finance, Warsaw.

Kornai, J. 1980. *Economics of Shortage*, Amsterdam: North-Holland.

———. 1990. *The Road to a Free Economy*, New York: W. W. Norton.

Li, J. 1993. "The Characteristics of China's Economic Reform in Comparison with Russia," Paper presented at the Conference on the Transition of Centrally-Planned Economies in Pacific Asia, San Francisco.

Lipton, D., and J. Sachs. 1990a. "Creating a Market Economy in Eastern Europe: The Case of Poland," *Brookings Papers on Economic Activity*, vol. 1, pp. 75–147.

———. 1990b. "Privatization in Eastern Europe: The Case of Poland," *Brookings Papers on Economic Activity*, vol. 2, pp. 147–208.

McKinnon, R. 1993. "Financial Growth and Macroeconomic Stability in China, 1978–92: Implications for Russia and Eastern Europe." Mimeo, Stanford University: Stanford.

Murrell, P. 1991. "Can Neoclassical Economics Underpin the Reform of Centrally Planned Economies?" *Journal of Economic Perspectives* 5, no. 4, (Fall), pp. 59–76.

———. 1992. "Evolution in Economics and in the Economic Reform of the Centrally Planned Economies," in C. Clague and G. Rauser, eds., *The Emergence of Market Economies in Eastern Europe*. Oxford: Basil Blackwell.

———. 1993a. "Evolutionary and Radical Approaches to Economic Reform," in Kazimierz Z. Poznanski, ed., *Stabilization and Privatization in Poland* Boston: Kluwer.

———. 1993b. "What Is Shock Therapy? What Did it Do in Poland and Russia?" *Post-Soviet Affairs* 9, no. 2, (April–June), pp. 111–140 .

Murrell, P., and M. Olson. 1991. "The Devolution of Centrally Planned Economies," *Journal of Comparative Economics* 15, no. 2, (June), pp. 239–265.

Murrell, P., and Y. Wang. 1993. "When Privatization Should be Delayed: The Effect of Communist Legacies on Organizational and Institutional Reforms," *Journal of Comparative Economics* 17, no. 2, (June), pp. 385–406.

Nelson, R., and S. Winter. 1982. *An Evolutionary Theory of Economic Change*. Cambridge: Harvard University Press.

North, D. 1981. *Structure and Change in Economic History*. New York: Norton.

Nove, A. 1991. "'Allocative Efficiency': Can It be So?" *Soviet Studies* 43, no. 3, (Winter), pp. 575–579.

Osband, K. 1992. "Economic Crisis in a Shortage Economy," *Journal of Political Economy* 100, no. 4, (August), pp. 673–689.

Poznanski, K. 1992a. "Property Rights Perspective on Evolution of Communist-Type Economics," pp. 71–96 in K. Poznanski, ed., *Constructing Capitalism,* Boulder: Westview Press.

———. 1992b. "Market Alternative to State Activism in Restoring the Capitalist Economy," *Economics of Planning* 25, no. 1, pp. 55–77.

———. 1992c. "Privatization of the Polish Economy: Problems of Transition," *Soviet Studies* 44, no. 4, pp. 641–664.

———. ed. 1993. *Stabilization and Privatization in Poland*. Boston and Dordrecht: Kluwer Academic Publishers.

Przeworski, A. 1992. "The Neoliberal Fallacy," *Journal of Democracy* 3, no. 2, (June), pp. 45–59.

Rodrik, D. 1992a. "Making Sense of the Soviet Trade Shock in Eastern Europe: A Framework and Some Estimates." Mimeo, Hoover Institution.

———. 1992b. "Foreign Trade in Eastern Europe's Transition: Early Results," National Bureau of Economic Rresearch Conference Paper, Cambridge, Mass.

Rogowski, R. 1989. *Commerce and Coalitions*. Princeton: Princeton University Press.

Schaffer, M. 1992.*The Enterprise Sector and the Emergence of the Polish Fiscal Crisis 1990–91.* Centre for Economic Performance Working Paper No. 280 (August).

Schumpeter, J. 1950. *Capitalism, Socialism and Democracy.* New York: Harper.

Slay, B. 1993. "The Dilemmas of Economic Liberalism in Poland" *Europe-Asia Studies* 45, no. 2, pp. 237–257.

Spulber, N. 1966. *The State and Economic Development in Eastern Europe.* New York: Random House.

Trk, A. 1993. "Trends and Motives of Organizational Change in Hungarian Industry: A Synchronic View," *Journal of Comparative Economics* 17, no. 2, (June), pp. 366–384 .

Vienna Institute for Comparative Economic Studies. 1993. "Transition from the Command to the Market System: What Went Wrong and What to do Now?" Mimeo.

Whitesell, R. 1990. "Why Does the Soviet Economy Appear to be Allocatively Efficient?" *Soviet Studies* 42, no. 2, pp. 259–268.

Williamson, O. 1975. *Markets and Hierarchies: Analysis and Antitrust Implications.* New York: Free Press.

———. 1985. *The Economic Institutions of Capitalism.* New York: Free Press.

———. 1993. "Contested Exchange Versus the Governance of Contractual Relations," *Journal of Economic Perspectives* 7, no. 1, (Winter), pp. 103–108.

Winiecki, J. 1991. "The Inevitability of a Fall in Output in the Early Stages of Transition to the Market: Theoretical Underpinnings," *Soviet Studies* 43, no. 4, pp. 669–676.

Woo, W. 1994. "The Art of Comparing Centrally-Planned Economies: Comparing China, Poland and Russia," *Journal of Comparative Economics*.

Zhou, H. 1993. "Planning, Plan-Influencing and Market Fine-Tuning: Implications for Economies in Transition," *Journal of Comparative Economics* 17, no. 3, (Fall), pp. 560–580.

9

Triggering Evolution: The Case for a Breakthrough in Privatization

Irena Grosfeld

In 1989 economic theory found itself confronted with an explicitly formulated demand: New East European governments started to look for help in designing a virtuous sequence of transformation measures. The best Western economists were attracted by this unusual challenge, so an impressive number of papers on different aspects of "transition to the market" have been produced, and a great number of policy recommendations, often contradictory, have been formulated since this process started.

The greater-than-usual cacophony of policy recommendations addressed to the architects of transition probably resulted from the fact that the post–centrally planned economies are all but what economists are used to: Market institutions and private property are assumed as given in most economic analyses but in these countries they were systematically eliminated almost fifty years ago. So the real challenge of transformation is the establishment of institutions capable at the same time of dealing with the legacy of central planning and of gearing the engine of economic growth.

Therefore, the governments in Eastern Europe need some robust guidelines for institutional change. But although economists know (or can analyze) how institutions function, they are badly equipped to identify the minimal set of institutions that constitute the hard core of a

Financial support of the Ministère de la Recherche et de l'Espace and of the Commissariat General du Plan is gratefully acknowledged.

market economy and to design a way of introducing them. Unlike the system of a centrally planned economy, which was based on a common design and consistently imposed on East European countries, contemporary Western market-based economies were not consciously designed: They evolved over the years and are characterized today by great institutional complexity and diversity. If there are some basic features common to all economies—for example, a price system determined essentially by supply and demand, a legal liability procedure protecting property rights and assuring the respect of contracts, some form of capital market —it is not clear which of them should be considered as prerequisites of a modern economy. Some of them emerged in the course of development; others, having clearly facilitated development in one country, may appear as a product of development in another.

    In particular, a crucial and much-debated issue concerns the speed, scope, and methods of privatization. Even if it is today commonly accepted that a dominantly private economy should be considered the key characteristic of the "final state,"[1] the path leading to this long-term goal is hotly debated. How large should the private sector be to make its logic spill over into the state sector? Should privatization be considered the final effect of transformation or rather as its sine qua non?

    This chapter discusses different arguments used in this debate in light of the actual process of structural change in Central and Eastern Europe. It argues in particular that purely spontaneous transformation of the ownership structure through the progressive development of the new private sector and the slow withering away of the state sector, the strategy advocated by evolutionists,[2] may be an unfeasible "first best." It neglects the need for profound redeployment of assets in the situation of the unusual uncertainty about the value of and prospects for state enterprises. The evolutionist view of transformation is based on a number of assumptions that have been contradicted by recent developments. It supposes notably that the process of selection of good and the elimination of bad enterprises can be rapidly put into motion. I argue, on the contrary, that telling potential winners from unquestionable losers in the sector of state-owned enterprises comes up against the insurmountable problem of the lack of adequate information, incentives, and competence. Therefore, there is an urgent need for achieving a real breakthrough in transferring assets from the state to the private sector. But because of different constraints strongly limiting the set of feasible privatization methods, unorthodox solutions should be envisaged. Among them, programs of quasi-free distribution of assets (through the voucher scheme or through investment funds) appear as the most promising moves.

The Relevance of the Evolutionary Approach

The most powerful argument in favor of private enterprise is provided by evolutionary economics, based on the Schumpeterian vision of capitalism (Nelson and Winter 1982), but also by institutional economics and especially the work of economic historians such as Douglass North. They focus on the role of institutions in economic development. The latter being viewed as a process of permanent change, the capacity of adjustment and accommodation to the largely unpredicted changes is considered the single most important characteristic of institutions. They should be so designed as to allow for and stimulate the search for efficient organization and technological innovation. So, the accent is put not so much on improvement of the static efficiency (both productive and allocative) but on the dynamic process of creative discovery and permanent restructuring in response to changes in relative scarcities.[3]

Such a view of institutional design is what makes evolutionary and institutional economics particularly relevant to the countries in transition. It is crucial indeed to recognize that the central concern of the transformation process should not only be to improve the use of existing possibilities but also, and above all, to establish institutions capable of learning and of rapid adaptation in the face of new circumstances. In this perspective, it is less important, or even futile, to try to identify a priori "the best" system or a particular organizational setup; the understanding of what is "the best" will change with time (including the particular mix of public and private) depending on the learning process and individual preferences.

According to such reading of the evolutionary theory, the most important task of the transformation strategy is to rapidly create conditions favoring entry and survival of the fittest and elimination of those who fail; in other words, the objective is to start the process of its restructuring and adjustment of the inherited state-owned sector. This means, of course, to get incentives right. But it also means—given the heavy legacy of central planning and in particular the misallocation of resources, the absence of capital markets, and the lack of information about the value of and prospects for the state-owned enterprises—that the process should be so designed as to generate as much information as possible.[4] Let me stress, however, that I do not share some Western economists' opinion that the managers of transition should design the information system first and then bother about the principal-agent problem. According to this view, fragmenting large enterprises and other procompetitive decisions should be given priority because they could improve the quality of available information.[5]

To be sure, in many cases, state enterprises are excessively integrated and their breakup is clearly desirable (and is taking place in most of Central and East European countries where antitrust agencies have been established). However, in many other cases, the way the old enterprises should be divided into smaller units is not obvious and the corresponding decisions should be left to those who will become residual claimants. Otherwise, without appropriate incentives and appropriate forms of corporate control, the stream of information will be noisy and purposely distorted.

For incentives, privatization is the key. Its importance stems from the idea that the sensitivity to change is a hallmark of the entrepreneur and may be supposed to follow from the ownership of capital. To be sure, in a modern economy where the widely held corporation has become the dominant form of business organization, the impact of private ownership on incentives is less straightforward. Managers who are not the firm's security holders can be expected to appropriate perquisites out of the firm's resources for their own consumption and to devote a smaller effort to creative activities (learning about new technologies, and so on) than in the case of an owner-managed firm. The inevitable conflict between owner (shareholders who bear risk) and executives (managers who manage risk) over the use of corporate resources poses acutely the problem of monitoring and disciplining managers who, pursuing their self-interest, may fail to maximize the wealth of shareholders.

The impact of the separation of ownership and control on corporate performance has been carefully studied and written about by a great number of individuals. Although they disagree on the global assessment of the overall efficiency of such a form of economic organization, they recognize that the principal-agent problem, because of the separation of ownership and control, is alleviated by the existence of several disciplinary devices: remuneration tied to corporate performance measured by stock market prices, managerial labor market, market for corporate control, and finally a bankruptcy law allowing for reorganization of poorly performing borrowers under the supervision of their creditors transformed into equity owners.[6] So one might say that it is not so much private property as such that contributes to the limitation of the problem of moral hazard and asymmetric information; financial markets are what really matters. In a modern economy, they indeed play the role of nervous system: They generate and transmit information about companies, finance their development, and control managerial performance.

Naturally, the question is whether some forms of financial market could be reproduced and whether a bankruptcy procedure could effectively work in the framework of the state-dominated sector.[7] Although there is no theoretically well-founded negative answer to such a question, recent experience of Central and Eastern Europe offers some evidence that even in the countries where an adequate legal framework was established—a corporate law, a bankruptcy law, an antitrust law, a stock exchange—it often remains an empty shell: Formally appropriate financial contracts and financial institutions may not work as expected in the state-dominated economy.

Institutions and Organizations

At this point let me, following Pelikan (1987, 1992) and North (1990, 1991), make a distinction between institutions and organizations. Institutions are understood as laws and formal rules but also as informal constraints, such as conventions and norms of behavior. Organizations include different economic and noneconomic bodies, the former being firms, banks, family farms, or cooperatives, the latter including political parties, governmental agencies, churches, and associations. Institutions provide a framework within which organizations evolve. They also provide an incentive structure for individuals who at some point may consider that existing institutions are blocking certain opportunities and will consequently try to alter the binding rules. Their perception and reaction will certainly be constrained by "bounded rationality," and there is also important feedback between formal and informal constraints.[8]

The transition from central planning to the market requires the introduction of a whole package of new laws, rules, and regulations. This legislative work can be done by local parliaments (delaying the introduction of new rules), or "ready-to-wear" laws can be imported from the European Community (EC). The rules will change with time but a number of them can be introduced from the beginning. However, the informal part of institutions—ethical standards of behavior, habits, attitudes—will inevitably evolve slowly, through the learning by doing process, creating in each country a different environment for economic development.

The case for an institutional big bang would probably be recognized even by some radical gradualists and evolutionists, although those who advocate an evolutionary transition usually do not make a distinction between institutions and organizations. More problematic is the issue of the change of the organizational structure of the economy. In a well-established, mature economy, the organizational structure would progressively adapt to the new institutional environment: Some enterprises (whether private or state-owned) would disappear, others would enter, some would merge, some others would be broken up. Contrary to institutional revolution, organizational change would be an inherently evolutionary process.

A number of economists argue that also in the case of Central and East European economies we should rely on such a progressive adjustment of the organizational structure to the new market-type laws and rules.

The advocates of a purely evolutionary approach to transformation reject any rapid moves toward the market and in particular accelerated privatization. They argue that actively contributing to the creation of the private sector is contrary to the spirit of evolutionary economics—that only organic, spontaneous development of the private sector, emerging through a process of trials and errors, would have the virtue of being endogenous. There are a number of differences among proponents of this view: Kornai (1990), for instance, suggested that the private sector should get all kinds of preferential treatment stimulating its development; others rather consider that the two sectors should get equal treatment. But the common element is the stress put on the need for a dualistic development: It is argued that the new, dynamic private sector will inevitably coexist with a large, but progressively shrinking, state sector and that this parallel process of expansion and contraction should not be disturbed by the intervention of the government.

In what the economists call the "first best" world, I would be sympathetic to such a claim. Instead of looking for methods allowing a speedup of privatization and restructuring, it would be preferable to proceed slowly, relying on the organic development of the private sector "from below" through free entry. It would be preferable to assist a spontaneous withering away of the state sector and a progressive expansion of the private sector, hopefully bringing about, through a spillover effect, a rapid response in the form of increased dynamic flexibility of the entire economy. Progressively gaining social support and building up a constituency for further reforms would certainly be desirable.

It is to be feared, however, and recent developments in Eastern Europe confirm, that in the economy painfully emerging from the forty-five year period of central planning—which needs a profound redeployment of assets but is dominated by state ownership of the means of production, and by the rent-seeking behavior that replaced any entrepreneurial spirit—the forces of adjustment in the state sector work so slowly the extremely fragile process of transition may be jeopardized.

Lessons of Recent Developments

Initially, at the beginning of the transformation effort, the policy recommendations were based on the experience of developing countries: Stabilize and liberalize trade first, then proceed slowly with privatization. It was expected that price liberalization, increased product market competition, and restrictive fiscal and monetary policies would create an appropriate environment to which managers of state-owned enterprises would be forced to adjust and that the selection of healthy enterprises and the elimination of unprofitable ones would promptly start.

This expectation proved to be unrealistic, underestimating the inertia and what was called by Polish sociologists "learned helplessness" of post–centrally planned state-owned enterprises. These enterprises proved to be ingenious in building up different protections from pressures to change and to be much less innovative in corporate planning, reducing costs, developing marketing strategies, and reorganizing production. To be sure, important differences could be noted in the behavior of different firms: Some of them, especially small enterprises, appeared flexible enough and rapidly reacted to the new market conditions. Others, especially large enterprises in small towns, are passively waiting for a restructuring and/or privatization decision of the "center" (Dabrowski, Federowicz, Levitas 1992).

Responding to the growing problems of liquidity, the managers of state enterprises try to soften the budget constraint (by letting debts to the budget, to banks, and to each other accumulate) and to keep the enterprises afloat, using up the enterprises' resources to increase wages of workers and managers, usually at the cost of asset stripping. In 1991 in Poland, for example, the entire sector of state enterprises experienced losses; almost 40 percent of state enterprises failed to provide any positive gross profit. Although an increasing number of highly indebted enterprises qualified as bankrupt and there exists a law on bankruptcy (with the possibility of liquidation and reorganization), the implementation of bankruptcy procedure proved to be difficult.[9] Clearly, the reason for it can be found in creditors' passivity (Mitchell 1992). But it also results from the fact that, in the absence of well-developed financial markets and without "advocates for capital," judgment about the firm's value and, consequently, decisions on whether the firm should survive and be reorganized, or liquidated through piecemeal sale of assets, are extremely difficult and debatable.

It has been argued that the structural adjustment could have been facilitated if the "bad debts" problem had been tackled at an early stage. To be sure, financial restructuring is necessary for the sorting out of the hopeless cases from the potentially promising ones, uncertainty about prospects for an individual firm being magnified by the fact that the most indebted enterprises are sometimes those with the best chances for survival. Therefore, different solutions aimed at cleaning up the banks' and enterprises' balance sheets are most welcome (see, for instance, Begg and Portes 1992).

However, these solutions cannot guarantee that the same behavior of state-owned debtors and creditors will not be reproduced rapidly after. The recent initiative of the Polish Ministry of Finance, linking the writing off of the banks' debts qualified as "bad" with the banks' involvement in the working out of a program of restructuring for the enterprises in the banks' portfolios, is an ingenious attempt to make the banks play the role of "insiders," as in the German or Japanese financial systems. It is also an attempt to link financial restructuring with real restructuring and privatization. However, it relies heavily on the banks' involvement in the process of evaluating the prospects for individual enterprises and may come up against the lack of people with the right skills to staff special bank departments effectively. Similarly, the option available to creditors to convert debt into equity is difficult to exercise because banks do not have adequate expertise to suddenly become owners, especially in the situation where participation in the capital of indebted firms would imply a highly risky long-term commitment. Nevertheless, this proposal may prove to be better than any other way of financial restructuring and of forcing the creditors, who have until now been passive, to improve the selection mechanism and to become actively involved in the control of the managers.

Introducing the practice of management contracts is sometimes considered another important, but unexploited, policy measure capable of stimulating restructuring. The stripping of assets in state-owned enterprises could be avoided, it is argued, if correct incentives are provided to managers: They should be interested in increasing the value of their enterprises instead of running them down. Thus, private rationality could be imposed on public enterprises even though the transfer of the right to the residual income would be postponed.

To be sure, trying to modify the structure of incentives that managers face, by making their utility function more like that of shareholders, can strongly influence the managers' performance. It is regrettable, therefore, that even in the countries where a very sophisticated scheme for management contracts was designed, its implementation remains marginal. In Poland the program of "restructuring and privatization" was first announced in the middle of 1991 but remained a dead issue for the next eighteen months.[10] It is interesting to note that also in developing countries, the practice of management contracts is very limited (Berg and Shirley 1987). It is not clear what the reasons of this failure are (administrative inertia? lack of competence? the unwillingness to take risks in a very unpredictable environment?), but until now the idea of privatizing management in Central and Eastern Europe did not prove to be an easily applicable method of restructuring.

Implicit Hypotheses of the Purely Evolutionary Approach

The very weak positive response of the state sector to the restrictive fiscal and monetary policies and to the increased competition resulting from the opening of the economy presents an important challenge to the purely evolutionary view of transformation. This view is based indeed on a number of questionable implicit hypotheses.

First, it is supposed to be politically viable to keep for a long time a large inefficient public sector and a dynamic but small private sector.[11] But typically, financial conditions of state enterprises in transition rapidly deteriorate and the government finds itself under double pressure. On the one hand, as in any country undertaking profound restructuring, the employees demand financial protection (subsidies, credits, concessions, various exemptions, and so on); on the other hand, privatization is often considered by the employees as a solution, allowing them to escape "discriminatory" taxes and giving access to capital, foreign markets, and to management skills. These pressures will be even more difficult to resist as powerful interest groups are being formed around them.

Also the managers and employees of newly privatized firms may, in case of difficulty, exercise pressure on the government to obtain some form of help. In postsocialist economies with a legacy of deep-set expectations of different preferential treatment and an unusually high rate of unemployment, such risk is particularly high. But the resistance to such pressure may be easier after privatization because the credibility of necessary restructuring and layoff decisions is higher when they are undertaken by private owners under market conditions.[12]

Second, it is assumed that the state is sufficiently strong, competent, and has enough political will to exercise control over state-owned enterprises and to credibly precommit to their slow privatization and closure. This seems to be a particularly heroic assumption. From the previous regime, the state inherited a great number of conflicting claims and expectations that it is unable to satisfy. The quality of civil service is poor: It lacks adequate skills and administrative capacities necessary to play the role ascribed to it by the strategy of a lengthy phase of a dual economy version of transformation. Therefore, limiting the reliance on the state capacities should certainly be considered one of the guiding principles of the transformation strategy. Real restructuring decisions are to be taken in a very noisy and uncertain environment, typical for transition, and must be based on the evaluation of expected profitability of different business strategies. Admittedly, both civil servants and private investors will initially operate in the same kind of environment. But the expectations of civil servants are clearly different from those of private owners with direct stakes in the firm. The latter have better incentives and capacities to assess the value of and the prospects for the companies and consequently will also contribute to improving the quality of information generated by the system. They should therefore be given voice and the possibility of exit.

Third, it is supposed that the expansion of the private sector will not be hindered or altogether blocked by maintaining the inefficient large public sector. But empirical evidence shows that large loss-making enterprises are crowding out the private sector: For instance, banks, be they state or private, prefer lending to state enterprises (even those that are heavily indebted) than to private insecure firms. Given that "creative destruction" has until now worked much more in the private sector, such behavior is perfectly rational. Also, because existing large enterprises retain market power, especially in nontraded goods market and markets protected by tariffs, access of new firms to production factors is difficult.

More generally, one of the important arguments used by evolutionists in favor of slow changes is that the class of entrepreneurs has to slowly emerge before a market economy can really work. But perpetuating the existence of the large public sector will delay the adjustment of the informal part of "institutions." Obviously, norms of behavior, customs, and conventions will in any case change slowly, but the speed of adjustment of the mental and behavioral constraints and legacies of the period of communist rule, such as the importance of equity considerations, the level of understanding of the working of a market economy, attitudes toward foreign investors and to the new market-type institutions, will be higher if the logic of the market is made universal. Unless a "critical mass" of the private sector is attained, individuals may not live up to the new terms of contract. The spirit of market institutions will be long in coming.

Finally, the cost of slow restructuring of the state sector has to be considered. It would be a mistake to submit the strategy of structural adjustment and of privatization to the maximization of budgetary revenues; I would even argue that the separability of budgetary considerations and of privatization strategy should be another of the guiding principles of transformation.[13] But maintaining loss-making enterprises may prove to be excessively expensive: It will either fuel inflation or have to be financed through increased taxation. Both of these events will have a negative impact on the development of the private sector, on which all hopes of "pure evolutionists" are, however, concentrated.

Putting in Motion the Process of Selection

It is certainly crucial to create adequate legal and fiscal conditions stimulating the expansion of the private sector. But unfortunately, given the strong domination of the state sector, which needs a profound reallocation of resources, one can hardly rely on its self-generated restructuring and, eventually, withering away. In other words, it is doubtful whether the organizational structure of the economy will harmoniously evolve within the new institutional framework. The latter must be filled up with private agents capable of transforming the formal rules and institutions of the market economy into effectively functioning devices. Hence the case for some degree of imaginative intervention and in particular for accelerated privatization. The governments must actively manage divestment to attain a critical mass of ownership changes.

The Czecho-Slovakian voucher scheme, the mass privatization program in Poland, and other methods of free distribution (used in Russia, Latvia, Ukraine, Romania, and now even envisaged in Hungary) should be assessed in such a perspective. Instead of treating them as an expression of some ideological commitment, let us rather consider them a pragmatic response to the actual obstacles the privatization process is running up against. In each country the set of possible privatization strategies is determined by social, political, economic, and administrative constraints that progressively emerge as the process unfolds. (See Grosfeld and Nivet 1992.) Because of the great uncertainty as to the implementation of different programs, an eclectic approach, indeed a diversified portfolio of privatization methods, seems to be a rational strategy. All countries actually chose a combination of different methods: initial public offering, trade sale, leveraged buy-out, auction, liquidation, restitution, free distribution. The latter, however, appears as the most promising strategy to accelerate privatization and to put in motion the process of adjustment.[14]

Often presented together, as relying on a quasi-free distribution of assets to the population, these programs are indeed quite different. The main concern of the Czecho-Slovakian voucher scheme is to privatize rapidly. Other goals, such as restructuring or establishing a corporate governance, are considered secondary and are supposed to be realized through privatization. The participation of millions of investors is viewed as a crucial move in the creation of a market economy, allowing for a great number of trials and errors and providing the best possible guess about the future profitability of each firm. Initially widely dispersed ownership is supposed to become quickly concentrated and is seen as a desirable evolution. The concern with fairness is dismissed as utopian: Transition is considered an inevitably dirty, noisy, and risky process that should be rapidly brought to an end.

For each of the enterprises selected for the first wave of the voucher scheme, the Czech and Slovak Ministries of Privatization had to choose one of the "basic" (submitted by the incumbent managers) or "competitive" (submitted by outsiders) privatization projects.[15] The citizens were given a chance to choose companies themselves: Having paid a registration fee, they could bid for shares of any company privatized by the voucher method or entrust their investment points to one of hundreds of rapidly emerging investment privatization funds. The whole process that is under way is managed with great pragmatism, many decisions being made and much regulation being introduced in an ad hoc way. This was probably made possible by a spectacular commitment of the federal government to make a great leap forward in terms of the transfer of state assets to the private sector.

The Polish approach to mass privatization is much more careful. The authorities are afraid of an anticapitalistic backlash and thus stress fairness and restructuring. The shares of enterprises are to be distributed to a certain number of privately managed investment funds, individuals getting a share in each fund. Therefore, individuals are offered a perfect diversification of portfolios; an unexperienced population does not have to assess the future profitability of firms in a very uncertain environment. The funds are supposed to be managed by professional managers, essentially foreign but preferably in cooperation with local counterparts. It is expected that the foreign fund managers will bring their investment expertise and will have better access to capital markets than Polish managers.

The fund managers will have to assume an active role in overseeing the daily management of the firms (they will sit on the boards of the companies) and will have to engage in all kinds of activities tending to maximize the value of the firms: restructuring, issuing shares, making new investments, borrowing money, selling shares to foreign or domestic investors, and so on. Because restructuring is seen as the most urgent task, there will be some initial restrictions on trading in the funds' shares. But the companies' shares will be tradeable immediately.

Taking into account the incentive failure of public corporations with widely dispersed ownership, the allocation of enterprises will be organized so as to permit an individual fund to acquire a large block of shares (33 percent), giving it sufficient control to initiate restructuring. To be sure, the key question concerns the incentives for and control of the managers of such funds. Notably, the risk exists that the funds will not be insulated from political pressure. The incentive scheme and the regulatory framework should, on the one hand, stimulate active restructuring instead of passive trading of shares and, on the other hand, prevent excessive concentration and all kinds of opportunistic behavior. A natural remuneration structure would involve a flat fee and a performance-related element. The latter, however, must refer to some "basic value" that initially, in the absence of robust markets for shares of the companies, will be very difficult to determine. A solution chosen in Poland consists in supplementing the constant part of the remuneration with stocks (1 percent every year plus 5 percent at the end of the ten-year period).

It is too early to compare the relative advantages of the two schemes. More time is needed to assess their effective impact on long-term growth. Such a comparison will be fascinating per se but also because the two programs may be interpreted as being inspired by two different views of the financial system: The voucher scheme refers more to the Anglo-Saxon model with widely held equity and an active market for corporate control, whereas the mass privatization program appears to be strongly influenced by the German (and Japanese) system, with a stable core of majority equity owners exercising direct control on management. But given that in the first wave of voucher privatization the funds attracted 72 percent of all investment points,[16] the behavior of the funds in Czecho-Slovakia will also be crucial for the process. This is one of the unexpected developments of the voucher scheme, making it more like the Polish mass privatization program than it was initially thought to be.

Although the two programs are based on general distrust of the ability of the state to effectively manage transition, they rely on the governments' intervention at two crucial stages. In Czecho-Slovakia the Ministry of Privatization has to choose among privatization projects that make the selection procedure manipulable by insiders; in Poland the government will have to appoint the first supervisory boards of the investment funds. Again, one might compare the relative drawbacks of both solutions, but one or another form of intervention seems unavoidable.

The question is whether such an initial push will give way to further institutional and organizational changes. The authors of both schemes seem to be sensitive to the need of leaving options open and preserving a possibility of dynamic adjustment of institutions, which, anyway, will be inevitable. It is essential indeed that these radical privatization programs be implemented in an evolutionary spirit. It means that some degree of reversibility may be considered a virtue, but certain irreversible moves toward changing the property structure must be made.

In the same evolutionary spirit, I would contest as premature the case for establishing a particular form of the financial system (see, for instance, Corbett and Mayer 1991). Empirical evidence supporting the ongoing debate about the relative advantages of the stock market and of the banking system does not provide clear-cut conclusions about the impact of financial contracts on the behavior of managers. Admittedly, in Central and Eastern Europe the development of the banking system (through a free entry for new banks and strengthening, commercialization, and privatization of the existing banks) is rightly perceived as being of primary importance: Beyond providing finance for industry, the banking system can also play a role in monitoring and controlling the behavior of managers and in reallocating assets through corporate restructuring.[17] But given the starting point of the reforms—high concentration, lack of information about the value of capital stock, lack of competition, corruption, lack of managerial competence—a pure insiders' model does not seem to be a desirable solution. Nevertheless, desirable or not, the stock exchange will not play an important role for some time to come. Hence, some innovative solutions must be found, combining, for instance, control of a portion of shares by some intermediary institutions with the rest being actively traded and providing a competitive check on managers and insiders. Both the Polish and the Czecho-Slovakian programs go in this direction.

Privatization through free distribution of assets can be viewed as a way of realizing a number of objectives: assuring the irreversibility of reforms, accelerating restructuring, and contributing to the development of capital markets. Finally, it can be argued that the speed of adjustment of the informal part of institutions (attitudes, conventions, norms of behavior) to the new legal framework is positively correlated with the size of the private sector.

Can such an attempt at breaking up the status quo be called evolutionary? It appears indeed as the real paradox of transformation: To start an evolutionary search for efficient organization and an appropriate mix of public and private, a radical move has to be made toward establishing a new institutional and organizational order. Only then can an evolutionary process really start.

Notes

1. Several economists are committed to the idea that ownership is not the key issue and that the advantages of a market economy can be obtained within a framework of a dominantly state ownership; see, for instance, Bardhan and Roemer 1992. But here, I shall not discuss this issue and take the desirability of privatization of a dominant part of the state assets for granted.

2. The case for slow, organic changes was first built up by Kornai (1990). For an evolutionary approach to transformation, see Murrell 1991, 1992; Poznanski, 1992; and Stark 1992. In somewhat different terms, Andreff (1990); and Brabant (1992) present a similar perspective on privatization.

3. See, for instance, Pelikan 1987 and Grosfeld 1990.

4. The importance of information in designing privatization strategy is strongly underlined by Frydman and Rapaczynski (1991a, 1991b).

5. See, for example, Newbery and Kattuman 1992.

6. Several authors, for example, Aghion and Bolton (1988) and Dewatripont and Tirole (1991), stress the role of debt as a powerful mechanism forcing managers to restructure their companies and adopt value-creating policies.

7. Some proposals in this direction have been formulated. See Tardos 1986 for the idea of socialist holding, Nuti 1988 for the idea of socialist takeover, and Gomulka 1992 for a suggestion to create the German-type supervision of state enterprises by commercial banks.

8. For the sources of institutional change, see North 1990, 1991.

9. In Poland, for instance, the liquidation procedure started in almost 800 enterprises but ended in less than 10 percent of them. See "Przydaloby sie ... przyspieszenie" 1992. The difficulty of selling assets of the bankrupt enterprises is the most often quoted reason for such delay.

10. At the end of 1992 serious attempts are being made, with the help of foreign consulting firms, to revitalize the program and attract some professional managers. Management groups are invited to bid for a particular company and submit proposals for restructuring before privatization. The winner, who gives the highest initial value of the enterprise, has to make a security deposit according to some predetermined scheme, for example, 5 percent of the value up to 10 billion zlotys. The winner is offered financial incentives to increase the value of the firm: a monthly salary, an annual bonus based on net profits of the firm, and a capital gain premium payable in shares of the company. And if a management group realizes a sale of at least 51 percent of the equity, it gets 70 percent of the real capital gain on the sale, that is, the difference between the sale price and the tender price, adjusted for inflation; 20 percent goes to the employees and 10 percent to the supervisory boards. For more details, see Grzegorzewski, 1991, and more recently "Setting it Right" 1992.

11. Obviously, the sector of state-owned enterprises will not disappear overnight. There is a difference, however, between, on the one hand, admitting its existence and trying to improve its performance but undertaking at the same time an important privatization effort and, on the other hand, entirely leaving the development of the private sector to the spontaneous forces and concentrating all available skills and resources on the control of the state sector.

12. The strategy of Czecho-Slovak authorities is clearly based on such an analysis. That is why the implementation of the bankruptcy law was postponed until spring 1993 when the first wave of voucher privatization ended.

13. An overhaul of public finance and social security requires careful treatment and should be dealt with in the early stages of transition. But mixing budgetary considerations and privatization may hurt both objectives: the macroeconomic equilibrium and the development of the private sector.

14. For small firms, an alternative can certainly be an auction in which cash and noncash bids are allowed. See, for instance, Bolton and Roland 1992. But for large enterprises, admitting a high debt-equity ratio would imply the risk of renationalization (see Buchi 1991 for the Chilean experience). Moreover, it would be

226   *Irena Grosfeld*

administratively cumbersome and would come up against serious moral hazard problems.

15. The projects had to specify the value of assets to be privatized, overall liabilities and total employment, the method of privatization (portion of shares designated for vouchers, sold directly to foreign or domestic buyer, transferred to the employees or to municipalities, left permanently or temporarily in the fund of national property), and, in the case of sale, the price and the terms of payment.

16. For details see several issues of *Privatization Newsletter of Czechoslovakia*, 1992.

17. Banks can actively intervene in corporate activities as equity owners or, if the bankruptcy law provides appropriate incentives, participate as senior creditors in reorganizing defaulting firms. See Aghion and Bolton 1988 and Dewatripont and Tirole 1991.

References

Aghion, P., and P. Bolton. 1988. *An Incomplete Contract Approach to Bankruptcy and the Financial Structure of the Firm*, MIT Working paper 484, Cambridge.

Andreff, W. 1990. *Techniques et Experiences de Privatization: la "Success Story" des Privatisations en France et les Besoins Actuels des Pays d'Europe de l'Est*, Paris: ROSES.

Bardhan, P., and J. E. Roemer. 1992. "Market Socialism: A Case for Rejuvenation," *Journal of Economic Perspectives*, 6, no. 3.

Begg, D., and R. Portes. 1992. *Enterprise Debt and Economic Transformation: Financial Restructuring of the State Sector in Central and Eastern Europe*. CEPR Discussion Paper No. 695, London.

Berg, E., and M. M. Shirley. 1987. "Divestiture in Developing Countries." Mimeo, World Bank, Washington, D.C.

Bolton, P., and G. Roland. 1992. "The Economics of Mass Privatization: Czechoslovakia, East Germany, Hungary, and Poland," *Economic Policy*, no. 15.

Brabant, J. M. van. 1992. *Privatizing Eastern Europe: The Role of Markets and Ownership in the Transition*. Dordrecht: Kluwer Academic Publishers.

Buchi, H. 1991. "Practical Aspects of Privatization: The Case of Chile," Lecture held at CERGE, Charles University, Prague, September 28.

Corbett, J., and C. P. Mayer. 1991. *Financial Reform in Eastern Europe: Progress with the Wrong Model*, CEPR Discussion Paper No. 603, London.

Dabrowski, J. M., M. Federowicz, A. Levitas. 1992. "Przedsiebiorstwa Panstwowe w Drugim Roku Transformacji Gospodarczej Instytut Badan nad Gospodarka Rynkowa," Gdansk.

Dewatripont, M., and J. Tirole. 1991. "Managerial Incentives, Corporate Control, and the Diversity of Securities." Mimeo, Harvard Institute of Economic Research, Harvard University, Cambridge.

Frydman R., and A. Rapaczynski. 1991a. "Privatization and Corporate Governance in Eastern Europe: Can a Market Economy be Designed?" in *Central and Eastern Europe Roads to Growth*. Washington, D.C.: International Monetary Fund, Australian National Fund.

————. 1991b. "Evolution and Design in the East European Transition," *Rivista di Politica Economica* 81, no. 11.

Gerschenkron, A. 1962. *Economic Backwardness in Historical Perspective.* Cambridge: Belknap Press of Harvard University Press.

Gomulka, S. 1992. "How to Create a Capital Market in a Socialist Country for the Purpose of Privatization," pp. in A. R. Prindl, ed., *Banking and Finance in Eastern Europe.* London: Woodhead-Faulkner.

Grosfeld, I. 1990. "Reform Economics and Western Economic Theory: Unexploited Opportunities," *Economics of Planning,* 23, no. 1.

————. 1991. "Privatization of State Enterprises in Eastern Europe: The Search for a Market Environment," *East European Politics and Societies* 5, no. 1, pp. 142–161.

Grosfeld, I., and J.-F. Nivet. 1992. "Les Enjeux des Privatisations," pp. in G. Mink and J.-Ch. Szurek, eds., *Cet Etrange Post-Communisme. Ruptures et Transitions en Europe Centrale et Orientale.* Paris: Presses du C.N.R.S./La Decouverte.

Grzegorzewski, Z. 1991. "Kontrakty menedzerskie," *Zycie Gospodarcze,* no. 12, p. 12.

Kornai, J. 1990. *The Road to a Free Economy.* New York: W. W. Norton.

Mitchell, J. 1992. "Creditor Passivity and Bankruptcy: Implications for Economic Reform." Mimeo.

Murrell, P. 1991. "Evolution in Economics and in the Economic Reform of the Centrally Planned Economies." Mimeo, University of Maryland Press: College Park.

————. 1992. "Evolutionary and Radical Approaches to Economic Reform," *Economics of Planning,* 25, no. 1, pp. 79–96.

Nelson, R., and S. Winter. 1982. *An Evolutionary Theory of Economic Change.* Cambridge: Cambridge University Press.

Newbery, D., and P. Kattuman. 1992. *Market Concentration and Competition in Eastern Europe,* CEPR Discussion Paper No. 664, London.

North, D.C. 1990. *Institutions, Institutional Change and Economic Performance.* Cambridge: Cambridge University Press.

————. 1991. "Institutions," *Journal of Economic Perspectives* 5, no. 1.

Nuti, D. M. 1988. "Competitive Valuation and Efficiency of Capital Investment in the Socialist Economy," *European Economic Review,* 32, ns. 2–3.

Pelikan, P. 1987. "The Formation of Incentive Mechanisms in Different Economic Systems," in S. Hedlund, ed., *Incentives and Economic System.* Croom Helm: London and Sydney.

————. 1992. "The Dynamics of Economic Systems; or, How to Transform a Failed Socialist Economy," *Journal of Evolutionary Economics* 2, no. 1.

Poznanski, K. 1992. "Market Alternative to State Activism in Restoring the Capitalist Economy," *Economics of Planning* 25, no. 1, pp. 55–78.

Privatization Newsletter of Czechoslovakia. 1992. Various issues.

"Przydaloby sie … przyspieszenie." 1992. *Rzeczpospolita,* November 27.

"Setting It Right," 1992. Privatization Update, *The Warsaw Voice,* No. 2 (November).

Stark, D. 1992. "Path Dependence and Privatization Strategies in East Central Europe," *East European Politics and Societies* 6, no. 1.

Tardos, M. 1986. "The Conditions of Developing a Regulated Market," *Acta Oeconomica* 36, nos. 1–2, pp. 67–89.

About the Book and Editor

In this timely work, renowned scholars provide a provocative view of the transition to capitalism in formerly socialist economies. The contributors consider the experiences of Eastern Europe, Russia, Mongolia, and China, most arguing that an evolutionary approach to the transition has a greater chance of succeeding than does shock therapy. Their evolutionary theoretical paradigm provides constructive alternatives to the conventional thinking on transition and on institutional change in general.

Kazimierz Z. Poznanski is professor of international studies at the Henry M. Jackson School, University of Washington.

About the Contributors

Maria Blangiewicz teaches in the department of economics at Gdansk University.

Josef C. Brada is professor of economics at Arizona State University.

Wojciech W. Charemza is professor of economics at the University of Leicester.

Irena Grosfeld is a researcher at the department of applied economics at CRNS, Paris.

Janos Kornai is professor of economics at Harvard University. He is also professor and chairman of the economics department, Institute of Economics, Hungarian Academy of Sciences.

Ronald I. McKinnon is professor of economics at Stanford University.

Peter Murrell is professor of economics at the University of Maryland.

Barry Naughton is professor of economics at the University of California-San Diego.

Jozef M. van Brabant is Section Chief at the United Nations, New York.

Index

240

Index

See also Models
Stock exchanges, 49, 214, 223–224. See also Financial systems
Structural vector autoregressive (SVAR) model, 58–70
Supply
diversion, 122–123, 132(n5)
and recession, 4
SVAR. See Structural vector autoregressive model

Taiwan, 98, 148–149
Taxation
Chinese internal revenue needs, 120, 121
and Mongolian reform, 89, 90
transition and instituting, 129–130, 131
Technology transfer, 146
Textiles, 148
TFP. See Total factor productivity
"Third road," 14, 31–32, 33, 186, 198
Time-varying parameters (TVP) model, 58–70
Total factor productivity (TFP), 144, 145(table)
Township and village enterprises (VTEs), 99, 118
Trade, foreign
and China, 99, 138, 142, 146, 148–149
collapse of CMEA, 103, 148, 172, 191, 204(n7)
cross-national comparisons, 187
and Mongolia, 84, 91, 92, 93
recession and destruction of, 3
Transition policy
Chinese, 138–145
cross-national comparisons and Chinese, 135–137, 145–151, 152(n1)
debate on price liberalization, 187–193. See also Price liberalization
gradual versus radical, 22, 97–104, 129–131, 157, 160–163, 176–180, 183–187

and industrial/privatization policy, 170–176, 194–201. See also Privatization
model, 119(table)
political issues in, 200–203
rhetoric versus implementation, 79–93
and role of market, 163–170
See also Evolutionary economics; Gradualism; Political power/leadership; Radicalism
Trk, A., 200
TVEs. See Township and village enterprises
TVP. See Time-varying parameters model
TVP-VAR nonstationary model, 58–70, 62(fig.), 65(fig.), 67(table), 69(fig.), 71–73(table), 73(nn 1, 2, 3, 4)

Ukraine, 101
Unemployment, 173, 189, 192
United States, 50, 54(n14)
Urban sector, 150

Vienna Institute for Comparative Economic Studies, 191
Vietnam, 98, 101

Wages
Chinese pre-reform, 145
controlling, 128–129
pre-reform explosion in, 193
and Russian reform, 125, 126
Wang, Y., 195, 196
Western Europe, 18, 146, 196–197
Whitesell, R., 188, 189
Williamson, O., 197
Wong, Christine, 123–124
World Bank, 121

Yugoslavia, 31, 158, 186–187

Zhejiang province, China, 149